THE
UNBEATABLE
MARKET

TAKING THE INDEXING PATH
TO FINANCIAL PEACE OF MIND

RON ROSS, Ph.D.

Printed by:

    Bookmasters, Inc.

    Mansfield, Ohio

    (800) 247-6553

    www.atlasbooks.com

This publication is designed to provide accurate and authoritative information in regard to the subject matter covered. It is sold with the understanding that the publisher is not engaged in rendering legal, accounting, or other professional service. If legal advice or other expert assistance is required, the services of a competent professional person should be sought.

Library of Congress Control Number: 2002092924
ISBN 0-9722230-0-2

First Printing

Editor and Project Manager: Ray Jones
Copy Editors: Judith Stephenson and Howard Seemann
Production Editors: Jenna MacFarlane and Katherine Poor
Cover: Jenna MacFarlane

For
my wife, Jan and our son and daughter, Garen and Carly.
The three most efficient sources of joy in my life.

Acknowledgements

One of the many things you learn when you write a book is that it is to a considerable degree a group endeavor. It is a profoundly humbling experience and greatly enhances your appreciation of everyone you know. For instance, the number of quotations in the book illustrates that I am much more a conduit than originator of ideas. So many people have been influential in my ability to write this book that I couldn't begin to thank them all, but the attempt has to be made.

My editor and project manager, Ray Jones, has given me the benefit of his extensive experience and sound judgement. It has been a true pleasure working with him. Jenna MacFarlane, our graphic artist, was also a delight to work with and is primarily responsible for the appearance of the book. Jenna possesses both aesthetic judgement and computer skills, both of which were crucial in making the book a reality.

The staff at Premier Financial Group not only liberated the time necessary to write the book, but gave me valuable support and assistance. Jeff Coontz, in particular, was a dependable source of ideas, encouragement, and inspiration. He spurred me on whenever my enthusiasm was flagging. My partners, John Gloor and Wayne Caldwell, have been especially helpful in making our firm a trusted provider of financial peace of mind for our clients. Ann Seemann, Howard Seemann, Frank Jewett, Jeff Secord, Loren Scott, Ann McDermed, Nancy Ross-Flanigan, Gerald Hoopes, Kenneth L. Fisher, and Saeed Mortazavi all read drafts of various chapters and generously provided both encouragement and suggestions.

I owe a special debt of gratitude to our clients, the nicest group of people I've ever known. They've helped me appreciate the frustrations people feel in dealing with the financial world. What I've learned from them has had a significant impact on the structure and tone of the book.

The research and educational efforts of everyone at Dimensional Fund Advisors have contributed enormously to the book's content. DFA continues to be the most sophisticated practitioner of passive management and the primary link between academic theoreticians and actual investors. DFA is committed to putting sound theory and evidence-based strategies into practice. That is the main objective of this book as well.

A central theme of this book is market efficiency. I am, therefore, deeply indebted to Professor Eugene Fama of the University of Chicago who formulated the Efficient Market Hypothesis, certainly one of the most elegant and useful economic theories ever conceived. Professor Fama continues to make significant contributions to the discipline of financial economics.

Throughout the time I've been writing this book my wife, Jan, has been her usual amazingly patient self. Throughout the years of our marriage she has been subjected to more economics lectures than any non-economist should have to endure. Above all, she and our children, Garen and Carly, make everything worthwhile. I am particularly indebted to Carly for inventing the title *The Unbeatable Market*. Until she did so, the lack of an appropriate title was one of my greatest frustrations as an author.

Ron Ross

Contents

✻

THE
UNBEATABLE
MARKET

CHAPTER 1

Wall Street: The Greatest Obstacle to Your Financial Peace of Mind

*If a man empties his purse into his head, no man can take it from him.
An investment in knowledge always pays the best interest.*
Benjamin Franklin

As an investor the first question you need to answer is, "Should I attempt to beat the market." Wall Street wants you to say yes. After all, Wall Street spends most of its time and resources attempting to beat the market. Don't assume, however, that Wall Street has valid reasons for its obsession.

Attempting to beat the market is called active management. The alternative—duplicating market rates of return—is called passive management, or more popularly, indexing. What you need to recognize is this: active management, attempting to beat the market, is not investing, it's gambling. What's worse—the odds are overwhelmingly against you.

The unambiguous conclusion of countless studies is that beating the market is the result of luck, not skill. There's no convincing proof that a single mutual fund has beaten the market through skill, although many randomly beat it through luck. Wall Street's favorite scam is pretending that luck is skill.

Why does the question of luck or skill matter? For this reason: unlike skill activities, the outcomes of luck-based activities are random. The problem with luck is that it is unpredictable, unreliable, and uncontrollable. Is it your intention to randomly invest your money?

About 90 percent of all mutual fund assets are actively managed. Actually, the use of the word managed is overly generous. It would be more accurate to call them actively mismanaged funds. The fundamental character of the beat-the-market game means that actively managed funds are closely akin to gambling casinos. The fund managers have maneuvered themselves into the enviable position of getting paid to gamble with your money.

Reprinted with permission from DOONESBERRY

Largely because of its flawed approach to investing, Wall Street is arguably the worst performing sector of the economy.

In no other part of the economy is there so large a discrepancy between what the consumer wants and what he gets. Wall Street is where there is the greatest gap between what's possible and what's offered.

Most investors' overall goal is long-term financial peace of mind. Unfortunately, Wall Street leads its customers in the opposite direction—toward stress, confusion, excessive activity, and unnecessary risk. No other industry could get away with such disregard of its customers' objectives. Ordinarily, competition assures that most consumers get value for their expenditures. As you will see, because of an unusual combination of factors and circumstances, the normal checks and balances have functioned inadequately on Wall Street.

The U.S. stock market has performed so well, especially during the past 20 years, that money managers have gotten away with mismanaging assets and overcharging their clients. That was true, at least, until about the second quarter of 2000. So far, the 21st century has not been kind to the active management practitioners, and the 2000-2001 performance of actively managed funds has served as a wake-up call to many investors.

Unfortunately, very few people know how to measure and evaluate the relative performance of investments, especially those made in mutual funds. Many, if not most, investors may be unaware that actively managed funds have underperformed the market as a whole. Index fund pioneer Rex Sinquefield has this to say about actively managed mutual funds and their managers: "If these guys were race horses, they'd be glue." It is easy to see which horse wins the race and which brings up the rear, but Wall Street managers successfully hide the fact that they're losers.

Investors would be furious if they were fully aware of how they've been abused, overcharged, and deceived.

Investors tend to assume they can trust brokerages and mutual fund companies to manage their money responsibly. However, the managers violate this trust in numerous ways. Some of the particulars (all of which will be examined more fully in subsequent chapters):

- *They're wasting your money.* Mutual fund managers unnecessarily increase your costs and decrease your net rate of return by more than three percent a year. The damage is even worse when the impact of unnecessary taxes is taken into account. Three percent is a conservative, educated guess. One of the biggest problems with active management is that there's no way to measure all the extra costs relative to indexing. The three percent per year handicap will do even more damage if stock market returns decline in the future. Taking three percent from an eight percent rate of return hurts a lot more than taking it from a twenty percent return.

- *Their investment strategies don't work.* Fund managers advocate and recommend you follow strategies with extremely low probabilities of success. By far the most relevant example is their persistent advocacy of attempting to beat the market. When probabilities are taken into account, their strategies are exposed as desperate long shots. The probability of truly beating the market is less than that of winning the lottery.

What I refer to as "Wall Street" is the active management/beat-the-market element of the securities industry. (About 98 percent—all but about 200—of the 12,000 mutual funds now in existence attempt to beat the market.) The term also includes the investment divisions of virtually all banks and insurance companies.

- *Fund managers unnecessarily increase the volatility of your portfolio, placing your financial security at risk and causing you significant stress.* This became especially evident during 2000-2001. Many investors experienced losses of 60 to 80 percent during a time when the overall market was down about 20 percent. An efficiently diversified portfolio would have declined much less than 20 percent. When an investment loses 80 percent of its value, it has to have a 400 percent growth just to get back to where it started.

- *Wall Street and the financial media do their best to inflame investor emotions.* Emotions—fear, impatience, panic, pride, overconfidence, overreaction, envy—are almost always detrimental to long-term investment success. Wall Street exploits these human tendencies for its own benefit, to the serious detriment of its customers. Wall Street professionals do their best to play on these emotions for the purpose of making an easy sale.

- *Wall Street has confused investors and unnecessarily complicated their choices.* For example, there are now over 12,000 different mutual funds. Why so many? This is product differentiation run amok. Do the names of the funds mean anything significant? No. It is impossible to distinguish one from another and the characteristics of each fund are continuously subject to change. Those 12,000 funds create a house of mirrors for investors. If you feel confused, you have a lot of company and, sadly, that is just the way the industry wants it.

- *They distract you from what matters most.* Wall Street focuses your attention on the issues of least importance and away from those of greatest importance—toward the short-term rather than the long-term, on elusive, extraordinary performance and away from what is realistic and attainable.

- *In order to promote sales, they ignore risk.* Risk and return are the two primary investment dimensions and are of equal importance. Wall Street places 99 percent of its attention on return because return is what sells. They do not grasp what risk means nor how to manage it.

- *They're reckless with your money and take on far too much risk.* Fund managers expose you to more risk than you or even they realize, primarily because they do not understand or advocate diversification, even though diversification is the single most effective method for reducing risk. For example, Peter Lynch, the closest thing Wall Street has to a poster boy, recommends owning no more than five individual stocks. (Lynch, 1993) If the guy Wall Street considers an icon is that irresponsible and clueless, what does that say about the rest of them?

- *They're bogus experts and false prophets.* Wall Streeters lead you to believe they're experts when they're actually grossly incompetent. If they faced facts about how markets work, they would follow totally different strategies. Their expertise is marketing and making you believe they're experts. Their strategies rely on an unfounded confidence in their superior ability to predict the future. Their predictive success is pathetic, but they manage to get away with it because most of us have short memories and don't take notes.
- *They've taken credit for something they had nothing to do with—the spectacular performance of the U.S. economy and stock market.* They're among the last ones who should be taking credit. They've retarded rather than enhanced investor rates of return and impeded investors from sharing in the fruits of economic progress.
- *They pursue a doomed strategy of high portfolio turnover.* The average portfolio turnover for mutual funds in 2000 was 150 percent, up from 80 percent in 1994 and 18 percent in 1955. Turnover amplifies costs and increases tax liabilities but is doomed to failure as a general strategy. For the most part, fund managers are trading among themselves. What one sells, another buys and vice versa. They all think they're smarter than all the others. If there were an Olympics for arrogance, all the gold medallists would be from Wall Street. The high and still rising turnover rates are another proof of gross incompetence and confusion and a classic example of the arrogance of ignorance.
- *They offer no decision-making guidance.* Wall Street gives investors little or no assistance in making decisions logically or systematically. Wall Street has made no serious attempt to explain to investors what their alternatives are or which decisions matter most. They especially don't want you to know the numerous advantages of indexed investing.
- *Wall Street over-promises what it can deliver.* Their claims are almost never backed up with objective, third-party evidence.

If you're mad as hell and you don't want to take it any more, these are your alternatives.

You basically have three choices: (1) You could wait for Wall Street to start feeling guilty and reform itself. As you might imagine, that is an exceedingly low-probability scenario. (2) You could hope for or lobby for government regulations to prevent consumer abuse. The various ways Wall Street abuses the public are not easily prevented by regulation, and anyway, the investment industry is already heavily regulated and has been for over 65 years. The existing regulations don't protect you, and no serious proposals have been offered to stem the abuses. (3) You could become a better-informed investor, particularly in regard to basic investment realities. The third alternative is both feasible and attainable. It doesn't mean going back to college and earning a degree in finance. Clarifying the third alternative is the basic purpose of this book. It will provide you the information you need to invest prudently and achieve long-term financial peace of mind.

As more investors follow the third solution, there will be some hope for the first solution. Wall Street will change when enough pressure is brought to bear by consumers who realize they're being offered an inferior product. Wall Street follows the path of least resistance. Investors have to become better informed and make that path lead in a more beneficial direction.

Wall Street has been able to take advantage of you because it knows more than you do, but you can tilt the playing field to your advantage.

By reading this book you can turn the tables on Wall Street—you'll become better informed than it is. You need to know what you're doing, because the experts don't know what they're doing.

Wall Street fleeces investors legally and without resorting to force. It all happens within the context of voluntary exchange. Nevertheless, it is an unequal contest. Wall Street has investors at a disadvantage because of its familiarity with the system. It's Wall Street's full-time job to keep investors off balance and to keep them coming. Furthermore, Wall Street has powerful incentives to keep it up as long as they can get away with it.

It's up to the investors themselves to break the pattern. They need to opt out of the game, to push themselves away from the table, and they can do it. After all, it's their money that's being squandered. They have the most to gain and, therefore, the strongest incentive for making a change. The good news is that clearly superior alternatives to the defective Wall Street model are available to investors.

Of course, it's not enough to advise you, to tell you what to do. I have to inform and convince I have to show you what serious, highly regarded researchers have concluded about how securities markets work. You need to grasp underlying logic to be firmly convinced.

The Wall Street/gambling model of the world has more surface plausibility than the academic/investing model. The academic model is counter-intuitive. If you don't make the effort to see below the surface, you will not have the resolve and ability to resist the siren song of those who want you to support their gambling habit.

The fund managers will, of course, vehemently deny that they're gambling. Some of them sincerely believe they can generate excess returns with the strategy they're using. However, they can continue believing this only by living in obstinate denial of clear, scientific evidence and even their own direct experience. Apparently, Wall Street is home to the world's slowest learners.

It's bad enough that they're gambling with your money. The danger is even greater when they don't even recognize that's what they're doing. Someone who doesn't know what he's doing is a far worse hazard than someone who does.

The active management form of gambling is even more uncertain than the variety practiced in the casinos of Las Vegas and Atlantic City. At the undisguised casinos you can, if you like, compute your odds (probabilities). You do not have that option when it comes to the beat-the-market game. There are simply far too many variables and unknowns.

This book is a distillation of what I've learned in two careers.

This book is a synthesis of principles of economics and practical investment advice. As such it is very much the product of my two careers. I taught undergraduate and graduate courses in economics at Humboldt State University in Arcata, California, for ten years. Then, in 1980 I decided to switch from teaching economics to doing economics. Since then I have earned my living as an investment advisor to individuals and trustees of pension plans.

In *The Unbeatable Market* you'll encounter the contrasting views of two communities—academia and Wall Street. As one of a relatively small number of people who have earned a living in both these cultures, I have learned firsthand how each of them operates and perceives the financial world. I've experienced the frustrations of attempting to construct prudent investment portfolios using actively managed mutual funds.

For most of the time since I stopped teaching, I have written either weekly or monthly columns in local periodicals. The columns have covered a wide variety of financial topics, all viewed from an economist's perspective. One of my favorite challenges is making economics accessible and useful to non-economists. Economic theory contains surprisingly practical lessons on how the world really works. Few people realize how much economics can help in resolving life's everyday challenges.

Efficiency is crucial.

The unifying theme of this book is efficiency—both your efficiency as an investor and the efficiency of securities markets. Your pursuit of efficiency is an essential part of making the right choices for the right reasons and achieving financial peace of mind.

A vital part of being good at anything is being efficient. As you improve at any endeavor, an increasing percentage of your effort goes toward accomplishing your objective. As you become more skillful in an activity—your profession, tennis, cooking, gardening, skiing, for example—you waste less effort. A skillful golfer hits the ball farther and straighter than an unskillful golfer and does so with the same or even less exertion. Skill and knowledge lead inevitably to increased efficiency. If doing it right is your goal, efficiency has to be considered. Describing someone as efficient is a true compliment.

Investment efficiency is about higher, more dependable rates of return, reduced risk exposure, liberated time, simplified financial affairs, reduced frustration levels, and greater confidence in making investment choices. Adopting an efficient approach to investing will provide you with a real opportunity for financial peace of mind. This book is based on the assumption that investing is not your hobby and that you would like to spend no more time than is necessary managing your finances. It will save you far more time than it takes to read.

Efficiency is a familiar word. It reflects the relationship between input and output, between costs and benefits. An efficient solution moves you farthest in your intended direction, or alternatively, accomplishes your objectives at the lowest cost. If your objectives are important and worthwhile, anything that makes you more effective in achieving them must be, too.

Suppose retirement is your primary investment objective. If you begin working at age 20, retire at age 65, and die at age 85, you will spend 30 percent of your adult life in retirement. During your accumulation years, say from age 30 to 65, the rate of growth you achieve on your investments will have a profound impact on your comfort and peace of mind during retirement, to say nothing of the stress you experience as the growth is or is not occurring. If the growth rate is sufficient, you may find you can retire early. Increasing your skill, efficiency, and understanding as an investor is an endeavor with a high rate of return and something that can have life-altering effects. On the other hand, improving your efficiency at loading your dishwasher or mowing your lawn would have relatively modest payoffs.

Investors face a number of constraints and dilemmas.

Lack of time—In the short run this results from the countless demands on a person's time. Almost everyone feels frustrated about a shortage of time. In the longer run, the problem is the limited amount of time we all have between the present and when we would like to be able to retire. If we had a hundred years to accumulate money for 30 years of retirement, investing would be a cinch and efficiency wouldn't much matter.

Information overload—We live in the Information Age, but the amount of information we're exposed to overwhelms our capacity to make sense of it or use it efficiently. It's not easy deciding which information we need to hear and which we can ignore. The problem of overabundance is severely aggravated by the fact that the information we receive is often contradictory, inconsistent, and self-serving. Wall Street and the media are seeming towers of babble, emitting far more noise than information. Investors may be unable to separate the signal from the static. There is no shortage of information—the problem is making sense of it and using the best of what's available. Information is simultaneously vital and confounding. A key purpose of this book is to help investors understand what information is and how to tell whether it is useful or useless. Information has become cheap, but wisdom and insight are still priceless.

Lack of a coherent strategy—Investing involves making choices, but few investors have a system for doing so and no system for distinguishing between what works and what does not. This leads to errors, inconsistency, and unnecessary stress when making choices. Valuable time is wasted going down blind alleys and following pursuits with low probabilities of success.

Poor grasp of the fundamentals—Relatively little effort has been made to provide investors with a basic understanding of how securities markets work or in helping them understand investment basics, such as risk or how to diversify. Knowledge of the fundamentals is ultimately the best self-defense against the misleading and counterproductive hype emanating from Wall Street and the media.

Dealing with these dilemmas is one of the paths to efficiency. Efficiency is not something that comes automatically. If it did, there would be no need for golf, tennis, or ski instructors (and especially no need for economists).

The key to investment success is understanding investment realities.

The more clearly we see the reality of the world, the better equipped we are to deal with the world...Our view of reality is like a map with which to negotiate the terrain of life. If the map is true and accurate,

we will generally know where we are, and if we know where we want to go, we will generally know how to get there. If the map is false and inaccurate, we generally will be lost. While this is obvious, it is something that most people to a greater or lesser degree choose to ignore.
Scott Peck, *The Road Less Traveled*

A fundamental premise of this book is that to be efficient you have to work with reality rather than against it. Knowledge of reality helps identify what's possible and what isn't, what works and what doesn't. Attempting the impossible or highly improbable is one of the world's leading time wasters. It acts like a black hole, capable of absorbing unlimited amounts of time and energy.

The psychiatrist and author, Scott Peck, has said that a mentally healthy person faces reality no matter what the costs and a mentally unhealthy person denies reality no matter what the costs. Pretty much the same distinction could be made in regard to the financially healthy investor. Fortunately, at least in the investment realm of life, facing reality is ultimately much easier than living in denial.

But how can you know reality? It doesn't speak to us in simple, unambiguous terms. Reality can never be known with certainty, but we can get closest to it by way of the scientific method.

There are two broad schools of thought on the behavior of securities markets. We'll call them the Wall Street model and the academic model. Although no mortal can say positively which of these models more accurately describes reality, the theory and evidence is overwhelmingly on the side of the academic model. The relative strength of the evidence is in the neighborhood of a thousand to one.

Academia is often perceived as being disconnected from reality and seen as life in an ivory tower. Ironically, at least in the investment arena, academia is far better grounded in fact.

The true value of academic research isn't that really smart guys who understand things better than we ever will come up with it—the true value is that it identifies what we need to focus on to succeed, and helps us to understand it. Investment theory simplifies things that are otherwise shrouded in mystery and confusion.
Eugene Fama Jr. "Factors in Practice,"
DFA newsletter, November 2001

Wall Street does not want you to know the academic model and especially doesn't want you to believe it. The leading players in the financial services industry have a vested interest in your ignorance. Even when it seems the players are trying to inform you, what they end up doing is beguiling you. Wall Street does its best to follow W.C. Fields' advice, "Never smarten up a chump." That also reflects their opinion of their clients.

Beating the market isn't nearly as easy as you've been led to believe.

Beating the market is the approach adopted by the vast majority of books, articles, and TV shows on investing. Here is a partial list of some of the best-selling investment titles during the past decade:

- *Beating the Street*
- *Outperforming the Market: Everyone's Guide to High-Profit, Low-Risk Investing*
- *Trouncing the Dow*
- *Beating the Dow*
- *100 Ways to Beat the Market*
- *The Motley Fool Investment Guide: How the Fool Beats Wall Street's Wisemen and How You Can, Too*
- *The Unemotional Investor: Simple Systems for Beating the Market*
- *Contrarian Investment Strategies: The Next Generation: Beat the Market by Going Against the Crowd*
- *The Beardstown Ladies Common-Sense Investment Guide: How We Beat the Stock Market and You Can, Too*

Despite claims of these and similar books, giving up the futile pursuit of beating the market is the surest way to increase your investment efficiency and enhance your financial peace of mind. You expend less effort and make more money. Increased efficiency is an attainable goal. Consistently beating the market is not. Furthermore, beating the market is not a requirement for achieving satisfactory long-term rates of return.

For the past 75 years the aggregate U.S. stock market has generated rates of return averaging between ten and twelve percent. At a ten percent rate of return your money doubles in a little over seven years, and quadruples in less than 15 years. As you will see, attempting to exceed market rates will decrease the probability that you will do as well as the market, and add a painful amount of additional risk.

Besides holding out the false promise of beating the market, another common deficiency of most investment books is that they provide virtually no third-party confirmation that the strategies they advocate actually work. Presumably, the authors believe their strategies will work, but that by itself means practically nothing in the context of basic, scientific protocol. In essence, they say, "Believe this because I believe this. Trust me." Or, "Because this strategy worked for me, it will work for you." That's definitely not enough. You should expect more and demand more.

Have active managers defined what it means to beat the market?

Beat-the-market hopefuls rarely say what they mean by "beating the market." Inconspicuously absent from all the books listed above is any specific definition.

Three conditions must be fulfilled before you can legitimately claim to have beaten the market:
1. Achieving an excess return relative to a passive, indexing approach.
2. Doing so with the same or lower risk exposure relative to a passive, indexing approach. (These first two conditions are simply to assure apples-to-apples comparisons.)
3. Doing so by way of skill, not luck. (A strategy based on luck is not a strategy. Luck is not something you can rely on or control in the future, and investing is about the future.)

A lot more people think they beat the market than actually do, mainly because of the simplistic, vague, and slipshod way it has been defined. If you don't define your terms, anything goes. Most people, even most of the professional money managers, think they've beaten the market if they fulfill the first condition. You will see later why that is grossly inadequate. The people who work in the active investment industry devote their lives to an objective that they haven't even bothered to define.

Let evidence be the arbiter.

Insistence on evidence is a fundamental recommendation of this book. Why is that so important? Look at it this way—if you don't insist on evidence, what are your alternatives?

The books listed previously advocate a number of different strategies. How can you decide which, if any, are valid? Should you believe them all? Since the advice in one book is inconsistent and contradictory to that in other books, it's not possible to believe every one of them.

Of course, you could try out all the strategies advocated in the various books. Alternatively, you could conduct your own experiments and develop your own strategy. I seriously doubt, however, that you have the time or money to do either of those things. It takes many years to allow a strategy to run its course and evaluate the results. Even if you had enough wealth to do the experiments, you will not live long enough to determine whether they are valid, at least with any degree of confidence. More importantly, if the strategy is wrong, you could lose your hard-earned money, as most of the so-called "day traders" have done. Fortunately, it's not necessary to go this route. More than enough research has been done, and it's more efficient to learn from the mistakes of others than your own. Let others suffer the losses while you learn from their hard-earned lessons.

The movie *Jerry McGuire* made famous the demand, "Show me the money." Whenever someone tells you about a surefire investment strategy, make this demand: "Show me the evidence." If you don't adopt the evidence standard, Wall Street will continue to have its way with you.

Evidence is the prime component of the "scientific method," which also entails "the systematic pursuit of knowledge involving the recognition and formulation of a problem, the collection of data through observation and experiment, and formulation and testing of hypotheses." (*Merriam-Webster's Collegiate Dictionary*) The "formulation and testing of hypotheses" is an aspect of the scientific method often overlooked, but is absolutely essential. You'll see why.

Science has given us longer life spans and greater comfort while profoundly expanding our knowledge of the world around us. However, it's not always easy to collect, quantify, and evaluate the evidence good science requires. It becomes even more difficult when we attempt to apply the scientific method to perplexing questions such as the following: What are the best techniques for raising children? What is justice? What's the best way to achieve happiness? But the scientific method can shed light even on riddles such as these.

The amount of data, evidence, theory, and research that can be applied to investment questions is immense. Financial transactions are, by their very nature, quantifiable, making it possible to analyze them statistically. So the scientific method is—or should be—particularly useful to investors.

> *Of all economic time series, the history of security prices, both individual and aggregate, has probably been most widely and intensively studied.*
>
> Harry V. Roberts, *The Random Character of Stock Market Prices*, Paul Cootner, ed.

I have not made any formal comparisons, but I suspect that over these twenty years, few, if any, hypotheses in economic theory have received as much empirical attention as the efficient market hypothesis.

Robert Merton, "On the Current State of the Stock Market Rationality Hypothesis," *Macroeconomics and Finance*, Stanley Fischer, ed.

Are securities markets efficient?

In order to be a well-informed and effective investor, you absolutely must address the following question: Are securities markets efficient? Investors rarely consider this all-important issue, but you must do so. The way you answer this question will profoundly affect nearly all your investment decisions.

Market efficiency is referred to formally as the *Efficient Market Hypothesis* or EMH. The EMH is a fundamental conclusion derived by means of the scientific method. An awareness and understanding of this theory can be enormously beneficial to you, and as you will see, the practical lessons derived from the EMH amount to good news for investors.

If these startling hypotheses are true, their practical importance is enormous. One cannot assert for certain whether these hypotheses are true or not, but one can confidently assert that the evidence regarding their validity is sufficiently persuasive so that all informed investors should be fully aware of the hypotheses themselves, the evidence regarding their validity, and their implications for investors.

James Lorie and Mary Hamilton,
The Stock Market: Theories and Evidence

The conclusion you reach on market efficiency is a critical fork in the road. If securities markets are efficient, then trying to beat the market is futile and you should employ passive management. Only if you think that markets are inefficient should you attempt to beat them. Inefficiencies offer the only hope for excess returns.

A primary purpose of this book is to make the EMH accessible to investors and investment advisors. This entails clearly defining what the EMH is (and what it isn't) as well as making the logic and evidence underlying it explicit and intelligible. If you don't understand the EMH, you probably won't believe it. On the other hand, if you do understand it, you will likely believe it.

Understand the EMH and you'll have fresh insight into how stock markets operate. You'll answer nagging investment questions and unravel market mysteries. And you'll take a major step toward achieving efficiency as an investor.

The EMH represents state-of-the-art research into securities markets. The 1990 Nobel prize for Economic Science was awarded to three economists for their contributions related to Modern Portfolio Theory, of which the EMH is a central element.

> *There is no other proposition in economics that has more solid empirical evidence supporting it than the Efficient Market Hypothesis...In the literature of finance, accounting, and the economics of uncertainty, the EMH is accepted as a fact of life.*
>
> Michael C. Jensen, "Some Anomalous Evidence Regarding Market Efficiency," *Journal of Financial Economics*, June/September, 1978

The Efficient Market Hypothesis is surprisingly simple and concise, at least on the surface. It says that *stock prices promptly reflect all available information*. Even if you accept that assertion, a legitimate question you might ask is, "So what?" Read on, and you'll be amazed at how widespread and significant the implications of that simple assertion can be.

Why does market efficiency matter?

For Wall Street, and especially the mutual fund industry, the implications of the EMH are devastating. Vast amounts of time, energy, and expense hinge on whether or not stock prices fully reflect available information, whether or not stocks are efficiently priced.

Usually, attempts to beat the market follow either one or both of two general methodologies: "securities selection" and "market timing." The success of these strategies depends on the existence of mis-priced securities and on the ability of investors to economically identify them. According to the EMH, however, mis-priced securities either do not exist or, if they do, cannot be identified in a cost-efficient manner. If this is true, any attempt to beat the market is an exercise in futility.

Active management or passive management?

Advocates of beat-the-market strategies subscribe to one or another variation of what's known as "active management." The alternative

DILBERT reprinted by permission of United Feature Syndicate, Inc.

approach is "passive management," and its objective is to duplicate market rates of return.

Active management or passive management? The question is a controversial one and a central issue in the investment world. Active management has no shortage of advocates. Their dogged adherence to a strategy that is at odds with vast amounts of empirical evidence is an interesting story in itself. Their error stems from a combination of faith, hope, arrogance, self-preservation, and the love of a challenge. The fact is, however, that if the EMH is correct, hundreds of thousands of people on Wall Street are getting paid to chase rainbows. Wishful thinking is Wall Street's stock-in-trade.

Nevertheless, as an economist I have to admit that Wall Street is behaving rationally. As Nobel laureate Paul Samuelson has observed, "This message (that attempting to beat the market is futile) can never be sold on Wall Street because it is in effect telling stock analysts to drop dead." The people on Wall Street simply can't imagine how they would make a living if they weren't trying to beat the market. But that's their problem, not yours. It's not your responsibility to provide livelihoods for stock analysts. What's rational on Wall Street isn't usually aligned with the best interests of you as an investor.

On balance, however, even actively managed funds have benefited investors. The availability of mutual funds is one of the greatest things ever to happen to the investing public. Mutual funds have made accessible to virtually all investors diversified, low-cost portfolios previously available only to the very wealthy. Actively managed mutual funds are generally superior to actively managed portfolios of individual stocks. It's past time, however, to move on to a far superior alternative— passively managed index funds. Actively managed funds have been rendered obsolete.

Are you trying to beat the market?

This book is intended to help you discover what is in your best interest as an investor. To determine that, you'll have to answer the question we asked at the beginning of this chapter: Should I attempt to beat the market? Although this question is a critical one for investors, it is not often asked. Wall Street rarely asks the question because they know the answer is unlikely to favor them. But it is essential that you ask it and answer it to your own satisfaction. The fact is you may not even be aware of whether or not you're trying to beat the market.

Here's the deal. If you have stock market-related investments and you're not investing in passively managed index funds, you are trying to beat the market. Every other stock market-related investment is designed to beat the market. So now that you know, what, if anything, should you do about it?

The first order of business is to equip you with the basic tools you'll need to understand how securities markets work. That's the objective of the next three chapters. Although I usually resist making predictions, I predict you will find the endeavor surprisingly enjoyable.

CHAPTER 2

Market Economics: Step One in Understanding the Stock Market

To see a World in a Grain of Sand,
And a Heaven in a Wild flower,
Hold Infinity in the palm of your hand,
And Eternity in an hour.

William Blake

Securities markets do not exist separately from the rest of the economy, nor do they operate according to their own separate set of economic principles. To understand securities markets, one needs to grasp the fundamental principles of a market economy and how it operates. As with any topic, seeing securities markets in their overall context will help you gain valuable understanding and perspective.

That's why, even though this is a book about investing money, you first need to make a small investment of a different type: your time. An investment is an outlay you make in the present in return for something providing a flow of benefits in the future. Eating corn is consumption; planting corn is investing. What you will learn in the next few pages will pay dividends in the form of usable information. It will increase your efficiency as you read the rest of this book and help you understand and evaluate other books and articles on investing.

19

Learning the fundamental principles of economics will make the world of investing much clearer to you. An awareness of basic economics is essential to understanding the investment world. Much of the misinformation and many of the myths about securities markets stem from a general lack of economic literacy. Make yourself familiar with these concepts and you will soon know more than the so-called experts.

This process requires no previous formal study of economics. However, if you have taken economics courses, you may consider this chapter a review. No one remembers everything learned in class, so the review will be worthwhile even if you have studied economics. Also, you may find that I have a different way of explaining things than the professor you had in school. Since our goal here is to make you a better-informed, more successful investor, we'll avoid exhaustive explanations and concentrate instead on those economic concepts most useful in understanding how securities markets operate.

Because you live in and interact with a free-market economy, you are at least intuitively aware of the dynamic forces that drive it: voluntary exchange, the price system, supply and demand, competition, efficiency, and incentives. Some of these we tend to take for granted, but all have important roles to play in our amazingly efficient economy.

This is going to be a fairly quick overview, so don't worry if you don't get it right away. The relevance of all the points covered may not be immediately obvious. All of the principles discussed in this chapter will be applied throughout the book, and as we put them to use, they will become clearer to you. It's a two-way street: the principles will help you understand the issues, and addressing the issues will make the principles more meaningful.

What is a market economy?

The way market economies work was first articulated in 1776 by Adam Smith in his classic: *An Inquiry Into the Nature and Causes of the Wealth of Nations*. Since that time mainstream economics has followed in the tradition of the *Wealth of Nations*, but some definitions have evolved over the years. Here is what economists now mean when they talk about a market economy:

> *An economic system in which decisions about the allocation of resources and production are made on the basis of prices generated by voluntary exchanges between producers, consumers, workers, and owners of*

factors of production. Decision making in such an economy is decentralized—i.e., decisions are made independently by groups and individuals in the economy rather than by central planners. Market economies usually also involve a system of private ownership of the means of production—i.e., they are capitalist or free enterprise economies.

MIT Dictionary of
Modern Economics (4th ed.)

I urge you to read this definition two or three times. The essence of what we usually refer to as a free market economy is summarized in two words: voluntary exchange. In fact, a "voluntary exchange economy" might be a better, more descriptive term than a "market economy." As we shall see, a market is actually more of a means than an end, and its main purpose is to facilitate voluntary exchange.

The concept of voluntary exchange has a number of profound implications.

Both words in the phrase "voluntary exchange" are crucial. A gift is voluntary, but it is not an exchange in the usual sense. Giving up one thing in exchange for another is fundamental to most free-market activity, and as we shall see, the fact that the exchange is voluntary has a number of profound implications.

Even in a market economy, not all economic interrelationships rely on voluntary exchange. Taxes are the most obvious example of involuntary exchange. Even if you think you get something in exchange for your taxes, paying them is not voluntary. Nevertheless, our economy is predominantly one of voluntary exchange.

If I buy a car from you, a voluntary exchange has taken place. An amazing thing about such a voluntary exchange is that we will both feel we have improved our respective situations. We both feel we have achieved a net improvement in our well being. In fact, that is a necessary aspect of voluntary exchange. It provides the motivation or incentive for the exchange to happen.

Let's say that we settle on a price of $5,000. You trade a car for money; I trade money for a car. You and I have different objectives and priorities. You value the money more than the car, so you end up better off. I value the car more than the money, so I also end up better off. Neither of us has experienced a pure improvement in our situations—I didn't get a free car, and you didn't get money for nothing.

Since each voluntary exchange causes a net improvement for the participants, the more voluntary exchange that takes place, the better off we all are. Anything that facilitates voluntary exchange is good for virtually everyone who participates in the economy. Some of the central features we see in the economy gain their importance from the role they play in facilitating voluntary exchange. Three particularly important examples are markets, money, and flexible prices.

A market is any arrangement that allows buyers and sellers to interact.

The *MIT Dictionary of Modern Economics* (4th ed.) defines a market as follows: "Generally, any context in which the sale and purchase of goods and services takes place. There need be no physical entity corresponding to a market—it may, for example, consist of the network of telecommunications across the world on which, say, shares are traded."

The Internet is an example of just such an arrangement, and this innovative new market has dramatically expanded the ways buyers and sellers connect. The Internet has greatly facilitated voluntary exchange and access to information. For instance, eBay allows sellers to search efficiently for buyers and buyers to search efficiently for sellers. Anything that reduces the cost of information or reduces search costs improves the overall efficiency of the economy. The basic purpose of this book is to reduce the cost of information about financial economics.

An economy is an exceedingly complex system composed of millions of participants whose objectives are frequently at odds with one another. Any such system must include some mechanism of checks and balances. By its very nature, voluntary exchange is the single most important check and balance mechanism in a free-market economy.

Voluntary exchange limits the power other people in the economy have over you. General Motors, as big and powerful as it is, cannot coerce you to buy its cars. If GM wants your money, it must offer you a car that is sufficiently appealing and competitively priced to entice you to buy it rather than the numerous other alternatives available to you, and that means not just other cars, but all alternatives.

Within the context of voluntary exchange, one person's power over another is inherently limited, especially when you have a variety of choices. If you have something I want, I must give you something you want. Voluntary exchange tends to create a balance of power. It limits one person's power over another.

Windmill fantails: a simple mechanical example of an equilibrium system.

My favorite example of an automatic check-and-balance mechanism is a simple device you have probably seen in action—the fantail on a windmill. Up until a few decades ago, small farms and ranches made widespread use of windmills to pump water. The wind rotated an elevated fan, which in turn, pumped water from the ground.

To make the most efficient use of the available breezes, the fan is allowed to swivel freely so that it always faces the wind. The key piece of equipment that makes this possible is the fantail, a flat piece of sheet metal protruding from the back of the fan. Mounted perpendicular to the fan itself, the fantail automatically points the blades directly into the face of the oncoming wind. That alignment allows the fan to take the maximum energy from the wind.

The fantail assures that the "equilibrium" position for the windmill is in the direction maximizing its power output. Only when it is parallel to the direction of the wind is the pressure equalized on both sides of the fantail. If there is a difference of pressure on the two sides of the fantail and if the windmill can swivel, it will do so until there is no difference in pressure. In that position there is a balance of forces which creates a position of rest. If you know the direction of the wind, you can predict the direction the windmill will face. That's because only when the fantail is parallel to the direction of the wind will it be in equilibrium. Because the windmill can rotate, it is a dynamic equilibrium system.

Allen Matheson

Equilibrium analysis is an especially useful and frequently applied tool of economic theory. A market economy is fundamentally an equilibrium system. All the accepted theories of how the stock market works are variations of equilibrium models.

Note that the reason the windmill has wind from which to take energy is also a question of equilibrium. The wind blows because there's a disequilibrium in the atmosphere—a difference in air pressure between two areas. Wind is the atmosphere's way of reestablishing equilibrium. When there's no disequilibrium, there's no wind. If you know the relative barometric pressures in two areas, you can predict the direction and velocity of the wind within some margin of error.

> The fantail of a windmill is an ingenious, efficient, and elegant device. It accomplishes its purpose nearly 100 percent of the time with little or no outside intervention or oversight. The same is true of checks and balances so crucial to a decentralized market economy—voluntary exchange, the profit mechanism, and competition, for example. Each of these systems serves to keep the economy headed in the most efficient direction. The foremost reason centralized economies fail is that they have virtually no automatic systems to maintain equilibrium.

Most decisions are made at the fringes of the economy.

Voluntary exchange is also intertwined with another characteristic that distinguishes a free market economy—decision-making is decentralized. Voluntary exchange and decentralized decision making are closely connected.

The decisions are made at the edges of the economy. You, not a central planner, decide if you will spend your money on a dishwasher or a computer. You are the one who is most aware of your preferences and priorities. It makes sense that, since you are the one in possession of critical information, you should be the one who makes the choices. The tradeoffs we make with ourselves—a computer rather than a dishwasher, for example—are a kind of internal voluntary exchange.

The number of personal computers produced and sold each year is determined by millions of consumers and hundreds of producers. The consumers aren't forced to buy, the producers aren't forced to produce, and the retailers aren't forced to connect the two groups. All these participants in the economy have voluntarily chosen these actions from a vast array of alternatives.

That you can make your own choices regarding how to invest your money is an example of decentralized decision making. You voluntarily purchased this book (I'm glad you did) and you are voluntarily reading it.

Amazingly, the actions of millions of producers, consumers, workers, and owners somehow fit together. A rough balance is maintained between production and consumption of computers. Producers are able to get a vast array of raw materials, machinery, and parts from suppliers pretty much as they need them, with few gaps in availability. Yet no one has to centrally coordinate all these intricate and delicate interconnections and interrelationships. Ironically, attempts to consciously coordinate the economy are almost always counterproductive and often result in chaos.

The poorest performing economies around the world—Cuba and North Korea, for example—are centrally planned.

How well all these countless decisions by millions of people stay coordinated is one of the most phenomenal aspects of a decentralized market economy. Because it works so well, most people take it for granted and never give it any thought. However, the fact that it's taken for granted is one of the perennial frustrations of economics professors.

Money makes voluntary exchange vastly more efficient.

Another economic feature that contributes immensely to voluntary exchange is money. By providing a reliable medium of exchange, money reduces the costs of voluntary exchange transactions. Money also contributes by acting as both a standard and store of value.

Without money, the only kind of voluntary exchange would be barter. Suppose the reason you were selling your used car is that you wanted a computer. Without money to serve as a go-between, you would have to find someone who both owned a computer he was willing to trade and who also wanted a car. Finding such "coincidences of wants" would be costly and time consuming. Voluntary exchange would be cut to a tiny fraction of its current level, and we would all be worse off.

Money also makes it possible to quantify transactions with a common yardstick. Because voluntary exchanges are made through the medium of money and expressed in standard units such as dollars or yen, we can compare the relative values of a whole universe of goods and services. They say you can't compare apples and oranges, but for practical purposes money allows us to do just that. Keep in mind, however, that monetary prices do not tell us the absolute value of anything.

The price system is primarily responsible for the extraordinary coordination that occurs in a market economy.

The relative values of apples and oranges expressed in terms of dollars serve as a minor example of another important feature of a market economy—something economists refer to as the price system. Among other things, the price system reflects the terms of trade or the bargains struck between people making voluntary exchanges.

The price you and I settle on for the used car is a compromise. I would like to pay less than $5,000; you would like to receive more. The $5,000 price we settle on is a balance point between opposing objectives. It's high enough to make you willing to sell, but low enough to make me willing to buy. If that compromise is unacceptable to either of us, the exchange will not take place. Remember, we are talking about voluntary exchange.

The economics courses contributing most to an understanding of how an economy actually operates are the ones focused on price theory or what's referred to as microeconomics. This is because the price system is absolutely critical and, more than any other economic mechanism, is responsible for the almost miraculous coordination that occurs in a free-market economy. Remember the market economy definition quoted earlier in this chapter: "an economic system in which decisions about the allocation of resources and production are made on the basis of prices...."

Consider the all-important role of prices in the dissemination of information. We have been reminded repeatedly that we live in the "Information Age." Although it's not often recognized as such, the price system is an incredibly effective and sophisticated information medium. Information is a recurring theme throughout this book, especially in regard to the connection between information and prices.

Our economic lives involve making choices, and prices give us crucial information about the costs and benefits of choices we encounter continuously. For example, what combination of land, machinery, labor, water, and fertilizer should a farmer use in growing his crops? To a degree these factors of production can be substituted one for another. For example, different amounts of wheat can be grown on an acre of land by adding water or fertilizer. There are an infinite number of combinations that could be used to achieve a given level of output. But what's the best, most economical, and efficient combination?

The relative prices of land, machinery, labor, water, and fertilizer provide the farmer with both the information and the incentive to make efficient choices. If the prices he pays accurately reflect the relative scarcities of the factors, the farmer will be led to efficient choices serving both his and the overall economy's best interests.

If the price of fertilizer is high, this sends the farmer a clear message: "This is a relatively scarce resource—economize on its use." Furthermore, it isn't just a message; it's a combination of message and incentive, both a carrot and a stick. The farmer is told: "Excessive use of this resource will be hazardous to your net income." It's a message that comes packaged with a natural consequence, an incentive to react appropriately to the message.

Most likely, the farmer will attempt to maximize the difference between the costs of production and the sale price of his product. His profits will depend on such things as his competition and his abilities. If he wants to produce 1,000 bushels of wheat, both his and the economy's best interest will be served if he uses the combination of resources with the lowest cost.

F. A. Hayek, in "The Use of Knowledge in Society," states: "We must look at the price system as such a system for communicating information. The most significant fact about this system is the economy of knowledge with which it operates or how little the individual participants need to know in order to be able to take the right action."

Since decisions are made primarily at the edges rather than the center, it is critical that the right information and incentives are provided to the millions of decision makers. The efficiency of the entire economy is fundamentally dependent upon the effectiveness of the price system.

Allowing prices to be flexible and uncontrolled increases the accuracy of the information they convey and, therefore, the effectiveness of the price system. Like the wind, conditions in an economy are ever changing, and flexible prices are analogous to a windmill's ability to rotate and adapt to changing wind conditions.

Einstein was right—everything is relative.

Regarding the price system, it is important to bear in mind that what matters are relative prices. Relative prices are what actually affect our behavior and our choices.

If all prices were doubled or multiplied ten or even a hundred times, there's no reason to think we would see significant changes in behavior— assuming a corresponding increase in the money supply. If, however, the price of a particular item doubles and others stay the same, you will almost certainly see changes in people's behavior and the choices they make.

Samuel Baily, in *A Critical Dissertation on Value*, wrote: "As we cannot speak of the distance of any object without implying some other object between which and the former this relation exists, so we cannot speak of the value of a commodity, but in reference to another commodity compared with it. A thing cannot be valuable without reference to another thing any more than a thing can be distant in itself without reference to another thing."

Einstein was right, of course—everything is relative. Without question, the price system is a relative phenomenon—the price of machinery relative to labor, the exchange rate between dollars and yen, the price of one stock relative to another, and the price of stocks relative to bonds. These relative values are what matter in evaluating alternatives and making choices.

The main tools used in the analysis of the price system are the concepts known as supply and demand.

Early editions of Paul Samuelson's *Economics* textbook included the anonymous quote, "You can make a parrot into a learned political economist—all he must learn are two words—supply and demand." Many a truth is spoken in jest.

The supply of a product tends to be positively associated with its price. The higher the price, the more of the product will be placed on the market (other considerations being equal). Demand for a product tends to be negatively or inversely related to price. In fact, some economists feel that the negatively sloped demand curve is the very crux of economic behavior. Some see this relationship as more a law than a theory.

The supply curve reflects the fact that at higher prices there is an increased willingness to produce and sell the product. Higher prices give sellers increased incentives to exchange their goods for money. The demand curve reflects the fact that, as the price rises, less of the product is purchased. Higher prices give buyers the incentive to buy less or switch to substitutes.

Figure 2-1

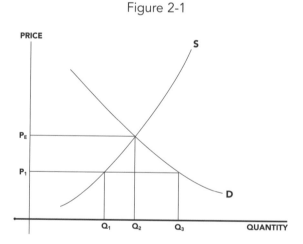

At price P_1, the quantity buyers would like to purchase is Q_2, but at that price sellers are only willing to sell Q_1. The gap between Q_1 and Q_2 is a shortage. If prices are flexible, they will tend to rise. P_e is the equilibrium price that brings into balance quantity supplied with quantity demanded. Higher prices result in surpluses (frustrated sellers) and lower prices result in shortages (frustrated buyers).

The concepts of supply and demand are especially useful when considered together. The intersection of the supply and demand curves identifies what is termed an "equilibrium price." This is the price at which quantity supplied equals quantity demanded.

The significance of an equilibrium price stems from the fact that any price other than the equilibrium price create problems that can be extremely harmful to an economy. Other prices create either shortages or surpluses of the good in question, and either of those situations creates costly inefficiencies.

If prices are flexible and uncontrolled, they will automatically tend toward equilibrium. For example, if there are a lot of homes for sale where you live, the asking prices are probably too high relative to the demand. Asking prices are too high for the quantity demanded to strike a balance with the quantity supplied. Prices will have to drop before enough sales can occur.

The above situation is sometimes described as a buyers' market. When there is an excess supply, buyers can afford to get choosy. They will tend to offer less than the asking price. Sellers will see their houses staying on the market for extended periods, and will eventually have little choice other than to reduce their asking prices.

Prices either above or below an equilibrium price result in short-circuited voluntary exchange. For example, a price lower than the equilibrium price means that there are frustrated buyers. At that price, there are more willing buyers than willing sellers. There are buyers wanting to trade money for the product but are unable to do so. Flexible prices, therefore, are another critical player in the process of voluntary exchange.

The existence of a shortage or surplus does not constitute an equilibrium condition. The *MIT Dictionary of Economics* defines equilibrium as: "A term borrowed from physics to describe a situation in which economic agents or aggregates of economic agents such as markets have no incentive to change their economic behavior." Whenever a shortage or surplus exists, someone will be unhappy enough to change prices and have an incentive to change his economic behavior.

A question that might occur to you is this: Are equilibrium prices determined on a supply-and-demand basis best for the economy? From an economic perspective, prices are right when they lead to the most efficient allocation of resources, to the greatest wealth creation possible from a given resource base, level of technology, and stock of capital. A well-structured price system maximizes the economy's productivity. The general conclusion of economic analysis is that supply-and-demand prices do in fact result in economic efficiency. The Nobel Prize for Economics in 1985 was awarded to Gerard Dubreau for his elegant mathematical proof of that conclusion.

Voluntary exchange makes specialization possible.

The *Wealth of Nations* opens with the statement, "The greatest improvement in the productive powers of labour, and the greater part of the skill, dexterity, and judgment with which it is any where directed, or applied, seems to have been the effects of the division of labour." The modern term for Smith's "division of labour" is specialization.

Without a highly evolved system of voluntary exchange, specialization would be impossible. If we couldn't trade our labor for a variety of goods and services, we would all have to be self-sufficient and so could not specialize. We could not, in other words, apply what Smith said accounts for "the greatest improvements in the productive powers of labour."

Incentives drive the economy.

According to the economist Steven Landsburg, "Most of economics can be summarized in four words: people respond to incentives." That may be an overstatement, but incentives definitely are an important aspect of economic behavior.

One of the most quoted passages of *The Wealth of Nations* is, "It is not from the benevolence of the butcher, the brewer, the baker, that we expect our dinner, but from their regard to their own interest. We address ourselves not to their humanity but to their self-love, and never talk to them of our own necessities but of their advantages."

Incentives are especially important in an economy relying on decentralized decision-making where all participants have their own unique priorities. If all of those self-determined actions have any hope of fitting together and if economic chaos is to be avoided, the incentive system has to be logical and internally consistent. The fact that such a large, complex, and decentralized system doesn't descend into chaos is a minor miracle.

The profit mechanism is the ultimate performance-based compensation structure.

The economic mechanism that most closely weds incentives with efficiency is the profit system. Profits represent the difference between a business's total revenue and its total costs.

In a fundamental sense, profits measure a business's efficiency. Profits reflect what the business's operation costs the economy relative to the value its operation adds to the economy.

The following question could be asked: Are a business's costs and benefits really a valid measure of society's costs and benefits? There is considerable justification for concluding the answer is yes. Remember, a business can only buy its supplies and raw materials by way of voluntary exchange, and it can only sell its products by way of voluntary exchange.

Because business owners have "rights to the residual," that is, they can take the profits home with them at the end of the year, there is a strong incentive to minimize costs and produce products desired by the public.

Profits are the primary reward for owning a business. There is not, of course, any assurance that profits will be positive, that revenues will exceed costs. The main reason companies go out of business is simply that they are losing money. In other words, their costs exceed their revenue and their profits are negative. Competition is the reality that makes it especially difficult to make and maintain profitability.

The profit system results in a kind of natural selection among businesses. While bankruptcies result in considerable pain for the parties involved, the alternative is the continued existence of companies costing the economy more than they're benefiting the economy. A major problem with government agencies, from the standpoint of economic efficiency, is there is no automatic mechanism for determining if their benefits justify the costs involved (since they do not have to rely on voluntary exchange). Private companies can continue to exist only if, through voluntary exchange, they can attract enough paying customers to cover and exceed their costs.

Competition puts the "voluntary" in voluntary exchange.

Competition is yet another important check-and-balance mechanism in a market economy. Competition is what forces sellers to keep quality high and prices low while giving you value for your dollar. Competition is what forces your employer to pay you what you're worth. If he doesn't and there is competition for your skills, you will seek employment elsewhere, or maybe even start your own business and go into competition against your old employer (sweet revenge). If there are several employers who need someone with your skills, none of them can take advantage of you. Conversely, if there are a number of people with your skills, none of you can take advantage of the potential employers.

The greater the degree of competition, the more power consumers have and the greater the degree of consumer sovereignty. As the late George Stigler, a Nobel laureate, said, "Competition is the patron saint of consumers." The greater the quantity and quality of your choices, the more meaningful is the term voluntary exchange. The more alternatives you have available, the less power any one of the providers will have over you. Competition does more every day to protect consumers than all the so-called consumer groups will ever do.

Competition also plays an important role in assuring efficiency. If you operate a business, you will not survive in a competitive environment if you allow your firm to become inefficient. Competition is a stern and unforgiving taskmaster.

At any given time there is an "equilibrium profit." It's essentially equal to the average profit prevailing in the economy. When profits in an industry are above average, that industry will tend to grow and attract new competitors, assuming the participants in the economy are seeking maximum profits. Below-average profit levels will tend to cause firms to contract in size or to exit that industry. The profit mechanism is a critical component of what Adam Smith described as an "invisible hand." Like the fantail on a windmill, it automatically directs resources where they will add the most value.

Excess profits attract new competitors, and increased competition squeezes out excess profits. It is a never-ending ebb and flow that occurs continuously in a dynamic economy.

Competition also plays a vital role in assuring the efficiency of the price system. Suppose you find a valuable antique chair at a garage sale that's priced at only $50. Since you happen to know something about antiques, you are aware that its actual value is more like $2,500. You have the ability to buy it for far below its real value because of a lack of competition from other buyers. If other antique collectors knew the item was for sale and had the opportunity to bid against you, the price would tend toward its full market value. This situation also illustrates the vital role of information in a voluntary exchange. In the garage sale example the seller failed to get the true value for the chair because of his lack of information.

The Internet allows consumers to seek the lowest price and firms to get quotes from more suppliers; it also reduces transaction costs and barriers to entry. In other words, it moves the economy closer to the textbook model of perfect competition, which assumes abundant information, many buyers and sellers, zero transaction costs, and no barriers to entry...Better informed markets should insure that resources are allocated to their most productive use.

"How Information Technology Can Boost Economic Growth," *The Economist*, September 21, 2000

If you have ever bought or sold a used car, you may well have referred the *Kelly Blue Book* that lists prices for most models and years (The *Kelly Blue Book* is now available over the internet at kbb.com). Did you ever wonder how the used-car prices listed are derived? The data are collected partly from car auctions. One of the interesting aspects of auctions is that there is at least a degree of competition among a number of possible buyers. The competition among those buyers minimizes the likelihood the car prices will be "too low." If there are a number of cars being auctioned, that will minimize the likelihood of prices being "too high."

The availability and cost of information are important aspects of how well markets work. The existence of resources such as the *Kelly Blue Book* is one of the things that decreases the cost of information and enhances the efficiency of markets. Having access to such information reduces the likelihood that a buyer will overpay for a used car, or that a seller will undercharge. The *Kelly Blue Book* is particularly interesting because it publishes information taken directly from the market, that is, prices derived from competitive, voluntary exchange auctions. It's an example of the market making itself more efficient.

Private property rights result in the decision maker bearing the costs and reaping the benefits of his decisions.

A critical legal institution of a market economy is private property rights. In a communistic system, there is no private property. In fact, the absence of private property could be described as the essence of communism.

Property rights are a prerequisite to the voluntary exchange process since what's being exchanged boils down to property rights. If I buy your car, what I'm buying is essentially the right to use the car, treat it as I like, and resell it when I wish.

It would be difficult to say whether private property rights or voluntary exchange lie closer to the heart of decentralized decision-making. Property rights are essentially the power to make choices regarding a particular piece of property or economic resource.

Private property rights are also a key component of the incentives operating in a market economy. Property rights imply that the owner reaps the benefits, or bears the consequences, of choices and actions taken with a given piece of property. One incentive you have for maintaining your home is that doing so will tend to increase its value should you ever want to sell it. In any economy, the resources that tend to get abused are the ones nobody directly owns, such as the air, rivers, public parks, and wildlife.

Private property rights allow the decision maker to experience the consequences, good and bad, of the choices he makes. Property rights are thus a critical element in the incentive system of a market economy.

The most interesting and challenging choices we face in our lives often are not simple yes or no questions but rather, questions of how much.

How long should you stay in school? How hard should you work at your job? How much should you spend on a new car? These are the kinds of questions addressed by something economists call "marginal analysis."

Marginal analysis is simply the measurement of incremental costs or benefits of some activity or product. Marginal costs (MC) and marginal benefits (MB) tend to have a characteristic pattern. In most cases, marginal costs rise and marginal benefits decline as you increase the amount of some activity. The first bite of food, for example, is more satisfying than the hundredth bite of food.

Let's say your pearl necklace breaks and the pearls spill onto the floor. It's fairly easy to find the first half of the pearls, but then they get progressively harder to find. Finding the last one might take as long to locate as it took to find the first 25. That's a simple but very typical example of the pattern of "increasing marginal costs."

The efficient quantity of something is reached when marginal costs equal marginal benefits. Up to that point, doing more of an activity adds more to your total benefits than it does to your total costs. When MC=MB, you've reached the point of maximum difference between total costs and total benefits. That's where net benefits are maximized. Going beyond that point adds more to costs than to benefits, and you lose ground rather than getting closer to your objectives. This is a fundamental and often used concept in economic analysis.

It's important to note that at the point where MC=MB, marginal benefits are almost always still positive. You would get increased benefits and pleasure by spending another $1,000 on a new car, but at some point the extra (positive) benefits are below the $1,000 extra cost.

Most people are familiar with the concept of diminishing returns. Usually, when they use that term, they are really talking about diminishing marginal returns.

Prices are determined at the margin.

A somewhat counterintuitive conclusion of economic analysis is that "prices are determined at the margin." To illustrate, assume you are a producer of an instructional video selling 10,000 units of your product for $12 each. Let's say you would like to increase your sales by 30 percent. Which of your buyers do you have to focus on in order to determine how much you need to reduce your price?

All of your current customers are willing to pay $12 per unit. If you want more buyers, you need to allure buyers who are not willing to pay that price. It's the marginal buyers, the wavering ones, who will determine your price. They think your product is worth somewhat less than $12.

Most of your customers probably think your product is worth considerably more than $12. The average value your product has in your customers' minds is probably well above $12. The pricing of your product, however, is determined not by average value, but rather by the marginal value. That's what's meant by prices being determined at the margin.

This is one of the numerous conclusions of economic theory that is counterintuitive. One important lesson of marginal analysis is that what happens at the edges of an activity often has more impact than what happens in the middle.

Off to the markets.

We have now reached the point where the marginal costs of additional time spent on basic economics is equal to the marginal benefits. (Even though I know more economics knowledge would do you a world of good and the marginal benefits are still positive.) It's time now to return to the major topic of the book—investing. The next chapter focuses on a basic description of securities markets.

Market economics summary.

- ► The main purpose of a market is to facilitate voluntary exchange.
- ► Since voluntary exchange causes a net improvement for the participants, the more voluntary exchange that takes place, the better off we are.
- ► Anything that reduces the cost of information or reduces search costs improves the overall efficiency of the economy.

- ▶ Within the context of voluntary exchange, one person's power is inherently limited, especially when you have a variety of choices.
- ▶ A market economy is fundamentally an equilibrium system.
- ▶ All the accepted theories of how the stock market works are variations of equilibrium models.
- ▶ By providing a reliable medium of exchange, money reduces the costs of voluntary exchange.
- ▶ Money makes it possible to quantify transactions with a common yardstick.
- ▶ More than any other economic mechanism, the price system is responsible for the almost miraculous coordination that occurs in a free-market economy.
- ▶ Our economic lives involve making choices, and prices give us crucial information about the costs and benefits of the choices we face.
- ▶ In a system where the decisions are made primarily at the edges rather than the center, it becomes critical that the right information and incentives are provided to the millions of decision makers.
- ▶ The price system is a relative phenomenon.
- ▶ Prices either above or below an equilibrium price result in short-circuited voluntary exchange.
- ▶ Flexible prices play a critical role in the process of voluntary exchange.
- ▶ A well-structured price system maximizes the economy's productivity.
- ▶ Without voluntary exchange, specialization would be impossible.
- ▶ The economic mechanism that most closely weds incentives with efficiency is the profit system.
- ▶ Property rights are a prerequisite to voluntary exchange since what's being exchanged amounts to property rights.
- ▶ Property rights allow the decision maker to experience the consequences, good or bad, of the choices he makes.
- ▶ Marginal analysis is simply the measurement of the incremental costs or benefits of some activity or product.
- ▶ The efficient quantity of something is reached when the marginal costs equal the marginal benefits.

CHAPTER 3

Critical Characteristics of the Stock Market

Wherever there are valuable commodities to be traded, there are incentives to develop markets to organize that trade more efficiently. In modern complex societies the securities markets are usually among the best organized and virtually always the largest in terms of value of sales. The prices of such securities are typically very sensitive, responsive to all events, both real and imagined, that cast light into the murky future.

The sensitivity of speculative prices and the huge volume of securities traded result in an impressive total of gains and losses in each trading day. The changes in wealth represented by these fluctuations have served as a constant lure to men who hope to earn fame and fortune by somehow unraveling the puzzle of price forecasting, who yearn for the discovery of a predictive formula which will unlock those gold-filled vaults.

Paul H. Cootner,
The Random Character of Stock Market Prices

Even though it is the topic of countless books, articles, and conversations, the stock market tends to perplex, confuse, and even intimidate people.

This may be due in part to a scarcity of basic descriptions. What exactly is the stock market?

While modern securities markets are sophisticated and highly evolved, they are in many ways like other markets. For instance, as is the case with the economy at large, the price system plays a critical role in stock markets. What's unusual about stock prices, however, is their extraordinary flexibility.

The differences between the stock market and other sub-markets within the economy are mostly differences of degree, but those differences have interesting implications. This chapter focuses on the distinguishing characteristics of securities markets.

What is a Security?

Step One in making sense of securities markets is to clarify the term "security." *Merriam-Webster's New Collegiate Dictionary* defines a security as "An evidence of debt or ownership." The textbook *Investments* (6th ed.), by William Sharpe, *et al*, defines a security as a "legal representation of the right to receive prospective future benefits under stated conditions."

A security is an intangible, a representation. It is also a kind of evidence. A bond is an evidence of debt; a stock is an evidence of ownership.

The title to your car is not your car; the deed to your home is not your home. The title can't be driven; the deed can't be lived in. The title and the deed are representations and evidence of who owns the car and house. Securities, deeds, and titles are all ways of associating specific property rights to specific individuals or institutions.

Ultimately, only people are capable of ownership. A corporation can be the registered owner of something, but the corporation, in turn, is owned by people.

How is buying a stock different from buying a car?

One way to grasp the distinguishing characteristics of stocks is to compare them to other assets we commonly encounter. Consider, for example, how buying 100 shares of IBM stock differs from buying a new car.

With anything you can experience directly, there is not as much need for communication or indirectly acquired information. When you buy a new car, it's relatively easy to evaluate what you're getting. You can see it, touch it, drive it, review the specifications, or read published road tests. The nature of the car, the flow of benefits it will provide you, its speed, and its size all remain basically the same over the time you own it. The car slowly wears out, of course, but even that can be forecast with a fairly high degree of confidence.

In contrast, when you buy shares of stock, the entity in question definitely does not remain constant. You become part owner of something that's similar to a living organism—an operating business that exists in and has to adapt to a dynamic environment. Consequently, determining the value of a stock and whether or not it is worth its price involves predictions. Making these predictions presents much more of a challenge than is usually the case when buying an automobile. Indeed, forecasting is one of the primary activities and challenges in the financial world. Most people buy stocks with the hope that they will change; that is, increase in value.

The very nature of investing makes prediction a necessity. The payoff for anything you consume is in the present. The payoff on an investment, however, occurs in the future.

The information contained in the price of a stock is an evaluation, not just of the company's current condition, but also of its likely condition in the future. You are buying the rights to future earnings, and those earnings are not likely to remain static. Consequently, there is no avoiding the need to forecast.

Future expectations are discounted in the current stock price. That's one reason news of seemingly little current importance often has a relatively large impact on the price of the stock. It's not just the immediate impact of what's implied by the information, but what it will mean in the long run. In an important sense, when you buy a stock, you're buying a prediction.

Consider also the difference between buying a stock and buying gold as an investment. Gold or similar precious metals pay no dividends or interest. Investing in such assets, therefore, is done in the hope that they will appreciate in value. Gold has been described as a barren asset. The fundamental nature of gold is fixed, especially in contrast to an operating company. The value of gold in the future will depend primarily on supply and demand. For example, in the 1890s the price of gold declined because of major discoveries in the Yukon and South Africa and the invention of the cyanide process which significantly lowered the costs of refinement.

You may have heard a commercial for a company selling gold coins that says, "There's only one investment that's been around for 5,000 years." I would ask the question my daughter sometimes asks me, "Your point is?" Gold has one of the longest histories in the investment world, but that history is not very impressive.

According to the data compiled by Jeremy Siegel in his book *Stocks for the Long Run*, the price of gold since 1800 has barely kept up with the rate of inflation. Its real rate of return (the gross rate minus inflation) has been zero for at least the past 200 years. By comparison, according to Siegel's data, the real rate of return for stocks has been 6.8 percent. A major factor in this discrepancy is that technological change has not been favorable to the price of gold. Technology has reduced the costs of discovering and refining gold—(leading to an increase in supply) and has made possible the development of substitute materials—(leading to a decrease in demand). On the other hand, technological change has been favorable to economic growth and, therefore, to stock prices (more about this in Chapter 10).

Also instructive is the comparison of stocks to bonds. Corporations issue both stocks and bonds, and these are the two primary components of many investment portfolios. Both meet the definition of a security. However, a stock is an evidence of ownership while a bond is an evidence of debt.

If you buy a $10,000, twenty-year bond that pays six percent interest, you know that you will receive $300 every six months for twenty years and then have your original investment returned to you, assuming the company issuing the security stays in existence. Even if the company has exceptional growth, you will not receive any more than what was originally agreed upon. For both the issuer and purchaser of the bond, there is little uncertainty. As you will see later, the cost of this reduced uncertainty is a reduced rate of return. Again according to Siegel's data, the real rate of return for bonds for the past 190 years has been 3.7 percent— a little more than half the return for stocks.

Bonds have a fixed maturity date and, therefore, a limited life span. Corporations, and therefore stocks, have a potentially limitless life span. Of course, corporations do occasionally go out of business, and in such instances, stockholders are the last in line in regard to claims on remaining assets.

Stock markets are one result of an essential feature of a market economy—private ownership of the means of production.

In the past several years, as a number of economies around the world have made the transition from communism to free market, one of the milestones, both symbolic and substantive, has been the establishment of securities markets. When the means of production are owned collectively, there is no role for stock exchanges.

In a market economy, owners of companies have wide latitude in deciding what to produce, how to produce it, and whether to expand or contract their scale of operations. Such decisions are another manifestation of decentralized decision-making.

Furthermore, the decision makers bear the consequences of their decisions. The net profits belong to the owners of the business. At the end of the year, if total revenues exceed total costs, the owners reap the rewards.

The corporate structure adds a number of interesting extensions to the institution of private ownership. Dividing corporations into literally millions or even billions of fractional shares reduces the cost of ownership for the person of average wealth and income. The corporate structure and the availability of publicly traded shares allows for a low-cost, wide dispersion of ownership of businesses, particularly large businesses. The critical mass for sharing business ownership has been getting progressively smaller. Less money is required, transaction costs are lower, and it's easier to be diversified, so the inherent risk is lower.

Compare the stock market and mutual funds to other forms of ownership. You probably know of a successful small business in your community, such as the Toyota dealership. Suppose you wanted to share in the profits of that business. It would probably involve quite an undertaking to make that a reality. It might be that your only option would be to buy the whole business, a transaction that could easily amount to millions of dollars. Even if you could raise that much money, would you want to invest it in only one business?

Limited liability means you can't lose more than your original investment.

A corporation's liability exposure is normally limited to the value of its assets. Consequently, its stockholders are protected against personal liability in connection with the affairs of the corporation. This is the famous doctrine of "limited liability."

Limited liability has major practical benefits for stock market investors. It effectively puts a floor under how much investors can lose, and that fact greatly increases the attractiveness of investing in stocks. If you could lose more than your original investment, which is in fact the case when you own an unincorporated business, you would be far more reluctant to invest. If a corporation gets sued or goes bankrupt, the shareholders know that the plaintiffs or creditors cannot come after any of their other assets. This creates a favorable asymmetry for the shareholders. There is no real limit to how far their investments can grow, but there is a limit to how much it can shrink.

Most stock markets are so-called "secondary markets," in which you purchase securities that have been "pre-owned."

A secondary security market is a "market in which securities are traded that have been issued at some previous point in time." (Sharpe, *et al.*, 1999) On secondary markets you buy securities that have been previously owned. The money you pay goes, not to the corporation itself, but rather to another investor like you. It's somewhat like buying a used car.

Of course, all the stocks on the secondary markets were at one time on primary markets, just as all used cars were once new. The way we most often hear about the primary market for stocks is in regard to "initial public offerings" or IPOs.

A legitimate question to ask is why would someone who creates a corporation want to share the ownership? Why wouldn't he just keep the ownership and all the profits for himself?

There are a number of answers to that question. One is that selling part of a company is a good way to raise capital. The alternatives would be to stay small, borrow the money, or grow by using earnings as they occur. When you borrow, it isn't necessary to actually give up part of the ownership so long as you repay the loan in a timely fashion. Borrowing all the money you need, however, is not always an option, especially for a young company or for a high-risk endeavor.

Another reason an owner of a corporation might want to share ownership is to make his investment more liquid and to allow himself to diversify. When an existing "closely held" company is "taken public," it means that in the future the shares will be traded on one of the stock exchanges. Someone who has created a successful corporation and watched it grow to a large size might very well have a high net worth. Unfortunately for him, the wealth is mostly concentrated in one asset. Going public typically means that the original owners remain as significant shareholders, but being publicly traded gives them the option of selling portions of their holdings in order to achieve the benefits of diversification and avoid having all their wealth concentrated in one enterprise.

There are also significant disadvantages to taking a corporation public. For instance, publicly owned corporations are subject to far more regulation than are closely held corporations. Under the Securities and Exchange Act of 1933, corporations whose shares are offered to the public must make full public disclosure of numerous details of their financial operation. They must make available their balance sheets and income statements, disclose officers' compensation, and reveal any significant purchases or sales of the company's stock by insiders. The Securities and Exchange Commission (SEC) is the government agency responsible for regulating securities markets and requiring full disclosure.

Earnings are ultimately the reason for buying and owning stocks.

The fundamental tangible benefit for being an owner of a company is to share in the current and future earnings or profits of the company. This is not just common sense, but a fact borne out by numerous research studies.

Of course, reality is never simple. If stock prices were determined strictly by a company's current earnings, all stocks would have the same "price/earnings ratio." The main reason there is a wide range of price/earnings ratios is that investors are always looking forward. Good and bad things can happen to the company, the industry, even the whole economy. When you invest in stock, you expect a flow of returns, but the rate of flow is not fixed.

Naturally, a company's stock prices will be bid up if its earnings are expected to grow, and the reverse will be true for a company with pessimistic earnings expectations. Earnings provide the ultimate motivation for stock ownership. Having said that, it should be noted that the main tangible benefit most people receive from stock market investments is not earnings but rather growth in the prices of their stocks. This will be discussed further in the next chapter.

Charities usually operate as non-profit corporations, and sometimes they own valuable assets, such as real estate. If you could buy shares in such a corporation, would you want to? If not, why not?

When trillions of dollars are at stake, it gets your attention.

The scale of the stock market is immense. A major portion of the productive power of the economy is continuously available for purchase. The current total value of the shares of all publicly traded companies in the U.S. is approximately $13 trillion.

This huge volume of wealth creates opportunities for the making of fortunes just by discovering and exploiting minuscule discrepancies in the market. The magnitude of the incentives created is enormous.

The scale of the market is a factor in another of its key characteristics—the intense competition among the participants. The stock market is possibly the most competitive economic environment that's ever existed. In this venue millions of highly motivated and well-informed buyers and sellers match wits against one another.

The amazing flexibility of stock prices produces a nearly perfect match of willing buyers and willing sellers.

One particularly noteworthy feature of stock prices is their flexibility. It's not uncommon for prices to change numerous times in a single day. This remarkable flexibility allows equilibrium prices to be established almost instantaneously.

As a result, on the major exchanges shortages or surpluses of stocks are relatively rare. Willing buyers are matched with willing sellers continuously. This allows stock exchanges to maintain inventories close to zero, a situation quite different from that faced by most other middlemen and dealers in the economy. For car dealers, super markets, or bookstores, price changes are infrequent and imbalances of supply and demand are reflected in inventory levels.

For relatively small companies (for example, a regional bank), temporary shortages and surpluses of a stock are not unusual. Such stocks are described as "thinly traded." The frequency and volume of transactions are relatively low, and prices change less often. Also, in the case of "initial public offerings," or IPOs, shortages and surpluses are fairly common because the underwriters have to make educated guesses about the stock's appeal before it is placed on the market.

Stocks are homogenous.

Another important characteristic of stocks is their homogeneity. One share of General Electric common stock is exactly identical to all the other shares (assuming the same class of common stock). All the shares are equal divisions of the same underlying entity. Contrast that to the real estate market. No two houses are identical. They differ, at the very least, in location, since two houses cannot be in the same place at the same time.

Partly as a result of this homogeneity, at any time all buyers and sellers of a particular stock pay or receive a uniform price (net of commissions and other necessary transaction fees). People buying IBM stock from San Francisco, New York, or London will pay essentially the same price if they place their orders at the same time. Typically, stock markets channel the trades for a particular stock through one trader or specialist, and this, too, promotes uniform pricing.

As a matter of fact, the enormous scale of the market drives price uniformity to very close tolerance levels. In other words, because of the magnitude of money involved, profits can be achieved with very small price discrepancies. As those profit opportunities are pursued, the price discrepancies are squeezed to almost zero.

The price uniformity prevailing on securities markets is an indication of highly evolved and efficient markets. In modern securities markets, what's known as the "law of one price" prevails, since price differences would create an arbitrage opportunity. In the *MIT Dictionary of Modern Economics* (4th ed.), arbitrage is defined as an "operation involving simultaneous purchase and sale of an asset, e.g., a commodity or currency in two or more markets between which there are price differences or discrepancies. The arbitrageur aims to profit from the price difference; the effect of his action is to lessen or eliminate it." The logic and implications of arbitrage play important roles in explaining how securities markets operate.

Stocks are highly liquid.

The flexible prices and uniform character of stocks contribute to another important feature of the stock market—its liquidity. Liquidity is the ability to convert an asset into cash quickly and with relatively little loss of value. (Loss being defined in relation to the current price, not the purchase price, of the asset.) To appreciate the market's advantage in regard to liquidity, compare again common stocks to real estate. It often takes months to sell a piece of real estate. If you want to sell it quickly in a so-called distress sale, you may have no choice other than to significantly reduce the price.

Even with stocks, of course, liquidity is not perfect. If a large number of people decide to liquidate their stocks rapidly, the value of a particular stock or the overall market can drop rather suddenly. The desire to convert to cash quickly and with little loss of value is not always an option. Thinly traded stocks also have limited liquidity. On the major stock exchanges, however, lack of liquidity is a relatively rare problem.

Obviously, liquidity is a highly desirable attribute for an investment. When you make an investment, it's nice to know you can convert it back to cash if you so desire. Our highly evolved securities markets have contributed enormously to the liquidity of stocks and have consequently increased the appeal and accessibility of ownership in the economy.

In this way and others securities markets have made it possible for more people to own stock in more and more companies. You can buy shares in most of the 8,000 or so largest corporations in the U.S. However, some large corporations are not publicly traded. Rather they are closely held by a relatively few people or by the employees of the business (as with Levi Strauss, Inc.). Being closely held is the usual case with most smaller corporations and unincorporated businesses.

How much is a stock or a company worth?

From an economic standpoint, what is something worth? The favorite answer of economists is "what a willing buyer will pay a willing seller."

According to that measure, the value of a house like yours might be $200,000. Of course, yours may be worth much more than that to you, and if it is, you will live in it rather than putting it on the market.

However, when you are evaluating goods and services relative to one another, it would be very difficult to find a better measure than the willing-buyer-willing-seller standard. What is your house worth relative to other houses and what are houses worth relative to, for example, cars? On the other hand, saying something is worth $5,000 says nothing about its absolute value. The absolute level of a stock's price, $15, for example, is less significant than its price relative to other stock prices.

This measure is also consistent with the fundamental nature of voluntary exchange and of a market economy. After all, what do we mean by the phrase "what a willing buyer will pay a willing seller?" That's simply another way of expressing the phenomenon of voluntary exchange, the interplay of supply and demand, and the establishment of a market-clearing, equilibrium price.

The most reliable measure of a company's value is its price per share multiplied by the number of shares outstanding.

As the interplay of supply and demand determine a company's price per share, so too do they determine the value of the entire company. It turns out that the most reliable measure of a company's intrinsic value is its price per share multiplied by the number of shares outstanding. This could be considered two ways of looking at basically the same phenomenon. In other words, the overall value of the company is what determines its price per share (taking into account the number of shares outstanding).

There is necessarily a large degree of subjectivity inherent in determining a stock's market value. Consider the difference between a stock's market value and its book value. If you do research on a company, a basic piece of information you might look at is its book value. This is the liquidation value of a company: the value of its tangible assets such as its buildings, machinery, cash, and accounts receivable. As I write this, the share price of General Electric is $38. Its book value per share is $12.60. That means GE's book-to-market ratio is .33. Book value takes no account of intangibles, such as the skill and experience of the company's management and workers, the value of its reputation and brand name, its established relationships with its customers, or the value of its existing contracts.

A company is much more than a collection of buildings and machines, but just how much more is a judgment call. As was explained above, a large part of the judgment relates to future events and developments. The stock's price reflects the consensus evaluation of all the company's tangible and intangible assets. Whether or not that consensus accurately reflects reality is a crucial issue and will be discussed more fully in the next chapter.

Stock prices, incentives, and the "cost of capital."

An important side benefit of the securities market price system is the role stock prices play in guiding capital to the most promising firms and industries. When a firm wants to grow and expand its operations and capacity, it needs additional funds. These may be taken out of the profits from past operations or borrowed, but firms whose stock is publicly traded have a third option, that of selling more shares in the company. The more favorably the company is regarded by the market—the higher the price of its stock and the lower the "cost of capital" for the company.

By issuing and selling more stock, the existing shareholders are selling a portion of their ownership. Let's assume they are willing to sell ten percent of what they own. The higher the market price of the company's stock, the more money they will be able to raise by selling part of the company. Alternatively, if they want to raise a certain amount of capital, the smaller the percentage of the company they'll need to sell.

Because it reduces the cost of growth, a high stock price is an incentive for the owners to expand the company. Therefore, stock prices will either encourage or discourage growth. The price hierarchy on securities markets is a kind of automatic mechanism for directing resources and, as such, plays a critical role in any advanced market economy.

Stock prices also affect the behavior of companies because management often has an ownership stake in the firm. Especially for upper-management, compensation packages typically include stock options or something similar. When management makes decisions resulting in more sales, growth, and profits for the company, it tends to result in higher prices for the company's stock. Insofar as they own shares themselves, or at least options to buy more shares at a predetermined price, management effectiveness is rewarded. For corporate managers, stock prices represent an important example of consequences. The stock market rewards companies and their managements when they make effective and profitable decisions and punishes them when they don't.

This is another example of decentralized decision-making and the far-reaching role of the price system. Even though the company only receives the proceeds when a stock is first issued, it is nevertheless affected by the secondary-market price of its shares.

The stock market has an impersonal influence on which companies grow and which contract, but some countries, Japan for example, attempt to augment this process through what is known as industrial policy, the purpose of which is to encourage the growth of industries the government judges to be especially important to the overall economy. As a result, the country was often referred to as Japan, Inc.

Industrial policy is a partial step away from decentralized decision making in the allocation of capital. It has not been an unqualified success, and some observers cite it as one of the causes of Japan's chronic economic malaise. Even the United States exercises industrial policy in various ways. Subsidies, import restrictions, and government loan programs are all examples of political rather than economic allocation of resources. It's the government and the political system, rather than voluntary exchange and flexible prices, picking the winners and losers. The scale of industrial-policy programs, however, is still relatively small compared to that of the securities markets.

Betting point spreads—Part One: Point spreads are like stock prices.

Many non-economists, I'm sure, would be surprised if they saw some of the places economists go in applying and testing economic theories. One instructive application we will make use of in the next three chapters is wagering on sporting events.

In a survey article titled "The Economics of Wagering Markets," the author, Raymond Sauer, states "Although these markets are a tiny feature of most economies, they present significant opportunities for economic analysis. These stem from the fact that wagering markets are especially simple financial markets, in which the scope of the pricing problem is reduced. As a result, wagering markets can provide a clear view of pricing issues which are more complicated elsewhere." (Sauer, 1998) The bibliography for Sauer's survey article lists ninety-nine articles on the subject, and that's by no means exhaustive.

Gambling is what economists call a zero-sum game, meaning that what one player wins, another loses. Investing, because of economic growth, is a positive-sum game. There are, however, a number of interesting parallels between the dynamics of wagering and investing in the stock market.

Our focus will be betting on National Football League (NFL) and National Basketball Association (NBA) games. One aspect of wagering that researchers like is that the data are relatively neat, tidy, and accessible. Each week contains a complete cycle of data. By comparison, the stock market is vast and open-ended. There is rarely a nice, neat closure.

If you have done any wagering on NFL or NBA games, you know that it's very difficult to be a consistent winner, even though most of the time the favored team wins the game. Since the likely winner is known, why not just bet on the favored team all the time? That way the more you bet, the more you would win—or so it would seem.

The answer, of course, is it's not that simple. There's the little matter of what's called the point spread. If the Chicago Bears have a better record than the Detroit Lions, you will not be able to bet on the Bears without giving up some points.

The bookies, who act as go-betweens, match bettors backing one or the other competing teams, and have no interest in taking a net position. In other words, bookies prefer to have none of their own money at risk. Their main responsibility is to set the point spread at a level that will balance the bets on each team.

The bookies set this spread on the Monday preceding the game to take place the following Sunday. Sometimes they set it wrong, and too many people bet on one or the other of the teams. When that happens, they adjust the spread and you might see it change as the week progresses. Their challenge is similar to that faced by the underwriters who set prices for IPOs. If the Bears' star quarterback dislocates his shoulder in practice during the week, the spread will probably change.

D14   San Francisco Chronicle

SUNDAY, OCTOBER 28, 2001

LATEST LINE

NFL

TODAY

FAVORITE	SPREAD	UNDERDOG
CHICAGO	2½	49ers
PHILADELPHIA	1½	Raiders
BALTIMORE	7	Jacksonville
TAMPA BAY	3	Minnesota
DETROIT	3	Cincinnati
ST. LOUIS	12	New Orleans
N.Y. Jets	2½	CAROLINA
Arizona	3	DALLAS
DENVER	7	New England
SAN DIEGO	7	Buffalo
Miami	2½	SEATTLE
N.Y. Giants	7½	WASHINGTON

TOMORROW

FAVORITE	SPREAD	UNDERDOG
PITTSBURGH	3	Tennessee

Source: Glantz-Culver
Home team in capitals. NL: No line.

The point spread is like a flexible price. It's also like an equilibrium price. It balances two opposing forces and equalizes two populations, for instance, people betting on the Bears and other people betting on the Lions. More precisely, it equalizes the dollar amount wagered on each team.

The equilibrium spread "clears the market"—meaning there is no surplus or shortage of Bears bettors or Lions bettors. The two sides of the wagers are analogous to supply and demand. As flexible prices equalize quantity supplied with quantity demanded, the point spread equalizes the amount wagered for and against a particular team.

Stock market summary.

- ► Simple descriptions of the stock market are hard to find.
- ► Modern securities markets are the most sophisticated markets that have ever existed.
- ► Securities are representations of ownership.
- ► Unlike a car, securities are intended to provide future or prospective benefits.
- ► A stock is an evidence of ownership. A bond is an evidence of debt.
- ► The availability of publicly traded shares allows for a wide dispersion of businesses ownership.
- ► Limited liability means you can't lose more than your original investment.
- ► Stock markets deal primarily with pre-owned securities.
- ► The fundamental benefit of owning a company or stock in a company is to share in current and prospective profits.
- ► The extraordinary price flexibility found in securities markets has far-reaching implications.
- ► In modern securities markets, the law of one price prevails.
- ► All the shares of a company are equal-sized divisions of the same underlying entity—they are homogeneous.
- ► Liquidity is the ability to convert an asset to cash quickly and with relatively little loss of value.
- ► As is the case with prices in general, what matters is one stock's price relative to other stock prices.
- ► A company's share price times the number of shares outstanding determines the value of the company.
- ► Because it reduces the cost of capital for the company, a high stock price is an incentive for its owners to grow the company.
- ► The higher the market price of a company's stock, the greater the amount of money that can be raised by selling part of the company.
- ► The stock market rewards companies and their managements when they make effective and profitable decisions and punishes them when they don't.
- ► The stock market helps determine which companies grow and which contract.

CHAPTER 4

Market Efficiency:
Stock Prices
Embody Information.
How So and So What?

A hypothesis is important if it "explains" much by little, that is, if it abstracts the common and crucial elements from the mass of complex and detailed circumstances surrounding the phenomena to be explained and permits valid predictions on the basis of them alone.

Milton Friedman,
"On the Methodology of Positive Economics"

The cornerstone of Modern Portfolio Theory is a concept known as the Efficient Market Hypothesis (EMH). First defined by Eugene Fama of the University of Chicago, the EMH has profound implications for both markets as a whole and for you as an investor. Understand the EMH and you will understand how stock markets work.

> ***Efficient market hypothesis*** *The view that the prices of shares on the stock market are the best available estimates of their real value because of the highly efficient pricing mechanism inherent in the stock market. First, the market is held to be "weak form efficient" if share price changes are independent of past price changes. Second, "semi-strong form efficiency" is present if share prices fully reflect all publicly available information. Third, "strong-form efficiency" will imply share prices will have taken full account of all information whether publicly available or not.*
>
> MIT Dictionary of Modern Economics

It's doubly appropriate that the EMH includes the word efficient because it happens to be an extremely efficient theory. In Friedman's terms, "it explains much by little," and the EMH does this about as well as any economic theory ever has. In fact, Professor Fama's elegant hypothesis is almost too concise. Because it says so much in so few words, it's easy to overlook its significance.

In this chapter we'll have a close look at the EMH and try to understand what it tells us about investing. A good way to begin is with the so-called semi-strong form of market efficiency. Of the three versions of the EMH, the semi-strong is the one most commonly discussed and the one with the most practical significance. This version of the EMH makes the following deceptively simple assertion: stock prices fully reflect available information.

In an efficient market stock prices fully reflect available information.

The soul and significance of the hypothesis is in three words—prices reflect information. Why does it matter whether or not that's true? As you will see, prices and information are the two dimensions of investing in securities that matter most when it comes to pursuing excess returns.

Consider how active money managers attempt to reach their objectives. How do they go about trying to beat the market and achieve excess returns? Primarily, they rely on securities selection or market timing.

Securities selection (popularly called "stock picking") involves searching for stocks that will rise in price faster than the overall market. When stock prices in general are going up and you want to outperform the market, you've got to identify stocks that will rise even faster. Your objective is not to generate average or normal returns, but rather excess or abnormal returns. Otherwise, you could simply replicate market returns by buying an index fund that would include all the stocks in a designated asset class.

In other words, what you're hoping to find in your effort to beat the market are mis-priced securities. (That might not be obvious to you yet, but stick with me.) You are searching for bargain-priced stocks. How do you find mis-priced securities? The usual technique is to gather, filter, and process information.

Analysts pour over the balance sheets, income statements, industry characteristics, and competitive positions of the company in question. Some money managers do on-site visits to get firsthand knowledge of the company and its management. There's simply no alternative to collecting and processing information when pursuing excess returns. If you doubt that's true, I challenge you to suggest an alternative.

The success of your attempt to beat the market will depend on how well others in the market have already done what you're attempting to do, that is, process information. Your success, in other words, will depend on the validity of the EMH. The fundamental conclusion of the EMH is that there is no way to find information that hasn't already affected the price. This means you can't reliably identify mis-priced securities, at least not without spending more than the discovery yields in excess returns. A mis-priced security is one that does not fully incorporate relevant information.

Market timing also turns out to be an issue of appropriate pricing. Market timers attempt to identify key turning points in overall market levels. From time to time the market suffers significant drops in value. For example, in October of 1987 the market lost over 20 percent of its value in less than a week. It would be a marvelous thing if you found someone who could see those kinds of events coming so that you could get out before the drop.

You would also want him to tell you when it had bottomed out so you could re-enter at the opportune time. Knowing when to exit is not particularly useful if you don't know when to return. You would sell when the market is over-priced, sit on the sidelines while it drops, and re-enter before it starts to rise again. That kind of advice could turbocharge your rate of return. There are plenty of newsletters claiming the ability to do just that for you, but they have the same pathetic success rate as active managers (Jaffe and Mahoney, 1999).

The overall level of the stock market is itself a kind of relative price. It's the price of an asset category relative to the price of other asset categories, e.g., bonds, money-market funds, real estate, etc. To say that the market is about to drop is the same as saying that stocks, on average, are mis-priced and are about to correct. Only incorrect prices, after all, are capable of correction. You can't correct something that's correct to begin with. The point to be made here is that market timing is another strategy that hinges on whether or not securities are priced appropriately at any given time. For example, is the current level of the Dow Jones Industrial Average appropriate in light of current economic conditions?

Why place so much emphasis on stock prices?

The EMH focuses its attention on stock prices. Why? If you're going to beat the market, you must do it by way of stock prices. Prices define the playing field. You enter the market by way of prices, and you exit the market by way of prices. You win or lose by way of prices. Although dividends are a significant element of stock returns, those current and future dividends are reflected in the prices, and you buy the dividends when you pay for the stock.

A stock's price is the actual contact point and the primary interface between an investor and the market. Prices are the medium, and as you will soon see, the medium is the message.

How does information get into the stock's price?

Stock prices absorb information primarily by way of the basic dynamics of the stock market. The information is in the price of the stock because anyone who possesses it can potentially profit by acting on it. The information does you no good unless you take action. If you have favorable news about a company, you will want to buy the stock. As you do so, because stock prices are highly flexible, the price will tend to go up, which is just another way of saying that the price now includes the new information. When there is an increase in the demand for some item, the price tends to rise.

The price of a stock is like an adjustable container. Favorable news makes it larger, while unfavorable news makes it smaller. The total information about any company is never uniformly positive or negative. The size of the container is a function of the net difference between the positive and negative information. The degree of flexibility of stock prices allows the container to change in very small increments. Consequently, the container's size incorporates the information and is accurate to very close tolerances. The flexibility of stock prices and the intense competition among the participants make securities prices high-fidelity transmitters of information.

A major breakthrough in technology has been the ability to digitize information—the compact disk for recording music or storing computer software, for example. Twenty volumes of an encyclopedia can be stored on a single compact disk. The efficient market performs a similar kind of translation, condensation, and conversion of information, storing it in the form of prices.

All owners will be affected by the knowledge of a few.

> *Why does informational efficiency matter? The capital markets channel funds from savers to firms, which use the funds to finance projects. Informational efficiency is necessary if funds, allocated through the capital market, are to flow to the highest valued projects... A related reason for caring about efficiency is that investors who do not have the time or the resources to do extensive analysis will be more willing to invest their savings in the market if they believe the securities they trade are accurately priced.*
>
> Steven Jones and Jeffry Netter, "Efficient Capital Markets," *Fortune Encyclopedia of Economics*

It's critical to recognize that it doesn't really matter whether or not all or even most buyers and sellers of the stock know all the information that is reflected in the price of the stock. Each stock's price is a distillation of an enormous amount of information. Many of the people who buy and sell stocks are totally naive and poorly informed. Nevertheless, the price they pay or receive is the same as the most sophisticated investors pay or receive.

Recall from the last chapter that everyone who buys a given stock at a particular time pays essentially the same price. The price they pay is not related to their sophistication or lack of it. This is the main reason why the issue of asymmetric or differential access to information is much less significant than many people seem to believe. The information resides not with any particular investor, but rather within the stock's price. This is a specific example of what F. A. Hayek referred to as "quantitative indices in which all the relevant information is concentrated."

It is not necessary, therefore, that all investors be well informed for the market to be efficient. Ironically, it takes a relatively small fraction of participants to generate an efficient price. If a stock is selling at $8 a share, and its true value is $10 it will be bid up to $10 even though only a small number of buyers know its true value. As long as the stock can be purchased for less than what it's actually worth, there's excess-return potential that will motivate additional purchases. *All the owners of the stock will be affected by the knowledge of a few.* The information known by a few effectively becomes a common good, similar to a radio signal that can be accessed by anyone in the area with a radio. Furthermore, the price is set at the margins by the smartest, best-informed participants.

Everyone pays or receives the same price for a stock at any particular time, so all the participants get the full benefit of all the incorporated information. The information is digested, analyzed, evaluated, condensed, and placed in the public domain by way of the price. The stock's price is an equal opportunity provider and dispenser of information. The stock market is the closest thing you will find in the real world to a level playing field.

> *Each investor, using the market to serve his or her own self-interest, unwittingly makes prices reflect that investor's information and analysis. It is as if the market were a huge, relatively low cost, continuous polling mechanism that records the updated votes of millions of investors in continuously changing current prices. In light of this mechanism, for a single investor (in the absence of inside information) to believe that prices are significantly in error is almost always folly. Public information should already be imbedded in prices.*
>
> Mark Rubenstein, "Rational Markets: Yes or No?
> The Affirmative Case," *Financial Analysts Journal*,
> May-June 2001

The sophistication of one investor relative to another is not the issue, and even if it were, why would some prices be more affected by it than others? What matters is one stock's price relative to another. Prices of stocks, and prices in general, are, above all, relative phenomena.

All the relevant information is right there in a single number. The stock's price is like a super-efficient statistic. It doesn't matter whether or not some of the investors are clueless. It is important to recognize that active managers compete not with other investors, but rather with the stock's price and the accumulated volume of information contained therein. We will see later that most of those who attempt to beat the market utterly fail to grasp the true nature of the contest. Attempting to beat the market is a battle, not between one investor and other investors, but between an investor and stock prices.

Securities markets are said to be efficient because of how well and how rapidly they absorb information and concentrate that information in prices.

Prices and information are the two most critical aspects of investing in stocks. If the market is efficient in regard to these two factors, any attempt to make abnormal returns is likely to be a futile endeavor.

> *Large numbers of investors forsake the buy-and-hold strategy that efficient markets theory dictates in favor of betting their information against other investors' information… The majority of traders appear to reflect belief on the part of each investor that he can outwit other investors.*
>
> Stephen Leroy, "Efficient Capital Markets and Martingales," *Journal of Economic Literature*, December 1989

In the end, the quest for a market-beating strategy boils down to an information-processing contest. The entity you are competing against is the entire market and the accumulated information discovered by all the participants and reflected in prices. The efficiency of market prices will define whether or not you have any realistic hope of winning the contest. The more efficient the market, the less chance you have of beating it. The contest is between an individual player—a portfolio manager or individual investor, for example—and the entire market. In this game it's one against all.

Competing against the market, in other words, is not like one National Football League team against another. Rather, it's much closer to one team playing all the other teams at the same time. What chance do your eleven players have against 319 players? The probability of your scoring any points would be extremely low. Just getting off the field in one piece would be an achievement.

Conclusions reached on Agate Beach.

Not far from where I live is a stretch of Pacific Coast shoreline known as Agate Beach, which is located within Patrick's Point State Park. The beach is comprised of pebbles rather than sand, and among those pebbles people who spend a little time can find agates. Agates are kind of interesting, but they really aren't worth much. People don't go very far out of their way or spend much time looking for them.

Suppose, however, that agates became worth $100 each. In that case, people would devote far more time and energy to finding agates. Of course, then there would be competition, and after a while it would become considerably harder to find them. The price of the agates would strongly affect the degree of difficulty because the price would determine the payoff and incentives for searching.

There would be a payoff for searching as long as you could find an agate in less than a $100 worth of your time. If it took you longer than that, looking for agates would not be an efficient use of your time. Because of this, there will always be agates left on the beach, that is, assuming that agate searchers behave rationally. No matter what the price of agates, the optimal or efficient number of agates will never be zero.

If agates had more value, one thing we would notice is that not everyone is equally effective in finding them. As a matter of fact, I've already noticed that, since my wife always finds more than I do.

Which agate finders would define how hard it is to find agates? The most proficient searchers would determine the degree of difficulty. The degree of difficulty would be determined at the margin, rather than by the average skill of the searchers. Furthermore, in equilibrium, the marginal cost of finding agates would be driven to equality with the price of agates.

A mis-priced security has enormous potential value equivalent to agates having values of thousands or millions of dollars.

Stock market participants have strong motivation for identifying mis-priced securities. With incentives that powerful the logical conclusion is that although the number of mis-priced securities will never be zero, they will nonetheless be extremely difficult and costly to find—a prediction overwhelmingly confirmed by the evidence. Those incentives are the main force causing successful strategies to self-destruct. (An extra challenge faced by people trying to find mis-priced securities is that, unlike agates, you can never be sure that what you've found is actually what you think it is.)

Betting Point Spreads—Part Two: Point spreads predict accurately.

In Chapter 3 we discussed how, in wagering, point spreads play a similar role to stock prices in the way they equalize the amount wagered on the two teams in athletic contests. The point-spread phenomenon is also instructive in the context of understanding an efficient market.

An interesting question that's been tested empirically is how accurate the point spreads are in predicting the actual outcomes of games. The conclusion of the research is that the point spreads are, in fact, effective predictors of the outcomes.

In statistical terminology, point spreads turn out to be "unbiased estimators." For the sake of simplification, let's say that the point spread for all the games on a Sunday was three points. Chicago was expected to beat New York by three points, Atlanta over New Orleans by three points, and so on.

For an estimator to be considered unbiased, it has to meet certain characteristics. An unbiased estimator is not expected to be correct in every instance, but when it's not, the errors are randomly distributed with a zero mean.

Unbiased estimator A statistic which is on average neither too high or too low. The method of estimation does not always produce estimates which correspond to reality, but errors in either direction are equally likely.
Oxford Dictionary of Economics

In the case of point spreads, you can be reasonably certain that most of those predictions would turn out to be wrong. Maybe Chicago beat New York by nine points. Maybe Atlanta lost to New Orleans by six points. The point spread can be only a single number, but the actual outcomes are spread over a range of possibilities.

Researchers have found that, on average, the point spreads are accurate. The actual outcomes are above the spread about the same number of times they are below the spread. After the fact, when you subtract the point spreads from the actual scores and add them up for all the games, you will find that the number is not significantly different from zero. Raymond Sauer looked at six seasons of NBA games, for example, and found the average difference between point spreads and actual point differences was .24. (Sauer, 1998)

This is significant because it's what determines how hard it is to win when you bet. If you bet on a number of games, you will typically find that you win about half the time. When that happens, you will not feel particularly successful, unless you consider breaking even is success. If you win half the time you actually lose money because the bookies insist on being compensated for their efforts. Their cut is called "vigorish."

On average the point spreads accurately reflect the relative difference in scoring abilities between the two teams. This is amazing when you consider how the point spreads are derived. Ultimately it's the bettors who determine the point spreads. The point spread reflects the consensus of their opinions as to the relative differences in the two teams' scoring abilities.

The point spreads are set in something akin to a democratic vote. The bookie's foremost concern is to equalize the number of bets on each team in a particular game. He wants the "election" to be a draw. He doesn't really care if it's an accurate prediction or not. He couldn't care less who wins and who loses their bets. He mainly wants to avoid having any of his own money riding on the outcome of a game. He's a go-between, a matchmaker, and ironically not himself a gambler or risk taker. As he facilitates other peoples' risk taking, he prefers to play it safe. The point spread divides the population of bettors on a given game into two equal parts—those who think the spread should be less and those who think it should be more.

Seemingly by magic, this process creates point spreads that result in half the scores being higher, half being lower. The point spreads do, in fact, turn out to be unbiased estimators, making wagering a "fair game" or what game theoreticians term a "martingale."

This results in an interesting irony. If the game were not fair, far fewer people would play. That's because you would have trouble finding someone willing to take the other side of a bet, i.e., bet on the underdog. The fact that the game is "fair," however, means that you will not win more than about half the time, except by chance. The spread has the effect of both increasing the population of willing bettors as well as making it impossible to win on a consistent basis. It's another process that results in a leveling of the playing field.

Much like point spreads in sports, stock prices are correct on average.

Research has also confirmed that stock prices are unbiased estimators. With stocks, every investment is expected to be a winner. You wouldn't bother buying a stock unless you thought its value would increase and give you a positive rate of return.

Let's assume that stock prices in general are expected to increase at ten percent a year. In retrospect, we will see that some increased much faster than ten percent, others by much less, or even declined in value. Market efficiency says that stock prices incorporate all currently available information. Efficiency is not about information accessible with a crystal ball.

What we will discover, nevertheless, is that the errors are about evenly distributed on each side of the market's prediction. The predictions embodied in the prices are not perfect. There are errors. Remember, however, that every imaginable alternative system will have errors as well. This is essentially what's confirmed by the numerous contests between stock-picking "experts" and someone throwing darts at a stock listing. As those experiments have demonstrated, the experts win only about half the time.

Every month for fourteen years the *Wall Street Journal* actually conducted an experiment, comparing choices made by market professionals and those made by throwing darts at stock listings. In the first 100 of those contests, from 1990 to 1998, the pros beat the darts 60 times. From those results you might conclude that doing well in the market is more than a matter of chance. However, the pros beat the Dow Jones Industrial Average only 51 times. The pros might be able to beat the darts 6 out of 10 times, but against the market they do no better than break even (*Wall Street Journal*, October 7, 1998).

Furthermore, the pros' strategy is far riskier than the market since each pro selected a single stock for respective six-month periods. As we will discuss further in Chapter 6, a portfolio with only one or a few stocks is much riskier than the diversification represented in a broad asset class. As you know, if you've studied statistics, even winning 60 out of 100 times is not statistically significant. It is well within the range of the likely total of heads or tails when you flip a coin 100 times.

The *Journal* calculated the rate of return for the pros to be 21.6 percent for the 100 contests. For that period of time the return for the S&P 500 was 16.6 percent. To achieve the pro's rate of return would have meant holding each of the stocks for only six months. One of the problems with that strategy is that all your gains would have been short-term and taxed at twice the rate of long-term gains. The pro's rate of return also did not take into account buying and selling commissions. It's unlikely the net rate of return would have been any higher than the much simpler and safer strategy of buying and holding an index fund.

In April 2002 the *Journal* announced it would no longer conduct the dartboard contests. Among the reasons it gave was the following:

> *For years there was a waiting list for professionals who wanted to participate, although interest has tapered off as the market has been beaten down in the past couple of years, and picking winners has become tougher even for pros.*
>
> "Putting Away the Darts After 14 Years,"
> *Wall Street Journal*, April 18, 2002

In other words, not only are active managers extremely slow learners, they are also wimps.

A systematic error contains information that can be exploited.

The EMH happens to be a specific application of a more general economic theory known as "rational expectations," although the two theories were developed about the same time. The theory of rational expectations is the theoretical context for the Efficient Market Hypothesis.

> ***Rational expectations.*** *The application of the principal of rational maximizing behavior to the acquisition and processing of information for the purpose of forming a view about the future. It suggests that individuals do not make systematic forecasting errors. Thus the theory suggests that individuals use all the available and relevant information when taking a view about the future and at a minimum use information up to the point at which the marginal costs of acquiring and processing information equal the marginal benefits derived from this activity.*
>
> *MIT Dictionary of Modern Economics* (4th ed.)

The 1995 Nobel Prize for Economics was awarded to Robert Lucas of the University of Chicago, primarily for his work in developing the theory of rational expectations, a concept that has become a central pillar of economic theory. The core insight of the theory of rational expectations is the conclusion that systematic forecasting errors are rare, and even when they occur, market dynamics minimize their impact.

What, you might ask, is a systematic error? Suppose, for example, you're shooting arrows at a target. After shooting about five arrows, you notice that they are clustered above and to the right of the bull's-eye. That clustering of misses is an example of a systematic error. What is your likely course of action?

If the archer's objective is to hit the bull's-eye, he will aim low and to the left. The payoff will be more bull's-eyes. A critical characteristic of a systematic error is that it is predictable. A predictable error can be avoided by an adjustment in behavior.

The archer can predict that if he aims directly at the bull's-eye, he will hit high and right. It's possible for him to improve his success rate at a very low cost. If he has a high-tech bow, he could correct the problem by simply adjusting the sight.

Your ability to correct that kind of error is very different from correcting misses scattered around the target and more random in nature. A systematic error contains information that can be exploited. Scattered shots contain relatively little information as to what corrective action to take.

Notice as well that the archer needs to be able to see where his shots have hit the target. This illustrates why information and feedback are critical issues in how well a system operates.

Information has a cost, and this is a primary reason we make errors in our lives.

When you think back on the mistakes you've made in your life, one of the thoughts you probably have is, "I wish I knew then what I know now." In other words, if you had had more information, it would have reduced the likelihood of your error. One reason you didn't have the information is that it would have taken time and effort to obtain it. In other words, it's a problem of the cost of information.

Part of the underlying logic for the theory of rational expectations is simply that, since errors are costly or painful, there is an incentive for minimizing them. The people who have the strongest incentives for discovering and minimizing errors are the participants. They are the ones who suffer the consequences and bear the costs of the errors. "Once burned, twice learned." It's the burn sufferer who has the strongest incentive for detecting and avoiding the painful behavior in the future. This is another example of our system of decentralized decision making, and decisions being made by the person with the most direct knowledge and the most to win or lose.

The fact that people make errors is not necessarily a violation of rational expectations. Usually it's simply the result of the fact that, since information has a cost, it's entirely possible that the cost of the information (especially for non-systematic errors) is greater than the cost of the error. It's also important to bear in mind that you can never be sure you've identified a true error. You are, after all, making a guess about the uncertain future.

The theory of rational expectations is reflected even in the animal kingdom. We have two dogs and our house has a more-or-less circular hallway. When the dogs are feeling energetic, they like to chase each other around that circle, especially when one of them has a bone of contention. Each time they start by one simply chasing the other in the same direction. It isn't long, however, before one anticipates what the other is doing and reverses direction to intercept the other one. Often they both try the ploy and they reverse the reversals. In other words, even animals take advantage of predictable events and adjust their behavior accordingly in order to have more success.

Successful market-beating strategies have an inherent tendency to self-destruct.

One of the fascinating aspects of an efficient market is that whenever a way is discovered to beat the market, it spontaneously leads to its own demise. Successful market-beating strategies have an inherent tendency to self-destruct. They synthesize their own poison pill. In fact, this is part of the dynamic process that creates market efficiency. "The basic reasoning behind the EMH is that in a competitive financial environment successful strategies self-destruct" (Bodie, *et al*, 1996). "Profitable trading strategies are self-limiting and self-destructive, eventually discovered and eliminated through overuse" (Rubenstein, 2001).

Suppose you notice that the stock price of a suntan lotion company went up for three consecutive summers. You decide that next spring you will buy it and take advantage of the rise in value. You think you could see a ten percent increase in your money in just a few months.

If there had been a pattern that had been that regular and had such a simple cause and effect, don't you think other people might have noticed it too? Insofar as any such pattern existed, other people would want to buy the stock in the spring too. As they did, its price would go up at that time. Also, why would anyone want to sell in the spring if they knew its price would be higher just a few months later?

If a stock's price is expected to be higher tomorrow, it will be higher today. The stock market is an arena populated with serious and sophisticated players where huge amounts of money are at stake. Anyone who

"Stock prices fell sharply today on the fear that stock prices would fall sharply."

The Wall Street Journal

thinks he's discovered a surefire, low-cost way to fleece those other players is deluding himself. He's suffering from a hazardous overconfidence. Do you think you could discover a pattern of other investors repeatedly shooting themselves in the foot that they haven't noticed?

In securities markets, the cost of making errors can be enormous, as well as the benefits of finding and exploiting other peoples' errors. Of course, some of the players in the market are none too bright, but as other players compete to take advantage of the errors, the errors will be eliminated and their impact will be minimal and transitory. A good working assumption to make is that no easy money is left on the table. People invest because they want to make money. They don't just carelessly leave profit-making opportunities lying around in plain view. That's contrary to human nature.

Nature abhors a vacuum, and efficient markets abhor incorrect prices. A vacuum draws matter, a low-priced stock draws buyers, and a high-priced stock draws sellers. Neither a vacuum nor a mis-priced stock represents equilibrium conditions.

The theory of rational expectations has been criticized from the standpoint that people aren't always rational. That's obviously true. However, in order for the theory to be rejected, you essentially have to assume that everyone is asleep. Only a small number of alert investors need to detect the pricing error in order for it to be corrected.

If people are so dumb, how come more of us smart people don't get rich?
Peter Bernstein

The self-destruction of successful strategies is similar to the proverbial pot of gold at the end of the rainbow. The end of a rainbow is a perfect example of something that's always out of reach even though it appears to be reachable. As is the case with trying to take advantage of mis-priced stocks, the act of moving toward the objective makes it move farther away. Investor behavior is not as dependable as the physics of light refraction, but the tendencies are very powerful nonetheless.

The risk-adjusted rates of return for all stocks tend toward equality.

Investors buy stocks that they expect to have a higher-than-average return and sell those that they expect to have lower returns. When they do, they bid up the prices of the stocks expected to have higher-than-

average returns and drive down the prices of those expected to have lower-than-average returns. The prices of the stocks adjust until the returns, adjusted for risk, are equal for all stocks.

Thomas Sargent, "Rational Expectations,"
Fortune Encyclopedia of Economics

One of the most counterintuitive, but nevertheless important, conclusions of Modern Portfolio Theory is that the risk-adjusted, expected rates of return for all stocks are approximately equal. Most people's reaction to that assertion is disbelief. "What? You mean to tell me that the appreciation potential for Microsoft is the same as Consolidated Edison? You must be crazy!" Assuming the two stocks have the same risk level, they basically have to have the same expected total return. Why? If, at current prices, the expected return for Microsoft is obviously higher than for Consolidated Edison, why would anyone buy Consolidated Edison? The only way the market can be in equilibrium is for the relative prices of the two companies to have already incorporated the inherent differences in the companies. In a voluntary exchange environment, that's the way it has to be.

Envision a market consisting of two securities of approximately equal risk. Security A is expected to grow at a 10 percent rate. Security B is expected to grow at a 20 percent rate. Such a situation would not last for long. If the market consensus were that stock A would grow at 10 percent and stock B at 20 percent, investors would attempt to sell A and buy B. This would put upward pressure on the price of B and downward pressure on the price of A.

When would the adjustment process stop? Not until the new slopes of the expected growth lines were the same, that is, parallel. Only then would shifts from one stock to the other stop. Like the fantail on the windmill facing in the same direction as the wind, only parallel growth expectancies represent a position of rest. That's what's meant by market equilibrium. Any other set of conditions will give the participants incentives to make changes.

In light of the price adjustments, from that point on, the two stocks have an equal expectation of future returns (taking risk into account). Any other set of conditions would not represent market equilibrium. There would be shortages or surpluses of one or the other of the stocks. The relative prices have to be such that the two stocks are equally promising from that point forward. Investors will adjust their portfolios until there's an approximately equal expectation for both stocks.

Figure 4-1

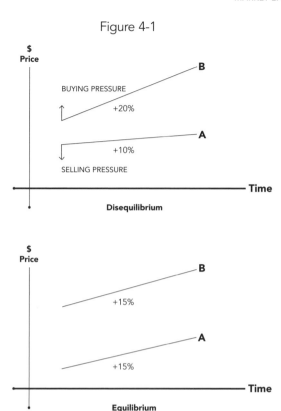

Mis-priced stocks are excess return opportunities and are not consistent with market equilibrium. Profit-making opportunities attract buyers, and the influx of buyers erases the opportunity.

Even a mediocre company has a positive price, which means that someone is buying the stock. Why buy the stock of a mediocre company when you could just as well buy an excellent company? The answer is simple: because the prices have adjusted to reflect the relative differences. If it weren't for adjustments in prices, all investment money would go to the companies with the most favorable outlooks and none to the worst companies. What would happen to relative prices if people invest only in companies with favorable outlooks? Recall how point spreads make betting on the poorer team a logical option.

It's an empirical question.

The theory of market efficiency is powerful in and of itself. Nevertheless, whether or not the theory accurately describes reality is, as economists like to say, an empirical question.

It's been said that there are an infinite number of hypotheses to explain any given phenomenon. The history of science is filled with discarded theories that once seemed imminently plausible. The population of hypotheses that sound good is many times greater than the number of hypotheses that can be supported by evidence.

Well into the 19th century physicians believed that bleeding patients was an effective treatment for a variety of ailments even though the opposite is true. They were able to hold that belief because of the poor state of empirical evidence.

As is true with all theories about the real world, whether or not securities markets are efficient is basically an empirical question. Empirically testing a theory is the rigorous process of comparing the theory to reality. Securities transactions occur in currency denominations and readily lend themselves to measurement. Such data are ripe for statistical analysis.

> *Tests of market efficiency demonstrate that U.S. securities markets are highly efficient, impounding relevant information about investment values into security prices quickly and accurately.*
> William Sharpe, *et al, Investments* (6th ed.)

> *The central message of the huge volume of literature on market efficiency is the supreme difficulty of earning abnormal returns making use only of publicly available information.*
> Lawrence Summers, "Does the Stock Market Rationally Reflect Fundamental Values?"
> *Journal of Finance*, July 1986.

"The cleanest evidence on market-efficiency comes from event studies."

Tests of the speed and accuracy of price adjustments to new information are known as "event studies." According to Eugene Fama, considered the foremost authority on market efficiency, "The cleanest evidence on market-efficiency comes from event studies, especially event studies on daily returns" (Fama, 1970).

The general conclusion of event studies is that market prices adjust rapidly to new information. Stock prices are quick studies. They learn and absorb information almost instantaneously. Keep in mind, however, that new information is inherently more uncertain than old information. It takes time before its significance and validity can be evaluated and confirmed.

One of the major pieces of evidence that is often adduced in favor to the hypothesis of market efficiency is the prompt response of stock prices to news. Countless studies have demonstrated that stock prices respond almost instantaneously to new information, and that no predictable excess returns can be earned by trading after the information has been released.

Lawrence Summers, "Does the Stock Market
Rationally Reflect Fundamental Values?"
Journal of Finance, July 1986.

Every actively managed mutual fund is an ongoing clinical trial of market efficiency.

In regard to Friedman's standard for a theory, the ultimate litmus test is the theory's ability to predict. Pricing efficiency implies it will be difficult to beat the market. The evidence indicates overwhelmingly that that is, in fact, the case. Ultimately, the most compelling and relevant empirical evidence of market efficiency is the basic fact that it is so difficult to beat the market.

Mutual funds shed considerable light on the active versus passive debate. No other investment structure offers as much easily accessible data that can be used to measure and evaluate actual results. Mutual funds put theory into practice while generating a treasure trove of evidence. They are ready-made and easily reachable tests of hypotheses, veritable test flights of an active manager's experimental aircraft. Once someone starts a mutual fund, he effectively makes himself naked to the world, and what's revealed is not a pretty sight.

Fortunately, for the brevity of this discussion, the results of the investigations of mutual fund performance are rather uniform.

James Lorie and Mary Hamilton,
The Stock Market: Theories and Evidence

If there is merit in a particular system or strategy, then the system ought to work when it's applied. If the system does not work in practice, that's a strong indication of problems or flaws in the strategy and underlying logic. Furthermore, if it doesn't work in practice, what good is it? You may be able to make a persuasive and compelling hypothetical case that the strategy is sound. However, how good it sounds is not what's relevant or useful. All money managers sound intelligent.

The Value Line mutual fund is a revealing case in point. If you've ever invested in individual stocks, you are probably familiar with Value Line's research reports on individual companies. It publishes detailed quarterly reports on 1,700 companies.

Value Line also offers its own mutual funds. According to the prospectus for the Value Line fund, "The fund makes investment decisions based on the Value Line Ranking System for timeliness. The system is based on historical prices and reported earnings, recent earnings and price momentum, and the degree to which the latest earnings deviate from estimated earnings." For the past ten years, the fund's performance has trailed the S&P 500 by 2.6 percent. The fund's extensive research capabilities apparently aren't enough to beat the market, and its timeliness ratings are of little or no value. Even the vast amount of research done by companies like Value Line is miniscule compared to the information embodied in a stock's price. Furthermore, the researchers can never be sure they've discovered a true pricing error.

The poor performance of the funds is powerful evidence that there is no payoff for market research. A common misconception about the market is that anyone who's willing to do some research can beat the market. Ironically, the reality is that no one can beat the market no matter how much research he does—at least not when "beating the market" is properly defined.

If there's anyone who could beat the market, it ought to be mutual fund managers. Managers of mutual funds provide themselves every imaginable advantage in their attempts to beat the market. They are highly trained and educated. The fund companies can afford to pay whatever it takes to attract the best talent. They have access to vast stores of research and data as well as the computer capacity to filter and analyze the data.

Yet the record demonstrates time and again that mutual fund managers do not make abnormal rates of return any more often than can be accounted for by pure chance. Each year only about one-fourth of active managers make excess returns relative to the appropriate index. Furthermore, the ones who beat the market one year have no significant likelihood of repeating in future years.

A number of comprehensive studies have examined the long-term performance of mutual funds. The studies by Jensen (1978), Sharpe (1966), Malkiel (1995), and Carhart (1997) are particularly noteworthy. Carhart evaluated 1,892 equity funds for the period 1962 to 1993 for the equivalent of 16,109 "fund years." He concluded, "The results do not support the existence of skilled or informed mutual fund portfolio managers."

These results are consistent with the EMH. It is what the EMH predicts will happen. If you don't believe the market is efficient, how do you explain those results?

"If you're so smart, why aren't you rich?" has to be one of the most revealing and illuminating questions ever invented. Furthermore, if you believe you are capable of beating the market, you should ask yourself why you think you can do so when mutual fund managers cannot. What advantage, specifically, do you possess that they don't? If you think you can beat the market by doing research, you need to have an answer for the following question: why can't Value Line, perhaps the most powerful and well-funded research service in the industry, beat the market? Why do you think you will be successful when it wasn't? What mistake is it making that you're going to avoid?

Some researchers argue that the evidence of mutual fund performance is a confirmation of the "strong form" of the EMH. Because of their extensive research efforts, it could be argued that mutual funds discover non-public information. Unfortunately, there is no clearly defined line between public and non-public information.

> *Several studies of the performance of mutual funds, whose performance*
> *is visible, support the contention that professionally managed portfolios*
> *do not outperform randomly selected portfolios of equal riskiness. These*
> *findings are consistent with the strong form of the hypothesis.*
> James Lorie and Mary Hamilton,
> *The Stock Market: Theories and Evidence*

The numerologists of the financial world.

> *The roulette wheel has no memory.*
> Peter Bernstein

The "weak form" of the EMH is also something investors should know about, if for no other reason than to be amused. The EMH definition earlier in this chapter said "The market is held to be 'weak form efficient' if share price changes are *independent of past price changes*." (emphasis added)

The weak form posits that a stock's price history contains no useful information relevant to its future price behavior. "Previous price changes cannot be used to predict future price changes." (Lorie and Hamilton, 1973) Or, if you want to get technical, "stock prices exhibit no serial dependencies." (Merton, 1987)

The conclusion of numerous studies is that price changes are permanent—they leave the past behind. There is no information regarding future price changes in past stock price changes; price changes have no memory.

The current price of a stock is the best attainable summary of all that's now knowable. What was knowable in the past has now been superseded and rendered obsolete—it's no longer state-of-the-art.

The weak form of the EMH is particularly relevant to a variation of active management known as "technical analysis." Practitioners of technical analysis are known as technicians, chartists, or "elves" (on the PBS show "Wall Street Week"). Such people believe there are discernible and exploitable patterns in graphs of a stock's price history. They even have names and categories for the patterns—support levels, trading ranges, bear traps, head-and-shoulders, necklines, trend lines, break-out points, up flags, down flags, resistance levels, bull traps, channels, support zones, and congestion zones, for example. They calculate various aspects of pricing history, such as "sixty-day moving averages."

> *Technical analysis is anathema to the academic world. We love to pick on it. Our bullying tactics are prompted by two considerations: (1) the method is patently false; and (2) it's easy to pick on. And while it may seem a bit unfair to pick on such a sorry target, just remember: it's your money we are trying to save.*
> Burton Malkiel, *A Random Walk Down Wall Street*

Technical analysis readily lends itself to hypothesis testing, and all the research conclusions point uniformly in the same direction. Nevertheless, many of the elements of technical analysis have great intuitive and emotional appeal. For example, if a stock once priced at $40 a share is now priced at $20, there's a natural tendency to think that it will someday be drawn back to the $40 range. You hope that it has some kind of homing instinct pulling it back to where it's supposed to be. That's particularly true if you yourself paid $40 for it.

Belief in technical analysis stems from a profound confusion about the basis of stock prices. It proceeds from a premise that stock prices are entities separate from other realities.

Technicians seem to believe that prices themselves have their own behavior characteristics. In other words, they basically deny that prices reflect information or that prices result from supply and demand dynamics. They apparently believe that prices levitate. When you get to the crux of technical analysis as a theory of stock price determination, it essentially says that stock prices determine stock prices.

Technicians give physical characteristics to prices, talking in terms of momentum, support levels, and breakout points. They act as though prices have mass and lives of their own. Technicians are the numerologists of the financial world. The more you think about technical analysis, the more ludicrous it becomes.

Malkiel points out that some technical analysts deliberately avoid examining other factors that might affect a stock's price. Do they just think that the price went up or down for no reason? Might there have been other determinants of the price history? Do they think that prices adhere to various patterns regardless of what else is going on? What is the strength of the pattern relative to other factors affecting the price?

The fact that they've named so many patterns is strong evidence that there are no true patterns. Nevertheless, many investors believe in technical analysis, and numerous books and newsletters are devoted to the strategy. The book *Technical Analysis of Stock Trends* by Robert Edwards is in now in its eighth edition. It is 752 pages of unadulterated sophistry, and it illustrates how even asinine ideas may have remarkable appeal.

The book and movie, *A Beautiful Mind,* showed an extreme case of obsessing over the search for patterns whether or not any exist. I can't say for sure that technical analysts are clinically schizophrenic, but it's clear they don't have a good connection with reality.

Market efficiency or a random walk?

One of the unresolved issues among theoreticians is that of whether securities markets are best described as being efficient or as being "a random walk." Random walk discussions emphasize stock price behavior, while market efficiency focuses more on explaining that behavior. The differences between these two alternatives are relatively subtle, but an explanation of the differences is instructive.

In the discussion to this point the stock market has been described as being efficient—defined as stock prices fully and correctly reflecting available information. In his classic book, *A Random Walk Down Wall Street*, as quoted on previous pages, Burton Malkiel uses the random walk model to describe the behavior of the stock market. Malkiel's definition of random walk basically parallels market efficiency and has the same weak, semi-strong, and strong variations. The randomness of stock price changes is one of the most compelling types of evidence of market efficiency.

In an efficient market, investors will incorporate any new information immediately and fully in security prices. New information is just that: new, meaning a surprise (anything that is not a surprise is predictable and should have been predicted before the fact). Because happy surprises are about as likely unhappy ones, price changes in an efficient market are about as likely to be positive as negative...In a perfectly efficient market, price changes are random.

William Sharpe et al. Investments (6th ed.)

Price changes are random because news (new information) is random. The price already includes all existing (old) information. The randomness (unpredictability) is evidence of efficiency, i.e., that the price reflects all currently available information.

There is a relatively low level of uncertainty about many aspects of the future—it is highly unlikely that General Electric will declare bankruptcy tomorrow, for example. There is a large degree of momentum to its operations. But when something happens that we did not expect, that is news. News is the unexpected, the unpredicted, the unanticipated.

Unquestionably, one of the things that makes stock prices change is news. What is news, after all? News, by definition, is unpredictable. The sun rising in the east is significant, but since it is predictable, it is not news. There's no information content in predictable statements. You know no more following the statement than you did before. "It's always darkest at night," for example. Or, "Castro Predicts Communism Will Outlive Him" (an actual headline). Is anyone surprised he would say that?

Stock prices incorporate information as it exists at a point in time. News adds to and alters the existing stock of information. If it is judged to be significant news, the stock's price will change accordingly.

The EMH is a theory of price determination and price changes. It says that information determines prices, and consequently, that changes in information (news) will result in changes in prices. Think of information as our best available approximation of reality.

Note carefully what the random walk theory says: stock price changes are random. If the theory is not explained carefully, there is a tendency to think that it says stock prices themselves are random. Anyone who thinks that's what the random walk theory is saying will, of course, reject it as absurd. That's particularly true of someone who doesn't like its conclusions and implications. The price of a stock at any given time, and especially its price relative to other stocks, is definitely not random. It reflects information, and information incorporates all that's currently knowable about reality. It can often be seen in retrospect that prices were wrong about reality, but the errors cannot be identified before the fact because they are random in nature.

Superior predictive ability is the essential ingredient in beating the market.

Randomness has critical implications for investors. A distinguishing characteristic of a random variable is that it is not predictable. Attempting to beat the market, more than anything else, involves predictions. Without extraordinary prediction success there are no feasible opportunities for making excess returns. A stock's price already incorporates a prediction. What makes you think your prediction is better than that? Be careful about wishful thinking.

You have to know something before the fact in order to place yourself in a position to profit from it. To actually win money, you have to place your bet before the race is run. Identifying winners after the race is easy. The difficulty is finding anyone who will take your bet then. After the race has been run, the information has no profit potential. As Johnny Carson used to say, "Timing is everything."

Randomness fundamentally implies the absence of profit-making opportunities. If stock price changes are random, you will not be able to identify the above-average changes as opposed to the average or below-average changes. If you cannot do that, you will not be able to beat the market. You may very well make a positive rate of return, but that's not the objective of active management.

Whether securities markets should be seen as a random walk or as efficient is, in a sense, a rather arcane point. Both, however, lead to the same practical conclusion: Attempts to beat the market are doomed to failure.

No theory has all the answers.

Market efficiency is generally regarded as a given among academic financial economists. It goes a long way toward explaining how securities markets work and is heavily supported by numerous empirical studies. Nevertheless, no theory has all the answers and no theory is without its skeptics. The working motto of the experts on Wall Street is "often wrong but never in doubt." An implicit motto of the scientific method could be stated: "sometimes right, sometimes wrong, always in doubt."

Two questions in particular bear review. (1) Does the market overreact? (2) Why is there such a high level of trading activity on the securities markets?

The first question is one that even casual observers of stock market behavior have wondered about. In the short-run, at least, don't the wide swings in stock prices indicate movements away from their fundamental values? The price swings appear to be out of sync with general and company-specific realities. It certainly seems that the underlying realities and intrinsic values couldn't change as fast as particular prices or the market overall.

The evidence appears to indicate that the market does in some instances react out of proportion to the magnitude of the changes in underlying realities. Overreactions and under-reactions have been seen as evidence of irrationality, animal spirits, mob psychology, or contagious behavior. The studies of over- and under-reaction have been part of the impetus for a sub-group of financial economists who call their theory of markets "behavioral finance."

The assumption of rationality is one of the fundamental building blocks of economic theory. Still, I don't know of any reputable economist who's ever said that everyone acts rationally all the time—that is, unless the term is defined so broadly that it loses most of its meaning. The assumption of rationality is only an assumption of tendencies in behavior. Depending on how you define rationality, we all see or read about instances of irrationality almost every day. Whether or not the assumption is legitimate is measured by whether or not using it leads to reasonably accurate and useful predictions, especially in comparison to alternative theories.

Over-reaction and under-reaction in the stock market can be identified, but, so far at least, only retrospectively. As we discussed above, that restriction has significant practical limitations. Can you reliably identify when and if the market is overreacting or under-reacting? So far none of the people who emphasize the two extremes have shown an ability to exploit the tendency.

Behavioral finance advocates basically argue that stock prices are based on emotion as well as information. For the sake of discussion, let's say that's true. What are the implications?

If it's true, it probably doesn't change the conclusion that you can't beat the market. It just means that there's another reason why price changes are unpredictable. The so-called "contrarian" mutual funds are designed to take advantage of market over- and under-reaction. They're no more successful in generating excess returns than the more traditional actively managed mutual funds. Furthermore, as discussed previously, insofar as there is any regular pattern in over- and under-reaction, prices would adjust so as to cancel out the opportunities for excess returns. "The market, as we have seen, has many special features that protect it from aggregating irrationalities into prices" (Rubenstein, 2001). Because of the way the market works, and especially the fact everyone pays the same price for a given security at a given time, the irrationality or ignorance of some of the players is not particularly relevant.

If stock prices generally reflect underlying values of the companies, why is the volume of trading so high?

Another question not resolved by the EMH is, why is there so much buying and selling activity on the securities markets? If stock prices generally reflect underlying values of the companies, what's the point of the high volume of trading? You can neither consistently buy a stock for less than it's worth, nor sell it for more than it's worth. You might as well just buy and hold. The question becomes even more perplexing in light of the fact that there is a cost to buying and selling. One favorable result of the high volume of trading is that it makes stocks more liquid. It makes it easier for sellers to find buyers and vice versa.

Both the over/under-reaction and the high volume of transactions are mysteries that appear, at least, to be violations of the theory of rational expectations. They seem to be examples of systematic errors, especially in the excess activity case. Why don't the participants wake up to the fact that they are repeatedly shooting themselves in the foot? One of the objectives of the next chapter is to explore some possible answers to that question.

Market efficiency summary.

- ► The soul and significance of the hypothesis can be summed up in three words—prices reflect information. Prices and information define the nature of the contest.
- ► What you're hoping to find in your endeavor to beat the market are mis-priced securities.
- ► A mis-priced security is one that does not fully embody relevant information.
- ► Market timing is an issue of appropriate pricing. The overall level of the market is itself a kind of relative price.
- ► Only incorrect prices are capable of "correction."
- ► If you're going to beat the market, you do it by way of stock prices. You win or lose by way of prices.
- ► The information is in the price of the stock because anyone who has significant information can potentially profit by acting on it.

▶ The flexibility of stock prices and the intense competition among the players makes securities prices high-fidelity transmitters of information.

▶ The information is held, not by any particular investor, but rather by the stock's price.

▶ It is not necessary that all investors be well informed for the markets to be efficient.

▶ Everyone pays or receives the same price for a stock at any particular time, so all the participants get the full benefit of the incorporated information.

▶ Securities markets are efficient in regard to how well and how rapidly they absorb information and concentrate that information in the prices of securities.

▶ The quest for market-beating strategies boils down to information processing contests. The contest is between an individual player and the entire market—"one against all."

▶ An unbiased estimator is correct on average. It splits the population of errors down the middle.

▶ Research confirms that point spreads and stock prices are unbiased estimators.

▶ A predictable error can be avoided by an adjustment in behavior.

▶ A fundamental reason we make errors in our lives is that information has a cost.

▶ Successful market-beating strategies have an inherent tendency to self-destruct.

▶ Only a small number of alert players need to detect a pricing error in order for it to be corrected.

▶ Risk-adjusted expected rates of return for all stocks are approximately equal.

▶ The only way the market can be in equilibrium is for the relative prices of stocks to have already incorporated the relative differences of the companies.

▶ A common misconception about the market is that anyone who's willing to do some research can beat the market.

▶ Technical analysis proceeds from a premise that stock prices are entities separate from other realities.

▶ The current price of a stock is the best attainable summary of all that's now knowable.

▶ News, by definition, is unpredictable. News adds to and alters the existing stock of information.

▶ The EMH is a theory of price determination and price changes.

CHAPTER 5

Against All Odds: Why Do So Many Keep Trying to Beat the Market?

❧

This is one of the great mysteries of finance. Why do people believe they can do the impossible? And why do other people believe them?
Daniel Kahneman, Professor of Psychology, Princeton

An unexciting truth may be eclipsed by a thrilling lie.
Aldus Huxley

In spite of a consensus among researchers regarding market efficiency, most investors and money managers continue their quest for abnormal returns. Active managers keep trying to beat the market, and mutual fund investors continue choosing active managers. If they believed in market efficiency, they could be spending their time and money on something more productive or entertaining. So why don't they? In this chapter we examine several possible explanations for what Daniel Kahneman calls "one of the great mysteries of finance."

Some investors do appear to beat the market.

The most obvious reason people doubt market efficiency is that many money managers and individual investors do appear to succeed in beating the market. Have these apparent market winners somehow discovered a system or strategy for identifying mis-priced securities? Casual observers might very well be led to think that these managers and investors possess superior research capabilities or that they have some kind of indefinable intuition or knack.

However, producing above average returns isn't necessarily the result of having a winning strategy for beating the market. Quite possibly it's simply a matter of luck.

If you hear about a money manager making excess returns, the tendency is to assume it was the result of skill.

Was it luck or was it skill? A surprising number of investment issues hinge on that question. Answering it in an informed, well-considered way will help you evaluate investment alternatives and reduce wasted effort.

When a person achieves above average results in one activity or another, we may assume that it was the result of skill, luck, or some combination of the two. You might think it impossible to determine which of these factors—skill, luck, or both—were in play, but you would be wrong. Actually, there happen to be techniques designed to do just that.

One such useful technique is to chart overall results. If they fall into the pattern known as a bell-shaped curve, we may reasonably assume that little or nothing but raw chance was at work. At the very least, a bell-shaped

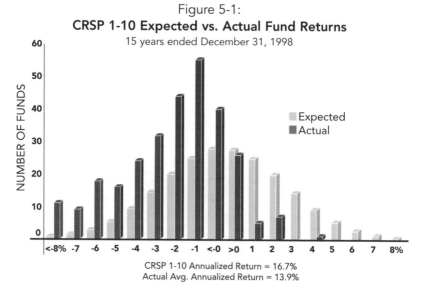

Figure 5-1:
CRSP 1-10 Expected vs. Actual Fund Returns
15 years ended December 31, 1998

CRSP 1-10 Annualized Return = 16.7%
Actual Avg. Annualized Return = 13.9%

Source: Micropal and Center for Research in Security Prices

"normal distribution" is strong circumstantial evidence of randomness. As a matter of fact, a bell-shaped distribution is what we observe when we examine the results of money managers.

Figure 5-1 shows the performance distribution for the 288 stock funds existing during the full fifteen-year period 1983 to 1998. The rate of return for the entire U.S. stock market for the period was 16.7 percent. The average return for the 288 actively managed mutual funds was 13.9 percent, a difference of 2.8 percent.

The returns are shown in comparison to the market, meaning that zero on the graph translates into a 16.7 percent rate of return. The "CRSP 1-10" returns includes all ten deciles of the U.S. stock market. The relative performance is skewed markedly to the left—showing that many more funds under-performed the market than out-performed the market. (For reference, the actual returns are compared to returns that would have resulted from nothing but chance.) In terms of annual compounded rates of return, many of the funds under-performed the market by six percent or more, a drag on performance that would make a profound difference over the fifteen-year period. Amazingly, as you will see later, this sorry record actually understates the real damage of active management because of something called "survivor bias."

The distribution of results, if anything, shows that active managers are unlucky. Active managers might well feel like singing the country and western lyrics, "If it weren't for bad luck, I'd have no luck at all." The presence of skill, intelligence, or intuition on the part of money managers is, as researchers sometimes say, an unnecessary hypothesis.

If you observed someone in a casino winning money at a roulette wheel, you would probably assume that he was just being lucky. If you hear about a money manager generating excess returns, however, the tendency is to assume that it's because of skill and intelligence. The conclusion of research and statistical analysis is that luck plays the same role in making excess investment returns as in winning at roulette.

If the excess returns generated by some money managers are due to luck, most research on mutual funds is a waste of time.

You might ask why it should matter if a money manager is skillful or just lucky? Who cares whether it was luck or skill, so long as the results were exceptional? When an event is the result of skill, it usually can be repeated in the future, but the presence or absence of luck at any particular time is random. Who knows when or if we're going to get lucky?

What we need to know is whether past performances can be repeated, and that is why the luck versus skill question is relevant. If performance cannot be repeated in any predictable way, why waste time researching the track records of mutual funds?

Past performance is used to determine the rankings on lists of the so-called best mutual funds and for the star system used by Morningstar, Inc., an investment research firm. If these past performances were the result of skill, they could reasonably be expected to recur, and this would give them predictive value. On the other hand, if the performances are the result of luck, the track records mean virtually nothing. Is there profitable, significant information in the track records, or just noise?

The evidence clearly indicates that mutual fund performance is determined by luck. Numerous studies have confirmed this. The top performers from past periods of one, five, or even ten years have no significantly greater probability of being top performers in succeeding periods than a fund randomly selected from the population of managers in the same asset class. While studies sometimes find a slight tendency for past winners to repeat and a somewhat stronger tendency for losers to repeat, these tendencies vanish after just one year. Extensive studies by Davis (2001), Brown and Groetzmann (1995), Ibbotson and Groetzman (1994), and Elton *et al* (1996) all confirmed there is no significant persistance in mutual fund performance.

Anyone who thinks mutual fund performance is the result of skill will find it hard to explain this lack of consistency. Are fund managers skillful in one year but not the next? That simply doesn't make sense. If the performance resulted from diligent research, did the managers just get lazy?

In skill activities such as golf there is considerable persistence and carryover from one period to the next. Golf talents are randomly distributed throughout the population, and there are more average golfers than either very good or very bad golfers. As a result, golf handicaps take on a normal, bell-shaped distribution. However, once a golfer's relative position in the distribution is established, there is a high degree of staying power.

Superstar Tiger Woods is one of about 300 touring professional golfers in the United States. These professionals consistently rank in the top one-one-hundred thousandth of one percent of the 25 million Americans who play golf, and they maintain their lofty rankings year after year. Their position on the extreme high end of the distribution during any given year is unlikely to change much during subsequent years. This is real information, not just noise.

Figure 5-2:
PGA Annual Scoring Average Rankings

1997	1998	1999	2000	2001
1 Nick Price	1 David Duval	1 Tiger Woods	1 Tiger Woods	1 Tiger Woods
2 Tiger Woods	2 Tiger Woods	2 David Duval	2 Phil Mickelson	2 Davis Love III
3 Greg Norman	3 Davis Love III	3 Davis Love III	3 Ernie Els	3 Sergio Garcia
4 Davis Love III	4 Jim Furyk	4 Justin Leonard	4 David Duval	T4 Phil Mickelson
5 Tom Lehman	5 Mark O'Meara	5 Hal Sutton	5 Paul Azinger	T4 Vijay Singh
6 Jesper Parnevik	6 Nick Price	6 Jim Furyk	6 Nick Price	6 Nick Price
7 Jim Furyk	7 John Huston	7 Nick Price	7 Stewart Cink	T7 David Duval
8 Scott Hoch	8 Ernie Els	8 Vijay Singh	8 Steve Flesch	T7 Bob Estes
9 Justin Leonard	9 Jesper Parnevik	T9 Dudley Hart	9 Tom Lehman	9 Scott Hoch
10 Phil Mickelson	10 Vijay Singh	T9 Payne Stewart	10 Loren Roberts	10 Chris DiMarco
11 Loren Roberts	11 Fred Couples	11 Chris Perry	11 Davis Love III	11 Scott Verplank
12 Ernie Els	12 Steve Stricker	12 Ernie Els	12 Jesper Parnevik	12 Bernhard Langer
13 David Duval	13 Bob Tway	13 Bob Estes	13 Vijay Singh	13 Charles Howell III
14 Lee Janzen	T14 Scott Hoch	14 Fred Funk	14 Fred Couples	14 Jim Furyk
15 Brad Faxon	T14 Payne Stewart	15 Tom Lehman	T15 Jim Furyk	15 David Toms
16 Mark Calcavecchia	16 Hal Sutton	16 Jeff Maggert	T15 John Huston	16 Tom Lehman
17 David Ogrin	17 Scott Verplank	T17 Carlos Franco	17 Hal Sutton	T17 Scott McCarron
18 Payne Stewart	18 Glen Day	T17 Phil Mickelson	18 Justin Leonard	T17 Mike Weir
T19 Steve Elkington	19 Mark Calcavecchia	19 Scott Hoch	19 David Toms	19 Jesper Parnevik
T19 Bob Estes	20 Justin Leonard	T20 Stewart Cink	20 Kirk Triplett	20 Jeff Sluman
		T20 Tim Herron		

Source: Professional Golfers Association (pgatour.com)

Figure 5-2 lists the top twenty professional golfers for the five-year period 1997-2001. The carryover from one year to the next is obviously persistent. Tiger Woods has been first or second all five years. Nick Price was first in 1997 and either sixth or seventh the other four years. Davis Love III has been ranked either third or fourth four out of the five years. The golfers' stroke averages and relative rankings are highly consistent.

If golf scores were random, the persistence of these winners is astronomically improbable. The improbability implies another explanation besides pure chance. The most obvious and plausible answer is that skill is involved.

Figure 5-3 illustrates the absence of persistence in mutual fund performance. The table shows two measures of the relative performance of five large actively managed mutual funds. Take, for example, the Janus Twenty Fund. Its performance relative to its peers, as measured by performance within category, went from the second quartile in 1990 to first, fourth, fourth, fourth, first, first, second, first, first, fourth, and fourth. That's equivalent to Tiger Woods' stroke average moving from 69 one year

Figure 5-3:
Mutual Fund Performance
American Century Ultra Inv

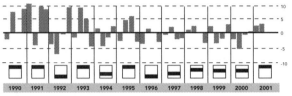

American Funds Growth Fund A

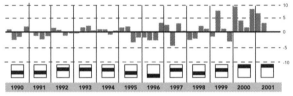

Fidelity Blue Chip Growth

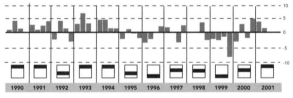

Fidelity Contrafund

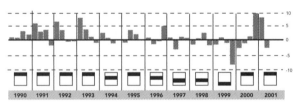

Janus Twenty

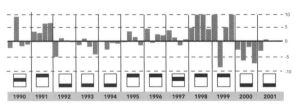

Source: Morningstar, Inc.

to 105 the next, 85 the next, and so on. Such rapid and extreme changes almost never occur in skill-based activities. Persistence proves skill; lack of persistence proves luck.

Of course, there is some degree of luck involved in golf—even Tiger Woods admits that—while there is arguably some degree of skill involved in active management. However, the enormous difference in the persistence of results shows the residual element in each activity is very small. Luck is a trivial factor in annual golf stroke averages, and skill is a trivial factor in active management results.

Professional golfers remain at the extreme high end of the probability distribution—a tiny sliver of one percent. In contrast, active managers can't even manage to stay in the same general range. The two patterns are polar opposites.

Also shown in Figure 5-3 are comparisons of fund performance versus category average. Again there is no consistency or persistence in any fund's performance. The funds spend about the same amount of time below the line as above.

The inconsistency of their performance proves they have no control over results and suggests that active management is nothing more than an elaborately disguised crapshoot. Just as you can't control dice, you can't control or predict random changes in stock prices. At a minimum it proves that the strategies followed by active managers are highly error prone. Since these managers make the right calls only about half the time, what possible assurance can we have that their correct calls will more than offset their errors? The inconsistency of their success reflects the high degree of risk and uncertainty inherent in active management.

Figure 5-4 shows another example of inconsistent performance. The data is from the article "Top Mutual Funds of 1998" in the February 1999 issue of the *Dow Jones Investment Advisor*. The magazine's editors preface the table with the following statement: "Once again, on the pages that follow, we present the top-performing mutual funds in each of twelve categories. Then, in the table below, we preface this historical data with a major caveat: Top funds don't usually repeat. Notice that only three of the 1997 top funds finished in the top quartile in 1998. In fact seven actually lost money last year...Be afraid, be very afraid."

To say that top funds don't usually repeat is an understatement. Three of the funds went all the way from the top percentile to the bottom percentile. Seven of the twelve funds actually lost money during a year when the market was up 28.6 percent!

Figure 5-4:
Top Mutual Funds of 1998

THOSE WHO ARE IGNORANT OF HISTORY...

Here's how 1997's top mutual funds performed in 1998. In the percentile rankings, 1 represents the top 1% and 100 the bottom 1%. The S&P 500 returned 33.4% in 1997 and 28.6% in 1998, and the Lehman Bros. corporate/government bond index returned 9.8% and 9.5%, respectively.

Category	Fund	Return in '97	Return in '98	Percentile in '98
Growth	American Heritage	75.00%	-61.22%	100
Blend	Hartford Capital Appreciation B	54.15%	2.52%	56
Specialty	Pilgrim Bank & Thrift A	64.09%	-1.83%	82
International Stock	Lexington Troika Dialog Russia	67.40%	-82.98%	100
International Bond	Fidelity New Markets Income	17.52%	-22.38%	32
Hybrid	Transamerica Premier Balanced Inv	35.38%	29.30%	2
Municipal Bond	Fundamental Fixed-Inc High-Yield Muni	15.67%	-0.29%	100
Government Bond	American Cent-Benham Tgt Mat 2025 Inv.	30.14%	21.92%	1
Convertible Bond	Davis Convertible Secs. Fund A	28.68%	-1.80%	70
Corporate Bond	Smith Barney Investment Grade Bond B	16.44%	7.89%	46
Corporate Bond-High Yield	Battery Park High-Yield A	18.02%	-0.03%	49
Value	Oakmark Select	55.02%	16.21	3

Source: Morningstar Mutual Funds

74 DOW JONES INVESTMENT ADVISOR *February 1999*

An interesting question that never seems to get asked is this: if the magazine's editors can see that the past means absolutely nothing in terms of future mutual fund performance, why do they continue doing their annual reviews of recent performance? Obviously the editors make no attempt to select their subject matter on the basis of what works and what doesn't. As long as subscribers read the articles, the magazine provides them.

The editor's words say one thing, but their actions say another. They attempt to distance themselves from the data, but the fact that they publish the surveys sends a misleading message that past performance really does mean something.

Ultimately, it's the responsibility of the investor to get the message that's made clear in the tables above. If you apply common sense to the facts they contain, you will come to the conclusion that there is no useful information in any mutual fund's past performance. In fact, common sense is really all that's required. You don't need a degree in finance, and you don't even need to believe in market efficiency.

One final example of inconsistency is the Profunds Internet Investors mutual fund. For the fourth quarter 2001, it was the best performing mutual fund out of approximately 12,000 mutual funds. For that quarter it had a total return of 94.3 percent! Unfortunately, for the entire year it was the worst performing fund! For the calendar year 2001 its total return was -76.3 percent (*Wall Street Journal*, January 7, 2002).

How is such extreme volatility possible? The managers of Profunds may have asked themselves this same question when faced with the brutal arithmetic and the heartbreaking results of their efforts at active management. In retrospect it's obvious they didn't have a clue.

Investing is about the future, not the past.

When you invest your money, what you care about is the future, not the past. That is why it's so important to determine whether past performances have been due to luck rather skill. If an active manager's positive results are due to luck, then he hasn't really beaten the market. More importantly, you can't rely on a continuation of his previous good luck.

Understandably, active managers who have done well recently never want their performance attributed to luck. No wonder. Luck is not a marketable commodity. If someone recommended you hire him because he's lucky, how would you react? Would you rather think of yourself as lucky or skillful? Which would be more favorable to your self-image?

Mutual fund companies would like you to believe they can give you good rates of return because they are skillfully managing your money. Certainly, they wouldn't want you to think they are counting on luck. No active manager ever comes right out and says, "Give us your money and we'll be lucky for you."

What's important for investors to remember is this—if you're relying on luck, you're gambling, not investing, and you're taking far more risk than you realize. What is your intention—investing or gambling?

What exactly does it mean to beat the market?

Another reason active managers and investors keep trying to beat the market is that many of them are confused about what that really means. They suffer from what Churchill called "terminological inexactitude."

For any debate to make sense, it's important to define terms. Too often, of course, that doesn't happen, and the result is a discussion that takes place on different planes or just goes around in circles. So it's essential that we establish a meaningful definition. To claim you've beaten the market, three conditions must be met:

1. Excess net returns relative to an index;
2. Same or lower risk relative to an index;
3. Results achieved with skill rather than chance.

Why make an index the benchmark? First, an index reflects the environment or backdrop, and its return reflects the average return for the entire population. It's also the rate of return you could get with almost no effort. Also, the reference points cannot be zero return and zero risk since meaningful comparisons only make sense relative to real-world alternatives.

In Modern Portfolio Theory, excess returns are termed alpha. In his book *Searching for Alpha: The Quest for Exceptional Investment Performance*, Ben Warwick defines alpha as follows: "The term alpha refers to that portion of an investor's return that is due to the skills of an investment manager, rather than the returns of the overall market."

When alpha is calculated for a mutual fund by a research service such as Morningstar, there is rarely any attempt to distinguish between luck and skill. The alpha calculation is simply based on historical performance. As you've seen, any excess returns of active management are probably luck-based. Simple track-record alphas, therefore, are misleading, as it may appear that many more managers have beaten the market than actually have.

Concerning the second condition, there's nothing inherently wrong with taking more risk to get higher returns. Nevertheless, it's important to keep in mind that risk and return are equally important investment dimensions. Both have to be taken into account in making apples-to-apples comparisons. You can't just assume that all investment alternatives are equally risky. If there's more risk involved with following one strategy over another, it should be taken into account. The next chapter is devoted to the topic of risk.

Efficient is not the same as perfect.

Another common source of doubt about market efficiency is the tendency to equate efficiency with perfection. That's a fairly natural mistake. Anyone who does believe that efficiency means perfection would likely reject the EMH.

Obviously, the market is not perfect. Nothing is. The market makes prediction errors up, down, and sideways. Some stocks rise in value much faster and some much slower than the overall average. You can observe all kinds of errors retrospectively or *ex post*. When you observe the market making errors, the natural conclusion you draw is that the pricing mechanism could not possibly be efficient—so, there must be profit-making opportunities for the savvy players.

When we look back at the market a year, a month, or even a week in the past, it's easy to see there were countless mis-priced stocks. However, there's a world of difference between what's knowable at one point in time versus what's knowable in another.

In the context of markets, it's hard to say what perfect means. How would it be defined? Would it mean that all predictions implicit in prices were always correct, that even in retrospect there were no pricing errors?

When you observe the market making errors, it doesn't imply that there's an opportunity for generating excess returns. Whatever alternative system you use to identify errors also will be prone to error. The evidence shows there is as much imperfection in all the alternatives as there is in the market. Nobel laureate Milton Friedman once asked an opponent in a debate, "What perfect solution on what perfect planet are you comparing this to?" Securities markets aren't perfectly efficient—they're just brutally efficient.

Perfect efficiency is a contradiction in terms. If this were a perfect world, we wouldn't even need to bother with efficiency in the first place. Efficiency is only relevant in an imperfect world—a world where we're constrained by limits. The basic economic reality is that our wants are greater than our ability to satisfy them.

Virtually every skeptical comment I've ever heard regarding market efficiency comes, at least in part, from a confusion between efficiency and perfection. Since perfection has little connection with the real world, it is not a particularly useful term or concept, and usually does more harm than good. Comparing yourself to perfection is an efficient way to make yourself miserable. Efficiency, on the other hand, is an extremely useful and practical concept.

Efficient does not mean perfect and perfect does not mean efficient. The only way to drive a market toward perfection would be to go beyond the point of efficiency in the search for bargains, that is, by spending more time and money searching than there is value in discovery. Perfection lies well beyond the point where marginal costs equal marginal benefits.

The American Economic Association once did a survey to measure the difference between economists and normal people. One of the questions they asked both economists and non-economists was, "Is anything worth doing worth doing well?" Most of the economists said no, most of the non-economists said yes. You can understand why there was a difference if you recall the lessons of marginal costs and marginal benefits.

You have to be aware of sub-par performance before you can get concerned about it.

It's fairly easy to see how self-interest drives active managers to ignore feedback and continue trying to beat the market. But why do their investors continue to tolerate the underperformance?

That's a good question, and no one has a complete answer. A partial answer lies in the fact that most investors don't know how to measure or evaluate the performance of their investments. The complexities of the investment world make it extremely easy to live in denial. This is part of the explanation for the continued existence of active management. Market-beating efforts would be viewed far more skeptically if investors got better feedback and had all the facts. The information problem is aggravated by the huge amount of information and misinformation generated by the investment industry. Wall Street is very good at obfuscating reality and distracting your attention.

Do you know the compound annualized rate of return on your investments? Probably you don't, especially if you own mutual funds or manage your own stock portfolio. How do I know that? For one thing, the calculations are not easy. In all likelihood you made your investments at various times, have made additions and changes, and do not calculate the performance at regular intervals.

It takes a financial calculator such as a Hewlett-Packard 12C or a Texas Instruments Business Analyst to compute the compound rates of return even if there is a single investment with no additions. To calculate compound rates of return with irregular contributions you need special software for your personal computer, that is, unless you are a math and computer wonk. Do you know your compound annual rate of return? If you do, I'm impressed.

Researchers Daniel Kahneman and Mark Riepe define a "well-calibrated" decision maker as one who doesn't make systematic errors when predicting.

> *Two groups of professionals have been found to be reasonably well-calibrated: meteorologists and handicappers at race tracks. Individuals in these professions learn to be well calibrated because of three characteristics of their trade: they face similar problems every day; they make explicitly probabilistic predictions; and they obtain swift and precise feedback on outcomes. When these conditions are not satisfied, overconfidence can be expected, for both experts and non-experts.*
> "Aspects of Investor Psychology,"
> *Journal of Portfolio Management,* summer 1998

An investment may appear to perform well even when its relative performance is poor.

The record shows that active management retards rather than enhances performance. Its negative impact generally goes unnoticed, however, and for a number of reasons you may not be aware of the damage done to your investments.

Part of the problem is that even if you know your rates of return, you probably don't regularly compare those rates to the appropriate benchmarks—large growth, small growth, international small, and so on. If you are working with irregular time periods, it may be very difficult to determine the benchmark. For instance, suppose you made an investment in June of 1992 and you want to see how you're doing in December of 2001. Do you know how to find the benchmark numbers for that time period? As will be discussed further in Chapter 8, an important practical advantage of passive management investing is that you eliminate the need to compare your performance to the benchmarks. You own the benchmarks.

Let's assume you discover your rate of return has been 11 percent over an eight-year period. That sounds pretty good, but once again, everything is relative, especially when it comes to evaluation. Did your strategy or portfolio manager add or subtract value? One of the commonest investment errors is confusing positive returns with excess returns.

If you achieved 11 percent but you were investing in an asset class that achieved a 15 percent rate of return during the corresponding period, your strategy or manager actually retarded your performance four percent. Furthermore, in all likelihood, more risk was incurred because of the lower degree of diversification inherent in active management.

The Beardstown Ladies—"Sorry, wrong number."

An illustrative and all too common example of confusion regarding rates of return is the experience of the famous "Beardstown Ladies." Some years ago a group of sixteen grandmotherly women residing in Beardstown, Illinois, formed an investment club. Unlike most other investment clubs, however, they became famous for their purported investment success and even wrote a best-selling investment how-to book. Titled *The Beardstown Ladies Common Sense Guide to Investing: How We Beat the Stock Market and You Can, Too*, this book laid out the investment strategies said to have generated a compound rate of return of 23.4 percent over a ten-year period. This impressive rate of return explains why the Beardstown Ladies became famous while most investment clubs toil in obscurity. For reasons that will become obvious, *The Beardstown Ladies Common Sense Guide to Investing* is no longer in print, but if you're interested you can probably still find a copy in your local used bookstore.

As is the norm with this genre of investment book, the claims made by the Beardstown Ladies had no third-party confirmation. In this instance someone did finally bother to check the record. Shane Tritsch, an editor at *Chicago* magazine, discovered that the book's rate of return calculation included the dues regularly paid by club members. In other words, the ladies calculated their rate of return based entirely on a comparison of beginning and ending values of their investment portfolio. They failed to take into account, however, the additions they had made to the portfolio, with the result that their apparent investment performance was greatly exaggerated (Gibbons, 2000).

The *Wall Street Journal* quoted the club's treasurer as follows: "I would not argue with anybody that we didn't have a 23.4 percent rate of return. But at the time we certainly thought we did." (*Wall Street Journal*, February 27,1998)

According to a later *Journal* article, "an independent audit found that the club's portfolio actually gained a market-lagging 9.15 percent annually. The Standard & Poor's 500-stock index gained an average of 14.9 percent annually over the same period" ("Investing Clubs Mostly Fail to Top Market," November 4, 1998).

This raises a number of questions. For example, why did they make such a gross and elementary error in evaluating their performance? How did they get away with it for so long? I have no way to know for sure, and I have no basis to believe the mistake was intentional. My guess is that it was mostly the result of wishful thinking leading to wishful measurement. But what about the people who bought their books and applied the advice primarily on the basis of erroneous and exaggerated information? Would the ladies have even bothered writing the book if they had known their actual rates of return?

The Beardstown Ladies story is unusual only because they were found out. The success of their book is a sad commentary on the gullibility of many investors. Their story illustrates the lack of scrutiny or verification that is the rule in the investment world. There is no system of accountability, and you can say virtually anything you want. Chances are no one will check out your story, and many people will take you at your word. Never believe any claim about investment performance without insisting on corroborating evidence.

Keep in mind, however, that even if the claims made by the Beardstown Ladies had been accurate, it would have meant nothing. There are thousands of investment clubs across the country. Some of them have undoubtedly experienced impressive rates of return, but was that performance the result of luck or skill? What's the most probable explanation?

Just as in the case of mutual funds, unusual performance of some investment club proves nothing about the reason for the performance. In all likelihood, their skill, strategy, or methods of stock selection had nothing to do with the excess returns. It's highly improbable that the Beardstown Ladies had anything useful to teach other investors. Even if they had been lucky, which apparently they weren't, you can't teach luck.

My intention is not to pick on the Beardstown Ladies. Their story just happens to offer a clear example of errors made all too frequently in the investment world. The real story is not what they did, but rather what it suggests investors are willing to believe and how easy they think it is to beat the market.

Stockbrokers easily avoid accountability.

The traditional relationship between stockbrokers and their clients adds to the difficulty of measuring performance. Typically, stockbrokers maintain a different portfolio for each client, and rarely do any two of them contain the same investments. This is true partly because clients have the final say in determining which investments are included in their portfolios. The composition of the portfolios is the result of a joint decision between stockbroker and client. Since the decisions are collarborative, the broker has no performance record that could truly be called his own. (In some instances the accounts are discretionary, which means that it isn't necessary for the broker to get approval for each individual investment. Relatively few brokerage accounts, however, are discretionary. An important disincentive for the broker is that such accounts place far more liability on him and his firm.)

Often the portfolio is influenced by what the broker's home office was pushing at the time the account was opened. The recommended list constantly changes, and the investments found in any given portfolio may depend on what the brokerage firm's flavor-of-the-month or hot stock du jour was at that time. Because there is no uniformity among his clients' accounts, calculating the broker's overall performance would be impossible.

The overwhelming majority of information used by active managers is redundant and therefore of no value.

In an important sense, the EMH is an application of information theory. This is indeed the Information Age, and ours is an information economy.

Not all information is created equal, however, and not everything dressed up like information actually is information.

Information assumes a variety of forms and characteristics and is not always useful for generating profits. For example, redundancy is one factor that will usually destroy the value and profit potential of information. Reinventing the wheel is a classic example of a waste of time. Although the information embodied in the wheel has enormous value to society, reinventing it is a useless exercise. Why? Because it is redundant.

The overwhelming majority of information offered or used by active managers is redundant and therefore of little or no value in generating excess returns. Redundancy transforms information into noise. In an efficient market public information and probably most private information are rapidly incorporated into the price of the stock. If the information is already in the price, you can't use it to enhance your rate of return. Active managers have simply come up with another way to reinvent the wheel. Redundant information is another issue that can be clarified by drawing parallels to point spreads in wagering.

Betting Point Spreads—Part Three: The challenge is identifying erroneous spreads.

So far we've seen how point spreads equalize the amount wagered on the opponents in a sports contest. The spread serves much the same role as flexible prices in equalizing the number of buyers and sellers for a given stock. Bookies are in a position similar to that of stock specialists. Both prefer to act primarily as clearing agents. Bookies connect and equalize the number of people betting on two opposing teams, while stock specialists connect and equalize buyers and sellers of stock. For stock specialists as well as bookies, happiness means having zero inventories and empty warehouses.

We also saw how point spreads prove effective in predicting the actual outcomes of games. Like stock market efficiency, point spreads are another reflection of rational expectations. In this way, point spreads fulfill the requirements of an "unbiased estimator." The point spread can only be a single number, while actual scores cover a range. Nevertheless, the point spread divides the population of errors down the middle, half above, half below. There are no systematic, predictable errors in the spreads, and on average they are accurate predictors.

Let's see how point spreads, like stock prices, reflect all public information. Point spreads reflect all that's known about the relative scoring abilities of two opposing teams. It's that fact that makes consistent winning a practical impossibility for sports gamblers.

You can do an immense amount of research on the two contestants in a particular game. You can look at their respective win-loss records. You can see how individual players match up against one another. You can see how well the two teams did against common opponents. Practically all the information you analyze is available to other bettors.

Just as efficient prices make beating the market extremely difficult, point spreads make winning with any consistency extremely difficult. It's critical to understand that in order to win money more than half the time you bet, it's simply not enough to identify the better team. Rather, what you need to discover are errors in the point spread. More specifically, you need to know something that has not already been taken into account in the spread.

Evaluating the spread is far more important and challenging than deciding which of the teams is independently good or bad in an absolute sense. Again, it's critical to bear in mind that everything is relative. To be a winner, you must identify point spreads that erroneously reflect the relative strengths of the two teams. Your search ought to be for a game with an erroneous spread—one where either the favored team is underestimated or the underdog is overestimated, one where other bettors are insufficiently optimistic about the favorite or insufficiently pessimistic about the underdog. The spread is your competition. This is a subtle but extremely important point. The point-spread errors define the moneymaking opportunities.

One stock's price relative to another is analogous to a point spread. Bear in mind that half the time the winning wager is on the losing team. If you always bet on the underdog you would win half the time, and if you always bet on the home team, you would win half the time. If the St. Louis Rams are the best football team in a particular season, should you bet money on them every week?

The profit potential is embodied in the errors.

One of the lessons of modern financial economics is that an investor must take care to consider the vast amount of information already impounded in a price before making a bet based on information.
Mark Rubenstein "Efficient Markets: Yes or No?"
Financial Analysts Journal, May-June 2001

A misconception seen with great regularity is thinking that the key to finding a buying opportunity is identifying a good company. This is Wall Street's most common logical error.

The following is a typical quote from the *Wall Street Journal*, "Mr. Campbell is going with Jones Apparel Group, the women's clothing maker in Bristol, Pa., which he says 'looks good' both as a value play and a growth play...'Management is highly respected in the industry,' he adds. 'They're doing the right thing to respond to customers.'" You can find similar quotes in every issue of the *Journal* or of similar publications, and you hear them repeatedly on cable TV financial shows.

Wall Street and the related media tend to work on the assumption that identifying strong companies is the secret to excess returns. In their typical fashion, active managers place all the emphasis on the factor with the least importance and virtually ignore what actually matters. You could make more money buying a mediocre company than a superior one if there's a greater error in the mediocre company's stock price, just as you can win a wager betting on the losing team if it loses by fewer points than the spread. You can make excess returns on a mediocre company if the consensus opinion reflected in the price exaggerates the company's negative qualities. If the information is already reflected in the prices, it's redundant and useless from a profit standpoint.

> *The most general implication of the efficient market hypothesis is that most security analysis is logically incomplete and valueless...The logical incompleteness consists of failing to determine or even consider whether the price of the stock already reflects the substance of the analysis. A very optimistic forecast of a company's future earnings is no justification for buying the stock; it is necessary that the analyst's forecast be significantly more optimistic than other forecasts. Such marked differences of opinion are the basis of abnormal gains and losses. A proper analytical report will include evidence of the existence of such a difference and support for the analyst's own view.*
>
> James Lorie and Mary Hamilton,
> *The Stock Market: Theories and Evidence*

Information about a company, good or bad, is useful only insofar as it's not already reflected in the price. Advice from a stock market whiz should include both information about the company and an explanation of why that information is not already incorporated in the stock's price. If you hear a piece of information about a particular company, do you think it matters whether or not that information is already reflected in the stock's price? Amazingly, that's a question that almost never gets asked.

Analysts often say something about a price being wrong, but they rarely offer any explanation for the market's oversight. They just say it's wrong with no explanation or evidence to back the statement. For example, an analyst quoted in the *Wall Street Journal* recommended buying Thermo

Instrument Systems. The price of the stock at the time was down 50 percent from what it had been a few months earlier, but the analyst said the price "seems unduly depressed in light of longer-term growth potential." What, specifically, caused it to be "unduly depressed?" How does he know that it's *unduly* depressed? What caused that particular stock to be inefficiently priced? The fact that analysts disregard these questions shows them to be abysmally naïve and profoundly confused.

Remember the critical role of prices in the investment process. The price represents the terms offered you for buying a piece of the action. What matters is not so much that one company is good relative to another, but rather that one stock's price reflects information better or worse relative to other stocks. It's not a matter of just the relative underlying realities, but rather the relative correctness of the prices reflecting those realities. If one company is twice as valuable as another company, buying its stock will not lead to excess returns if its outstanding stock is already twice as costly.

If you still have doubts about this ask yourself the following: is a good company a good buy regardless of the price? The typical stock analyst apparently thinks the answer is yes. Can a good company ever be overpriced? Isn't it possible to lose money by investing in a good company? Recall that half the time the winning sports wager is on the losing team. As you will see later, you're slightly more likely to make higher returns with out-of-favor companies because they involve more risk.

During 2000-2001 Amazon.com stock's price lost 95 percent of its value. It was a good company before and after the fall. In hindsight, that good company was vastly overpriced, and many people lost money investing in it.

There's an old story about the Paris police chasing a criminal through the streets of the city. They saw him run into a building and decided to seal off his escape routes by placing a policeman at each door. Unfortunately, there were four doors and only three policemen. Their solution was to cover the building next door, since it had only three doors.

Active managers have a lot in common with those policemen. What they need to do is identify pricing errors, but that's much too hard and they don't have a clue as to how to go about it. Instead, they do what they're equipped to do, even though it's the wrong job. Searching for pricing errors and analyzing why they exist isn't nearly as much fun as doing research and listening to gossip about the companies themselves. Determining whether or not a stock's price incorporates all relevant information is no fun because it's an impossible task. Maybe active managers know that, at least at an intuitive level, and that's why they avoid making the attempt. They are like three policemen trying to cover a building with a thousand exits.

There is a profound difference between looking forward and looking back.

> *If you can look into the seeds of time and say which grains will grow and which will not, speak then to me.*
> William Shakespeare, *Macbeth*

Another common error made by active managers is failing to appreciate the profound difference between looking forward and looking back, or what economists like to term *ex ante* and *ex post*. People who have visions of beating the market have a tendency to believe that the future will, for the most part, be a repetition of the past. They think that if they discover something that would have worked in the past, they can assume it will work in the future. It's not that simple. Falling into the trap of thinking the future will be a reproduction of the past has been given the name "hindsight bias."

The stock market and the economy are systems of mind-boggling complexity. Nothing occurs for a single reason. Stock prices are affected by the state of the economy, interest rates, regulations, taxes, corporate earnings, and countless other factors. These variables are never all positive or all negative. They are never aligned in the same way, and they never have the same relative strengths in any two or more time periods. As I write this, for example, the nation is in a mild recession (negative for stocks), but interest rates are historically low (positive for stocks), just to name two of the large number of factors that influence the market.

Furthermore, if you happen to detect a recurring pattern, it's logical to assume that it's already reflected in the price, unless you think you are the only one alert enough to see it. The starting assumption for anyone who wants to beat the market should be "the prices are right," but active managers blithely assume the prices are wrong.

Another reason there is a break between what we see happening *ex post* and *ex ante* is the tendency for successful strategies to self-destruct. As was explained in Chapter 4, the self-cancellation of successful strategies is one of the central forces that leads to market efficiency.

In some cases investors may see valid relationships but have no way to exploit them. For example, a strong relationship exists between interest rates and the stock market. Rising interest rates tend to depress the market, while falling rates stimulate the market. (We will explore the reason for this in Chapter 10.) Unfortunately, predicting interest rates is about as difficult as predicting the stock market itself. Predicting interest rates is equivalent to predicting bond prices, something no one has shown an ability to do.

Another example can be found in oil prices. If you could predict oil prices, it would help in forecasting the probable future prices of oil company stocks. Again, no one has demonstrated an ability to reliably predict oil prices. If you could forecast the weather months in advance and the severity of an upcoming winter, you might be able to predict the price of heating oil. Again, the answers to these riddles are beyond the reach of mere mortals.

If you're so smart, why are you selling your secrets rather than using them?

An obvious logical gap in the active management game is this: if a market beater actually had something valuable to sell, he wouldn't be selling it. He would exploit it himself. Anyone who has found an effective way to consistently identify mis-priced securities has two choices—either use the system or sell it so that other investors can use it.

If you had a system for making abnormal returns, you would continue using it until it stopped working. After all, why would you stop short of that? Would you grow tired of making money and accumulating wealth? Not likely. That's not how we observe people behaving.

Maybe you would run out of money to invest, but then you could borrow money and generate a net profit by leveraging. After all, beating the market by definition means that you can make a higher rate of return than prevailing interest rates. So if you had a system that did actually beat the market (excess returns with known risk), it would always pay to leverage. (Leverage simply means investing with borrowed money.)

If someone who had a market-beating strategy sold his system, sharing it with others, the returns would be dispersed among numerous investors. He would capture little or none of the value of the system in use. His income would depend mostly on selling the advice, not on the value of the advice itself. If his system worked and he believed in it, he would use it, not sell it. A possible exception might be a financial advisor who was charitably motivated, rather than a profit maximizer. It could be that this advisor had his eyes on sainthood rather than material wealth. My guess is it would be hard to find evidence supporting that hypothesis.

If you were a fisherman who knew of an excellent fishing spot, would you tell everyone about it or would you keep quiet and use it yourself? A fishing hole can't support an unlimited number of users. If you discovered a system for winning the lottery, what would you do with it? Somehow I doubt you would sell it.

Advice on how to beat the market is similar. Because of flexible prices, as the advice is used, it gets used up. Buying an under-priced stock pushes its price up until it's no longer under-priced. You can generate excess returns only as long as you can purchase the stock for less than it is worth. Remember, a fundamental reality of efficient markets is that successful strategies self-destruct. You need to take advantage of your secrets before that happens.

That's not the case with most other kinds of information or advice. For example, if I had a new way to stay physically fit, I could tell the world about it without affecting its usefulness to me. The world of fiscal fitness, however, doesn't work that way.

Market-beating advice is unusual in terms of its enormous potential value in use. It's not possible for its sale price to have as much value as its application value. (If I had a fantastic new physical-fitness regimen, on the other hand, I couldn't get rich just by making use of it myself.)

Active managers and investment newsletter writers claim to have ways of identifying mis-priced stocks. Ironically, what's mis-priced is their advice. Their willingness to sell rather than employ their advice proves that it's really worth little or nothing and, in fact, usually has a negative value because of how much time it wastes and the extra risks involved in following it.

Their willingness to sell their secrets is an implicit admission that their secrets are bogus—they are committing deliberate fraud. If their strategies were skill-based, they wouldn't sell them. On the other hand, they're willing to sell luck because it's worthless. It's a totally one-sided transaction—they get paid, you get nothing. Voluntary exchange malfunctions whenever there is an informational breakdown.

A hypothetical example might help illustrate the inherent dilemma. Assume there's a $1 million profit potential in a certain strategy. That strategy could be used by its inventor to generate $1 million in excess returns, or it could be sold and put to use by others. If the inventor sells the strategy for more than $1 million, he's better off selling it, but what about the buyers? As a group they pay more than the strategy is capable of generating in excess returns. In this context, the only way the inventor can be better off selling is for the users to be worse off buying. This example is based on the unlikely assumption of anyone identifying such a strategy.

Hypothesis? We ain't got no stinking hypothesis!

Among the reasons financial economists lack respect for active managers is that they offer no alternative hypothesis to the EMH. By the very act of trying to beat the market, active managers deny the efficiency of securities markets. They clearly demonstrate what they don't believe, but they say very little about what they do believe.

Of course, no one is legally or morally obligated to offer a testable hypothesis for everything he believes. However, if you tell people that the model you rely on is right and another is wrong, don't be surprised if they ask you to specify your model. People need some basis for deciding which version of reality makes the most sense. The EMH provides an internally consistent, logical, and evidence-based explanation of why it's difficult to beat the market. It also provides an explanation of how relative stock prices are determined and what causes changes in prices.

The people who reject market efficiency do not offer a coherent, testable alternative theory of stock price determination. Active managers, for the most part, have not joined the debate. Instead, they've ignored it. Even though they provide no explicit theory or hypothesis, it is possible to deduce some of their implicit beliefs.

The very fact that they attempt to beat the market indicates they don't believe stock prices correctly reflect all available information. They apparently believe it is possible, by collecting information, to reliably identify and purchase stocks for less or sell them for more than their intrinsic values.

Nevertheless, it does appear that stock pickers feel that the EMH is true to some degree. Otherwise, it would not be so difficult and take so much research to find bargain-priced stocks. If mis-priced stocks are difficult to find, the implication is that most stocks are correctly priced. They must believe, however, that the market is not consistently efficient across the board, i.e., some prices reflect available information while others don't. Such a belief raises further questions.

If information determines prices for the most part, but inconsistently and unreliably, how do you account for and explain the inconsistency? Why are some stocks appropriately priced while others are not? How do you go about distinguishing which stocks fully reflect available information and which do not? What, specifically, is their theory of errors? What is their *ex ante* error-identification system?

What is it about some prices that prevents them from absorbing and reflecting information? Is there an information barrier that exists under certain circumstances but not others? What are those circumstances? Are some stock prices wrapped in Goretex?

How do active managers explain what determines stock prices generally? You need a general theory of price determination before you can deal with exceptions to it. Why is this stock or company an exception to the general rule?

Whatever their theory of errors, active managers have to believe that the errors are only transitional. If you're going to generate abnormal returns by buying mis-priced stocks, a necessary condition is that the mis-pricing is only temporary. If you buy a stock that is under-priced, it will not appreciate faster than the overall market if it remains under-priced. If the market never wakes up to the stock's intrinsic value, it will only parallel the performance of the overall market, and this would result in only normal, market rates of return. In order for the excess returns to be realized, the information you think isn't reflected in the price must, within a reasonable period of time, become reflected in the price. You will make abnormal returns only if other investors wake up to the true value of the stock. What caused them to doze off in the first place? What would cause them to reawaken?

How do active managers explain this temporary error? Not only do they need a theory of errors, they also need a theory of error correction. They apparently believe that only some stocks are mis-priced, and even those only temporarily. What is the process by which the mis-pricing is corrected?

All active managers think they can beat the market. They think they are better, superior to something—but what is that something? Other managers? Why do they think they are better than other managers? Do they think they are smart and other managers are stupid? Aren't all active managers trying to do basically the same thing? How are they different?

The market consists of all investors, but not all investors can beat the market. If one of them does better than average, it has to be at the expense of someone who does worse than average. What is the active manager's vision of who that is?

> *After all, the market's performance is itself an average of the performance of all investors. If, on average, mutual funds had beaten the market, then some other group of investors would have "lost" to the market. With the substantial amount of professional management in today's stock market, it is difficult to think of a likely group of victims.*
>
> William Sharpe *et al, Investments* (6th ed.)

Wall Street is populated by people who see themselves as prophets. Everyone thinks he's above average. According to Mark Rubenstein, "It's clear that the average investor thinks he's above average." In Garrison Keillor's fictional Lake Wobegon, "all children are above average." Keillor's joke is no joke on Wall Street—it's a way of life. Everyone there thinks he's better than everyone else. Wall Street is a place where positive self-esteem has run amok.

A market analyst is doing well if he knows one percent of the relevant information.

Conventional "fundamental analysis" looks at the various details and characteristics of a company. Some kind of conclusion is reached regarding the intrinsic value of the company and that's sometimes compared to the market price for the company's stock.

Whatever analysis is done can only be a miniscule fraction of the analysis done by all the other participants. It's naive (and arrogant) to believe that such a partial and limited analysis actually means much in relation to the consensus analysis reflected in the stock's price. For any one company the relevant significant information would easily fill a 1,000-page book. Active managers read the proportional equivalent of two pages and act as though they know enough to judge the value of the company. Even if they do extensive research, they're lucky if they gather one percent of the relevant information. What they do know is only a drop in the ocean compared to what they don't know. The analyst knows something about the company in question. It never seems to occur to him to ask, "How much of the relevant information about this company do I not know?"

Essentially, active managers take a sample of information. Is it an unbiased sample? In other words, does it accurately reflect the characteristics of the entire population of information?

In securities markets there can be neither perpetual winners nor perpetual losers.

The underlying model active managers rely on is a logical impossibility. They seem to believe they are a sub-population of investors who systematically takes advantage of another sub-population of investors. That cannot be true.

A population of perpetual losers simply cannot exist. They would drop out of the game because of discouragement or because they ran out of money. Conversely, there cannot exist a sub-population of perpetual winners. They would want to continuously increase their investments either with the returns they've already generated or with borrowed money. They would not voluntarily quit until they owned all the wealth in the world.

Conceivably, you could invent a system capable of beating the house at a gambling casino. If you were allowed to continue using it, you would end up owning the casino, but long before that happened the casino would call your little adventure to a halt. They would not let you put them out of business. When someone invents what might be a winning strategy for beating the stock market, there is no one to tell him he can't play anymore. Instead, the market itself steps in with price adjustments that effectively reset the odds and cancel out the profitability of the winning strategy. If his success was purely a matter of luck, the market doesn't even have to adjust. The laws of probability will deliver his comeuppance.

When you hear money managers explain how they plan to beat the market, it becomes clear that many of them have an image of competing against other investors. As was explained in Chapter 4, the competition is not actually between investors of various degrees of sophistication, but rather between each investor and the consensus of all other investors, as reflected in the price of a stock.

No doubt, some managers are smarter than others, and if that were how markets work, the smart ones would fleece the dim bulbs. If inequality in the distribution of intelligence mattered, there would be an ongoing wealth transfer from the clueless to the savvy investors. It would be like a never-ending chain letter and that's simply not a realistic possibility. Markets could not operate that way for any extended period of time. Why not? If there were an ongoing transfer of wealth from the unsophisticated to the sophisticated investors, the unsophisticated investors would cease investing. Only if they were unsophisticated, masochistic, and have unlimited wealth would they continue playing the game.

There are those who make rates of return above and below market averages. However, because winning and losing in an efficient market is mostly a matter of luck, and because luck by its very nature is random, there is continuous turnover in the populations of winners and losers. Bob Dylan's lyrics, "the first ones now will later be last," are nowhere more true than in the active management world. This turnover is another reflection of luck-based results rather than skill-based results.

Even if you grant that incompetent investors influence stock prices, that's not enough to provide you with a way to generate excess returns. Do incompetent investors affect all stock prices or just some? If not all, then which ones specifically? If you're going to select from a population of stocks, you need a way to identify which stocks are being affected most by the existence of incompetence. What's the rule and what are its exceptions?

Why can't the best brains on Wall Street achieve mediocrity?

A popular refrain from the proponents of active management is that passive investing amounts to settling for mediocrity. That's a serious charge, especially for Americans. For most of us the idea of mediocrity is not acceptable. The settling for mediocrity charge scores rhetorical points, but what does it actually mean in the context of investing? When the charge is made in this context it is never clearly defined. Is acceptance of market rates of return actually equivalent to mediocrity? And even if it is, what are the available alternatives? And what if mediocrity, like par in golf, generates highly satisfactory results? If someone could show you how to shoot par golf, I'll bet you would be extremely interested. I certainly would be.

The strategy of passive management means duplicating market or asset class rates of return. Whether or not an investor should accept market rates of return depends on the costs and benefits of attempting to exceed those rates. Having the objective of doing better than average is definitely no guarantee of doing so. What if mediocrity is as good as it gets?

If securities markets are efficient, attempting to beat the market is a colossal waste of time involving unnecessary risk. The costs far exceed the benefits. In regard to the issue of settling for mediocrity, Nobel laureate Paul Samuelson observed, "Isn't it interesting that the best brains on Wall Street can't achieve mediocrity?"

Everyone, of course, would like to experience market-beating rates of return. For most, however, that isn't a necessity. For the past 77 years the S&P 500 has achieved a compound rate of return of almost eleven percent. At a ten percent rate of return, money doubles every 7.2 years. At that rate, it has multiplied eight fold in 22 years. If that's not sufficiently rapid growth, the problem is that you did not give yourself enough time. It's not a problem that can be adequately addressed by pursuing false hopes.

Whether or not market rates of return are sufficient to meet your needs doesn't really mean much anyway. Reality is what matters, not one's fantasies.

Playing the stock market is a form of gambling that's legal in all 50 states and can be done from the comfort of your own home.

There is one benefit of active management that's rather hard to deny: the entertainment value of attempting to beat the market. A *Forbes* magazine article titled "Amateur Hour on Wall Street" examined the phenomenon of five million ordinary investors doing stock trades over the Internet.

"I cannot wait to get up in the morning and trade," one especially eager investor told *Forbes*. "This is the most exciting thing in the world for me right now." (*Forbes*, January 25, 1999)

There's no question about it, for many people there is entertainment value in attempting to beat the market. Doing research on individual companies is so enjoyable for many people it's practically addictive, as is monitoring the daily prices of stocks.

An economist's role is not to argue with anyone's tastes and preferences or their priorities. Rather, an economist's responsibility is to identify costs and benefits so people can make better-informed decisions.

At least a part of the pleasure of attempting to beat the market is the perception that it's possible to do so or that the player has in fact been successful in the past. As has been discussed above, these issues are very much in doubt. If an investor could measure the entertainment costs of playing the market and recognize the extremely low probabilities of beating it, it might well have an impact on his choices. He might decide that taking up golf, tennis, or chess would be just as much fun and much less costly. In other words, there are more efficient, lower-priced ways to have fun. Is playing the market the only way you can think of to have fun?

Using your investments as entertainment is among the costliest and highest risk forms of recreation. So-called day trading on the Internet is the world's most expensive and dangerous video game. Furthermore, the more money you have to invest, the greater the cost. Your irresponsibility could easily be costing you five percent a year. That's $5,000 on a $100,000 portfolio and $50,000 on a $1 million portfolio. The damage is far greater when you measure the impact on the compound rate of returns over long periods of time. Are you getting your money's worth? Are you responsible only to yourself for this money? Are your children, spouse, heirs, or employees affected by the performance?

People in general and investors in particular succumb to hindsight bias and other psychological pitfalls.

The most rigorous work that's been done in analyzing investor behavior is within a field known as "prospect theory," developed by psychologists Daniel Kahneman and the late Amos Tversky. What they found in their research is that people in general and investors in particular succumb to the human weaknesses of overconfidence, hindsight bias, regret avoidance, and generalizing from small numbers.

The following is a partial list compiled by Mark Rubenstein (Rubenstein, 2001) of some of the logical errors made by investors. Probably we've all been guilty of the following behaviors, or we've observed them in people we know:

- Overconfidence about the precision of private information
- Illusion of knowledge: overconfidence arising from partial information
- Disposition effect: tendency to hold losers but sell winners
- Illusion of control: unfounded belief in being able to influence events
- Gambler's fallacy: need to see patterns when, in fact, there are none
- Ellsberg paradox: perceiving differences between risk and uncertainty
- Extrapolation bias: failure to correct for regression to the mean and sample size
- Excessive weight given to anecdotal experiences relative to large-sample statistics
- Overreaction: excessive weight placed on recent relative to historical evidence
- Failure to adjust probabilities for hindsight and selection bias
- Magical thinking: believing you can influence the outcome when you cannot
- Selective recall
- Disjunction effect: waiting for information even if it's not important to the decision
- Confusing probabilities with preferences
- Status quo bias: more to lose than gain by departing from current situation

Not all information is created equal—a summary of information issues.
There is a wide range of information content in what we read and hear. To make the best use of the information available to you, keep in mind the following:

- Is it redundant—a variation of reinventing the wheel? The marginal utility of redundant information is zero.
- When is it available? Does it arrive too late to be of value? There is a huge difference between the value of information *ex ante* and *ex post*.
- Is it predictable? Predictable information is already discounted in current prices. Predictable statements contain no information.
- How much does the information cost, particularly in comparison to the possible benefit? A primary reason we make mistakes in life is that information is not free.
- Probabilities are a critical component and dimension of information.

- "Probabilities are the very guide of life" (James Butler, 18th century cleric).
- Is it public or exclusive? If it's public, the logical assumption is it's redundant in regard to excess returns potential.
- What happens to the value of the information as it's put into use? What is the durability or half-life of the usefulness? Does its usefulness self-destruct?
- Are the prerequisites to using the information attainable? Do you, for example, need the ability to predict interest rates or make long-range weather forecasts?
- Skill-based positions in a frequency distribution contain information about future positions. Luck-based positions do not contain information about future positions.
- The price system in general and the price system in securities markets are information and communication systems.
- Systematic errors contain low-cost information.
- The degree to which information affects behavior depends on the feedback mechanism as well as the incentives involved.
- In efficient markets, past price changes contain no information concerning future price changes. Price history tells us nothing about future prices.
- If you know one percent of the relevant information about a company, which is about all you could hope to know, that information you have is extremely unreliable and error prone.

CHAPTER 6

Risk: the Realities and the Opportunities

❦

The revolutionary idea that defines the boundary between modern times and the past is the mastery of risk: the notion that the future is more than a whim of the gods and that men and women are not passive before nature. Until human beings discovered a way across that boundary, the future was a mirror of the past or the murky domain of oracles and soothsayers who held a monopoly over knowledge of anticipated events...The capacity to manage risk, and with it the appetite to take risk and make forward-looking choices, are key elements of the energy that drives the economic system forward.

Peter Bernstein,
Against the Gods: The Remarkable Story of Risk

Risk is more complex than return, harder for Wall Street to comprehend, and harder to explain to their customers.

What space and time are to the physical world, risk and return are to the financial world. Risk and return are the two key factors involved in every investment decision, and are equal in importance. Unfortunately, Wall Street refuses to recognize that. One of the Street's most irresponsible errors is that it puts such heavy emphasis on return it virtually ignores risk.

Return sells, and of course, that's what you hear about in advertisements. Return is a positive, while risk is a negative, and when you're trying to sell something, you focus on the benefits, not the costs. Return is what investors assume matters most.

The especially volatile performance of actively managed mutual funds during 2000-2001 exposed the risk inherent in their ill-conceived strategies, particularly the error of concentration (lack of diversification). The risk had always been there, it was just out of sight.

In this chapter you will learn why risk is just as important as return. You will also learn what risk is, how to use it to your advantage, and how to recognize and avoid unnecessary risk (referred to in financial economics as "uncompensated risk").

Make risk your investment servant.

You've no doubt heard someone say, or said yourself, "I took a calculated risk." In fact, taking calculated risks is a key to investment success. On the other hand, taking what's known as "uncompensated risks" is a recipe for investment failure.

Risk is a more critical and universal fact of life than you might realize. It's a factor in virtually everything we do. A recognition of what risk means and how you can manage it to your advantage can have a profound impact on your life. Gaining sophistication regarding risk is one of the surest steps for achieving superior knowledge and perspective compared to the pseudo-sophistication of Wall Street.

In 1952 Harry Markowitz published an article titled "Portfolio Selection" and launched what is now known as Modern Portfolio Theory. A major insight of the article was that risk is an inescapable aspect of investing and needs to be explicitly considered when evaluating and comparing investments.

Like many of the advances in knowledge, this insight seems obvious in retrospect. Of course, risk ought to be considered in making investment choices! Before Markowitz there was at least an intuitive awareness of risk as an investment issue, but nothing close to a systematic treatment of it. A fundamental element of Modern Portfolio Theory is something called "mean-variance analysis," which is in essence a rigorous way to examine the relationships between rates of return (mean) and risk (variance).

Unfortunately, investors and their advisors are not often rigorous in their evaluation of risk, preferring instead to focus most of their attention on return. After all, return is fun, risk is scary. But investors would be better off and have more financial peace of mind if they reversed the order of these priorities. Surprisingly, risk is more manageable than return. Our concern should not just be our target, but also the probability of successfully hitting that target.

Risk is a common term, and everyone has some understanding of what it means. It is, however, an incredibly rich and subtle dimension of life, one that is easy to overlook and take for granted. The definition and implications of risk are anything but simple.

If you want a higher return, the means to that end is the proper management of risk. Wall Street and the media rarely provide investors with meaningful guidance on how to trade risk for return. Misunderstandings about the risk-return trade off cause some investors to take more or less risk than they intend. A further problem is that investors often make investments unaware that extra risks have been taken. In many cases the extra risk occurs with no corresponding likelihood of higher returns.

Because the word risk is so emotionally charged, it's better to use the word uncertainty.

Theoreticians argue there is no meaningful difference between risk and uncertainty (Hirshleifer and Riley, 1992). However, risk is an emotionally charged term, while uncertainty is more precise and emotionally neutral. Thinking in terms of uncertainty rather than risk will help you evaluate your alternatives dispassionately and minimize the damage your emotions can have on your decision-making effectiveness.

When we take an action or make a choice, we can't be certain it will turn out as we expected. We can't control or predict all the variables. Risk tends to be thought of as the chance an action will turn out worse than we expected.

There is, on the other hand, the possibility that an action we take will have better results than anticipated. Significantly, there's no single word in the English language for that kind of favorable outcome. The English language (as well as a number of other languages) sets up a subtle bias against risk taking. Risk has a generally negative connotation and is nearly synonymous with the words hazard or danger.

The relationship between risk and reward is not unique to the financial world. There is a profound connection between these two realities in virtually everything we do. Having children, for example, is a choice that entails both enormous rewards and risks. Riding motorcycles is more fun than driving cars, but it is also more dangerous. In football, a long pass play has a high potential payoff, but a lower probability of success.

Risk could be looked at as a gate we have to pass through in order to reach whatever goals we set for ourselves in life. Insofar as risk is a reflection of uncertainty, it is inescapable. Risk is as ubiquitous and universal as time. Nothing happens without the passage of time, and nothing occurs without an element of uncertainty. Time is nature's way of keeping everything from happening at once, and uncertainty is nature's way of holding our interest. Hiesenberg's "uncertainty principle" is considered in the same league as Einstein's theory of relativity. It says that uncertainty is inescapable and that nothing is certain except uncertainty. The mathematician and author Jacob Bronowski called Heisenberg's uncertainty principle "one of the great scientific ideas, not only of the twentieth century, but in the history of science" (Bronowski, 1973).

There's no avoiding risk, so you're better off learning how to embrace it. Even if risk could be avoided, the price of avoidance would be too high.

Accepting the inevitability of risk is one of the keys to being a realistic investor.

Security is mostly a superstition. It does not exist in nature...Life is either a daring adventure or nothing.

Helen Keller

Too many people are thinking of security instead of opportunity. They seem to be more afraid of life than death.

James F. Byrnes

Since risk cannot be avoided, the next best thing is to manage it for our benefit. Risk should be seen as a tool. It's another way of working with reality rather than against it.

Out of necessity we have to make decisions and take actions, the consequences of which are in the future. The future, however, is not ours to know. We cannot foresee how the countless complex elements of reality will interact or what the net outcome will be. The future and uncertainty are inseparable and therefore the future and risk are inseparable.

Much of what has been addressed in this book, especially in Chapters 4 and 5, deals with the issue of information. One of the main reasons information has value to us is its role in reducing the degree of uncertainty of the future. Knowing the weather forecast (an analysis of information of current conditions and trends) for tomorrow reduces our uncertainty of what tomorrow's weather will be. As we accumulate and process more information about physics and meteorology, the accuracy of the forecast is enhanced.

A number of major university economics departments offer an upper division course titled "Decision Making Under Uncertainty." That an entire course could be devoted to that topic reflects the importance of the uncertainty dimension in the process of making effective choices. Uncertainty is what makes decision-making such a challenge.

You've probably heard people say, "You can never be too careful," but that advice is absolutely false. Of course you can be too careful. There is a cost to being careful, and you can take caution way past the point of efficiency. We all know that speed kills. That doesn't mean that we should all drive at 20 mph. Caution does have a cost, and there are optimal levels of caution and danger.

Our material progress has been profoundly enhanced by our willingness and even enthusiasm for innovation and risk taking.

Risking and living are inseparable.
Aaron Wildavsky

In recent years, there has been a growing appreciation of the subtleties and importance of risk. Two books in particular have contributed to defining and exploring the topic of risk: *Searching for Safety*, by the late Aaron Wildavsky, and *Against the Gods: The Remarkable Story of Risk* by Peter Bernstein.

Wildavsky demonstrated that the search for safety is paradoxical and ironic. He illustrated the general theme of his book with what he termed "the jogger's dilemma." There have been instances of people dying of heart failure or being killed or injured by cars while jogging.

In general, however, jogging improves physical and mental health and increases life expectancy. Wildavsky pointed out that "you cannot have one—a safer organism—without the other…. safety is the other side of risk." In other words, joggers increase their body's resilience by exposing it to a certain level of risk. The probability that jogging will lengthen your life is many times greater than that jogging will shorten it. A longer life span is in the fat middle of the distribution of outcomes of jogging; getting hit by a car while jogging is on the narrow tail of the distribution.

Wildavsky noted that life expectancy in the United States has shown a remarkable increase during the past century. A major reason is that we are a wealthy nation. Wealth allows us to afford such life-extending advantages as better nutrition, sanitation, refrigeration, and medical care. There are strong relationships between life expectancies and wealth, both among countries and among individuals. Wildavsky summarized, "wealthier is healthier."

During the twentieth century, life expectancy in the United States increased by almost two-thirds (from 47 years to 77 years). In the year 1000 the life expectancy in western Europe was only 24 years. By 1820 it had increased to 36 years (Maddison, 2001). Dramatically increased life expectancy is the single best summary statistic of the benefits of modern living and our material progress.

We are a nation of immigrants, and immigrants are almost by definition risk seekers. A primary reason the market system is so much more successful than communism is that it provides a far more hospitable environment for risk taking. The market economy offers rich rewards and, therefore, incentives for taking risks. Our future growth will be profoundly affected by these incentives.

Another ironic conclusion of Wildavsky's research is that "an ounce of prevention" is not necessarily "worth a pound of cure." Some hazards can be predicted, others can't. We can't prevent unexpected hazards, so our best strategy is to maximize our ability to cope—what Wildavsky called "expanding our resilience." A broad-based stock of knowledge increases our ability to solve the problems we encounter. A diversified, robust economy increases our resilience when meeting unpredictable hazards. Trees survive, not by preventing the wind, but by bending with it.

In general, our survival is much more the result of our defenses, such as antibodies and immune systems, than of our attempted avoidance of all potentially harmful microbes and infections. Our country has encountered countless serious problems in its history—wars, depressions, and terrorist attacks, but our strength and wealth have given us the ability to survive and prosper in spite of them.

Bernstein's *Against the Gods* shows how seemingly arcane topics, such as probability theory and statistics, have improved our ability to cope with uncertainty. We now have a much greater ability to manage the relationship between the past and the future. Before the concept of probability there was no way to apply the power and tools of mathematics to events yet to come. Probability is uncertainty quantified.

Either you think probability is the most fascinating topic in the world or you don't. If you don't I feel sorry for you.

Robert Solow,
Nobel laureate for Economic Science

We can't foresee or control the future, but all outcomes are not equally likely. Our knowledge of the world comes in the form of probabilities, not certainties. Knowledge of the differences in likelihood, however, can be extremely useful. Bernstein traces the intellectual history of risk and probability theory and demonstrates its importance in both science and practical issues. Statistical analysis is a vital tool for practically every imaginable discipline. One objective of statistical analysis is deriving probabilities for the purpose of making better predictions. Statistical analysis also helps in estimating the strength of relationships—the value of exercise in maintaining health, for example.

Probability is a major element in the science of decision-making. Successful decision-making involves not only the costs and benefits of the menu of choices but also the probabilities of possible outcomes.

Worrying is one of the greatest obstacles to peace of mind. Actually, worrying could be thought of as a probability disorder, since it usually results from placing unrealistic probabilities on potential problems. Of all the things you've worried about in your life, how many of them actually happened? Ten percent is probably an exaggeration. Were the ones that happened as big a problem as you feared? Did you cope better or worse than you expected?

The concept of expected value proves that risk and return are of equal importance.

In terms of practical significance, "expected value" is one of the most useful lessons derived from the science of statistics. It teaches that the true value of an event takes into account not only the value of a particular outcome, but the probability of that outcome as well.

Expected value is simply the combination of payoff and probability. What, for example, is the expected value of winning $5 in the flip of a coin if it comes up tails? As you've probably already guessed, the answer is $2.50, the potential winnings ($5) times the probability of getting tails in one toss of a "fair coin," which is .5.

When making decisions, it's surprising how often errors result from violating the simplest logic. Failing to recognize expected value is a good example of fundamental logic being overlooked.

What, for example, is the expected value of a lottery ticket? Since the sponsors of lotteries typically retain about half of the revenue from the tickets, the expected value of any one ticket is about half its purchase price.

Which is more important—the size (reward) of the lottery jackpot, or the probability (risk) of winning? Doubling the probability will have the same impact on the expected value of the ticket as doubling the size of the jackpot.

Greater uncertainty causes a reduction in the perceived value of any given outcome. For example, when an event occurs that causes an increase in the level of economic uncertainty, the stock market usually suffers a decline.

Investment risk is the possibility that your realized return will be less than what you expected.

The conclusions regarding risk reached by Wildavsky, Bernstein, and others are applicable to the world of investment and finance. According to Burton Malkiel, "When all is said and done, risk is the only variable worth a damn in the market" (Malkiel, 1997).

In the investment world, the relationship between risk and return is prominent and recurring. The connection between them is strong. However, it is important to keep in mind that it is neither fixed nor totally consistent. For example, there are numerous high-risk investments with relatively low expected rates of return, and of course, you want to avoid such investments—hedge funds and limited partnerships, for example.

In the context of investments, risk essentially translates into the possibility that your realized return will be less than your anticipated return. A leading investment textbook (Sharpe, et al, 1999) defines risk as "the uncertainty associated with the end of period value of an investment." In other words, what is the probability that an investment's value at the end of a period will be less than what was predicted at the beginning of the period? If the present is defined as t, what is the range and distribution of expected values at time t+1?

In general, if you want the opportunity for a higher return, you have to be willing to take more risk. In other words, you have to invest in securities that have more uncertainty in regard to their "end of period" values.

A probability distribution conveys the nature and limitations of our knowledge of the future.

The realities of risk and uncertainty can be seen using simple probability distributions. The uncertainty of the future means we cannot foresee precise, specific outcomes. In many cases, however, we do know something about the "probability distributions" of expected outcomes. Different kinds of events have different probability distributions.

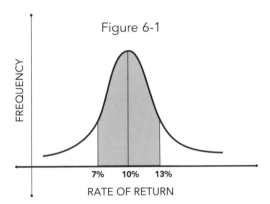

Figure 6-1

Figure 6-1 shows a probability distribution for a single, hypothetical investment. It indicates that the mean expected rate of return is 10 percent. This particular investment has a standard deviation of 3 percent. The standard deviation is considered to be the best measure of "central tendency." A larger standard deviation means the mean has less meaning. The smaller the standard deviation, the greater the probability density and, therefore, the *smaller the degree of uncertainty.* A normal distribution with a mean of 10 percent and a standard deviation of 3 percent means that two-thirds of the outcomes will be between 7 percent and 13 percent. (The mean, 10 percent, plus or minus the standard deviation or 3 percent.)

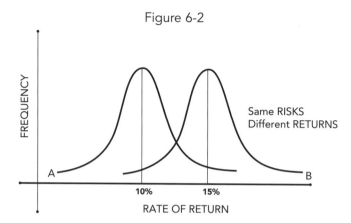

Figure 6-2

Figure 6-2 shows probability distributions for two different investments, A and B. The two investments have the same standard deviation, but B has a higher mean rate of return. If you are given a choice between the two investments, you should definitely opt for B.

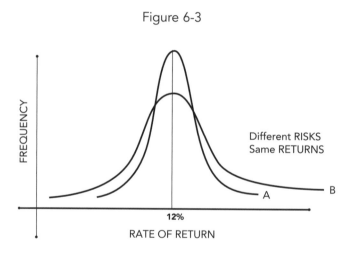

Figure 6-3

Figure 6-3 shows two more probability distributions, again designated A and B. In this case, the means for the two are the same, but A has a lower standard deviation. Investment B has a greater degree of uncertainty. It has less of a "central tendency." Given a choice, A is the better investment. The return is the same but the risk is lower.

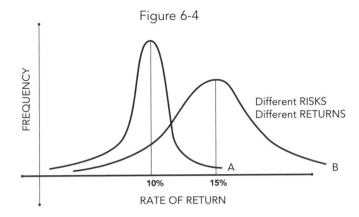

Figure 6-4

Figure 6-4 shows two more distributions. In this case both the means and the standard deviations are different. Investment A has a lower expected mean rate of return and a lower standard deviation than Investment B. If asked to choose between these two investments, the choice is not so simple. It requires a tradeoff. The choice would have to take into account your risk tolerance. How much uncertainty are you willing to tolerate to give yourself the opportunity for a higher return? Becoming familiar with your feelings about risk and return is an important step in getting to know yourself as an investor.

Figure 6-4 reflects the prevailing reality of the investment world and is essentially a picture of the risk-return tradeoff. In general, investments with higher expected returns require higher risk exposure. Higher risk exposure is the same as more uncertainty. Figures 6-2 and 6-3 reflect situations where a tradeoff isn't necessary. They represent situations where you can get either a higher return for no additional risk, or a lower risk with the same return.

Why higher returns for higher risks?

It's probably not news to you that if you want higher returns, it usually means you have to take more risks. Why this relationship exists, however, is rarely spelled out.

The risk/reward relationship is basically the result of a combination of two realities: (1) most people are "risk averse," and (2) ours is a voluntary exchange economy. A substantial amount of research has established the fact that people are "risk averse." All of my direct experience with clients and prospects is consistent with the rigorous research that's been done. As a general rule, people prefer to avoid risks. They don't like uncertainty, particularly in regard to investments. They are reluctant to put their hard-earned money in the fickle hands of fate.

Of course, human nature is anything but simple, and if people were uniformly risk averse, Las Vegas and Atlantic City wouldn't be so popular. Someone who likes bungee jumping or hang gliding doesn't necessarily enjoy casinos. Risk itself can be rewarding in terms of excitement and invigorating stress. In many instances, there seems to be an attraction to the risk taking itself, not just to the possibility of the potential monetary payoffs.

On the other side of the voluntary transaction are the people willing to pay you an enhanced return. Investing is a voluntary activity. If you need money for expanding your business, you don't have the option of coercing investors to provide you with the funds. Rather, you must make them an offer sufficiently enticing to get them to voluntarily commit their funds. Investing in a business expansion is inherently more uncertain than investing in, for example, treasury bills. If the potential investors don't like risk, you've got to offer them something to offset or compensate for that negative aspect of the investment. It is possible to entice people to do even something they prefer to avoid, if you compensate them sufficiently. That compensation usually takes the form of a higher return, or at least the possibility of a higher return.

In the context of voluntary exchange, there has to be a perceived payoff for both participants. Why would you be willing to offer a higher return? If you believe that expanding your business makes sense from a profitability standpoint, you expect the enterprise to be so lucrative there will be plenty left over for you even after you pay extra to get the necessary funding. Endeavors with the greatest return potential typically have a high degree of uncertainty.

Investment risks come in a variety of forms.

Books about investing typically list a number of types of financial risks— market risk, business risk, industry risk, interest rate risk, default risk, and purchasing power risk, among others. All of these subcategories of risk reflect specific sources of uncertainty regarding "end of period values."

Business risk, which is also termed specific, firm-specific, unique, idiosyncratic, or diversifiable risk, is the risk associated with investing in an individual company. There are events that might primarily affect that particular company, such as new competition, product obsolescence, changing consumer preferences, management incompetence, a lawsuit, a strike, or a plant explosion, and there is always the possibility that any specific company could go completely out of business. When that happens, its assets may not be sufficient to pay off all its creditors, meaning that stockholders will be left with nothing. If, on the other hand, you invest in an effectively diversified mutual fund with a portfolio of 100 companies in a cross section of industries, virtually the only way you could lose your entire investment is a collapse of the entire economy.

The bad news about business risk is that you get no extra return for taking it. Failure to diversify is the most prominent source of "uncompensated risk" and will be discussed in the next chapter.

Industry risk or sector risk is similar to business risk. Often an economic change affects most of the companies in an entire industry. In the 2000-2001 period, for example, technology companies suffered declines far greater than the overall market. The so-called "sector funds" provide the most accessible way to expose yourself to industry risk. Like specific risk, industry risk is uncompensated risk. *Wall Street Journal* columnist Jonathan Clements titled his column on the subject "Sector Funds Need a Warning Label."

> *These are the financial world's most dangerous products. The fund industry's response? They are pumping out the darn things faster than ever. That is bad news for investors. It has become an all too predictable cycle: A market sector turns hot, sector funds are rushed to market, investors pile in, the sector collapses and shareholders bail out, usually licking their wounds.*
>
> *Wall Street Journal*,
> August 14, 2001.

Market risk is risk that affects the entire market. Market risk is like a tidal change—a rising tide that lifts (or a waning tide that lowers) all boats. Changes in the market indexes, such as the Dow Jones Industrial Average or the Standard and Poors 500 or the Russell 5000, are reflections of market risk. Market risk is the one risk you don't avoid by broadly diversifying or investing in index funds. In fact, another name for market risk is "non-diversifiable risk."

In Modern Portfolio Theory, market risk is usually referred to as "systematic risk." That's a somewhat confusing and misleading malapropism. The appropriate word is systemic. In other words, market risk is something that affects the entire system. Market risk is not systematic in the usual sense of the word. Some of the literature has switched to using the word systemic. For example, the *Third Restatement* document discussed in Chapter 10 and Bernstein's *Against the Gods* both use the term systemic.

Default risk and interest rate risk are both aspects of bonds and other "debt instruments," a category of investments often termed "fixed." Default risk is almost self-explanatory. It's the possibility that whomever you lent money declares bankruptcy and fails to repay the debt. Default risk is a close relative to business risk.

Why do bond prices and interest rates move in opposite directions?

Interest rate risk is complex and somewhat counter-intuitive. If you've ever followed the bond market, you have probably noticed a rather curious relationship between bond prices and interest rates—when interest rates rise, bond prices fall and vice versa. Why?

First of all, it's necessary to note some of the basic features of bonds. A bond has a face amount, a maturity date, and a "coupon" rate. Assume the face amount is $10,000, the maturity date is June 15, 2020, and the coupon rate is eight percent. This means the issuers of the bond will pay you $400 every six months, and then pay you $10,000 on June 15, 2020.

At the time the bond is issued, the coupon rate will be approximately equal to prevailing interest rates for bonds having similar characteristics. The corporation will not want to pay any more interest than it must in order to sell the bonds, but it also has to pay enough to make the bonds sufficiently attractive to investors.

Let's say you buy one of these bonds when it's issued, but you decide you want to sell it five years later. How much can you expect to receive? Will you get more or less than $10,000? It will depend mostly on what's happened to interest rates in the interim.

If prevailing interest rates are higher than when you purchased your bond, you will find that you can only sell at a loss. Assume new bonds are paying ten percent. No informed buyer would pay you the face value. Remember, capital markets have to rely on voluntary exchange. The price prevailing in the bond market will be less than the bond's face value.

Your bond pays $400 every six months. For $10,000 an investor could now get a bond that pays $500 every six months. The only way you could sell your bond in a competitive market is for the price to be "discounted." In order for the existing bond to be comparable to newly issued bonds, its price would have to be reduced to approximately $8,000. On the other hand, if interest rates had dropped during the period, you could sell your bond for *more* than $10,000. Furthermore, the longer the bond's maturity, the greater the impact of interest rate changes on the bond's price.

This is the basic logic behind why interest rates and bond prices move inversely to one another. Fundamentally, interest rates and bond prices are two reflections of the same phenomenon.

Inflation: the invisible pickpocket.

Purchasing power risk could also be called inflation risk. Investments are denominated in currency. The purchasing power of a currency, dollars or yen, for example, is not fixed. Inflation is a decline in the exchange value of a unit of currency. Inflation reduces the purchasing power of money, and purchasing power is what ultimately matters when it comes to evaluating the success of an investment.

T-bills are generally considered to be the lowest risk investment available. But note that the reward for investing in T-bills is commensurate with the low risk. The 75-year compound rate of return for T-bills has been 3.8 percent. Inflation for that time period has averaged 3.1 percent, which means that the "real" rate of return for T-bills has been only .7 percent and even less than that if you consider taxes. The tax pain is aggravated because you pay taxes on the gross return. The IRS doesn't allow you to deduct losses suffered from inflation.

Even T-bills, federally insured bank accounts, and certificates of deposit are subject to purchasing power risk. You can never be certain about how much you will be able to buy with your investment when it matures. The so-called I-bonds, which are tied to the rate of inflation, come about as close as anything to eliminating that kind of uncertainty.

Is volatility an adequate measure of risk?

Although risk and return are without doubt the two most significant dimensions of any investment, they are definitely not parallel phenomena. An investment's rate of return is relatively easy to define, quantify, and measure. There are, of course, different components of total return, such as dividends, interest, and appreciation. Nevertheless, it is a fairly straightforward exercise to add these components together to derive a measure of total return. Even the impact of taxes can be taken into account if you need to calculate an after-tax rate of return.

Risk, on the other hand, is not so easy to measure. Although volatility is the variable most often used to represent risk, there are a number of reasons for doubting just how well it reflects the true meaning of risk.

From the perspective of what really matters to individual investors, there is also reason to question the *significance* of volatility as it relates to investments. Consider the distinction between temporary loss (volatility) and permanent loss.

If you invest $10,000 in the stock of a company that fails, the money you invested is gone forever. If you invested the same amount in a typical equity mutual fund in early October 1987, it was probably worth only about $7,500 a month later. However, six months later it was again worth approximately what you invested. Whether or not that would have created a problem for you is largely a question of timing.

Figure 6-5:
Reduction of Risk over Time
1926-2001

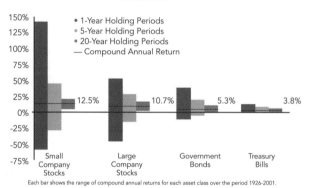

Each bar shows the range of compound annual returns for each asset class over the period 1926-2001.

Taking a long-range view is another effective way of narrowing the range of probable outcomes and, therefore, reducing risk. Figure 6-5 above shows range-narrowing effects over long investment periods. Twenty-year holding periods have far greater probability densities than one-year holding periods. The longer the investment horizon, the greater the chance for random shocks to balance out.

After having worked with hundreds of clients over the past twenty years, it's clear to me that most of the major investment objectives people have are long term in nature. Investing, by its very nature, tends to be long term. Retirement planning, of course, tops the list. Even for someone who is already retired, long-range planning is still the appropriate perspective.

As discussed previously, the investment that is generally seen as the benchmark for low risk is a 30-day treasury bill. These are short-term loans to the federal government, which have virtually no default or interest rate risk. There is almost no uncertainty as to the value of a T-bill at time t+one month.

T-bills put you in a good position if the economy does poorly. But what if the economy does well? It's OK to prepare for the worst-case scenario, but what about the best-case scenario? What about the highest-probability scenario?

SBBI—the research report that spawned an industry.

In 1974, while they were graduate students at the University of Chicago, Rex Sinquefield and Roger Ibbotson published the results of their research on historical rates of return for major investment categories. The research took advantage of a database compiled by the Center for Research in Security Prices (CRSP). Their findings consequently had a profound impact on the investment world. Unlike most economic research, their results were relatively easy to grasp and understand by a wide group of people. Their basic report continues to be updated annually and available through Ibbotson Associates in Chicago (ibbotson.com). What was the nature of their research and why has it had such impact?

Figure 6-6:
Stocks, Bonds, Bills, and Inflation
1925-2001

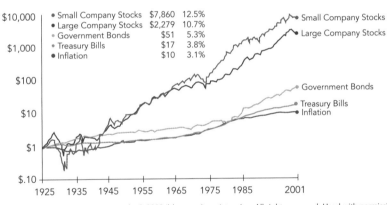

Sinquefield's and Ibbotson's basic data have been nicknamed "SBBI," which is the abbreviation for Stocks, Bonds, Bills, and Inflation. The SBBI data and graph show what the rates of return for these major asset classes and inflation have been since 1926. Before this report became available, no one knew what the long-term rate of return for the stock market had been. "So what?" you might ask.

Among other things, their study for the first time established a standard with which money managers could be measured and evaluated. Their results helped spawn a small industry of people and firms to do just that: the investment advisory industry.

If a picture is worth a thousand words, a graph is worth 100 tables of numbers. The SBBI graph above illustrates a number of important realities about the broad investment categories.

The rate of return on stocks (being an owner) is about twice the rate of return of bonds (being a lender). That fact could be shown in a table. The graph, however, illustrates the difference in the degree of volatility and uncertainty between owning and lending. The difference in the shapes of the stock and bond historical performance lines conveys the most important differences distinguishing the two asset classes.

The graph also illustrates that, although there have been numerous drops in the market during the past 75 years, the drops have all been temporary. There have been thousands of individual stocks that have suffered permanent loss, but never in this country has the overall market experienced permanent decline. Does this prove that future drops will be temporary? No. It does indicate that the probability of a permanent drop in the future is very small. The only honest statements we can make about the future are probability statements.

The graph shows the difference between the volatility of short- and long-term "fixed" securities—30-day treasury bills versus 20-year treasury bonds. The historical profile for 30-day T-bills is much smoother than for 20-year bonds. Both are obligations of the federal government. The only difference is the length of the maturities. The federal government has never defaulted on debt securities either short-term or long-term. The volatility and uncertainty of fixed investments increases as the maturity increases.

Figures 6-7 and 6-8 reflect the same data as the SBBI graph. The figures further illustrate the linkage of uncertainty and rates of return. They show that in order to attain a higher rate of return, it's necessary to tolerate wider ranges of outcomes.

Another important lesson the graphs illustrate is something called the equity premium. The long-term rate of return for long-term government bonds has been 5.3 percent. For the stock market, as measured by the S&P 500, the return has been 10.7 percent. That difference of over five percent, the equity premium, is the historical extra return resulting from being an owner compared to being a lender.

The much greater degree of volatility of stocks vs. bonds or stocks versus T-bills reflects the higher degree of risk (uncertainty). That volatility is the entry fee you have to pay to get that extra return. Economists are

Figure 6-7:
Asset Class Returns
Highs and Lows: 1926-2001

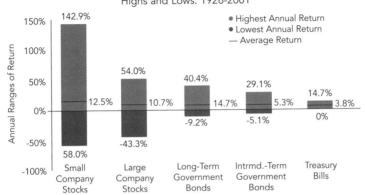

Each bar shows the range of compound annual returns for each asset class over the period 1926-2001.

Source: *Ibbotson Presentation Materials*, © 2002 Ibbotson Associates, Inc. All rights reserved. Used with permission.

Figure 6-8:
Summary Statistics and Returns Distributions
1926-2001

	Compound Annual Return	Risk (Standard Deviation)	Distribution of Annual Returns
Small Company Stocks	12.5%	33.2%	
Large Company Stocks	10.7%	20.2%	
Government Bonds	5.3%	9.4%	
Treasury Bills	3.8%	3.2%	

*The 1933 Small Comany Stock total return was 142.9%

Source: *Ibbotson Presentation Materials*, © 2002 Ibbotson Associates, Inc. All rights reserved. Used with permission.

somewhat perplexed why the equity premium is as large as it is, but it's clear that it exists and that it's been around for a very long time. In his book, *Stocks for the Long Run*, Jeremy Siegel shows that it has gone back at least as far as 1800 in the United States.

Eugene Fama and Ken French recently have made a persuasive case that the equity premium is unlikely to continue at its historical level (Fama and French, 2001). They also argue that the historical equity premium has probably been miscalculated and exaggerated. The policy implications of their findings are not clear. What does a lower equity premium imply in regard to the mix between equity and fixed investments? If you're a long-term investor, and the premium remains positive (maybe three percent rather than five percent), is that enough to continue with a 100 percent equities portfolio? At the very least, investors should not base their decisions on the assumption that the equity premium will always be as high as it has been in the past.

In an efficient market opportunities for making higher returns will exist if you are willing to give up some safety and certainty to get them.

Let's assume you see the value and necessity of taking risks. Unfortunately, you can't automatically increase your returns by taking on more risk. One of the problems is the issue discussed above—that of "uncompensated risks." Some risks are rewarded, while others are not. You don't always get what you pay for.

A major focus of research in financial economics has been the identification of factors that generate higher returns by way of tolerating more risk. How do you take more risk? According to the "three factor model" the paths to higher risks and returns are (1) invest in stocks rather than fixed investments, (2) invest in "distressed," high book-to-market companies, and (3) invest in smaller companies. As we will see, item (1) is the most powerful of the three. Historically, step 1 would have added about five percent to your rate of return, step 2 would have added about three percent, and step 3 would have added about two percent.

A "book-to-market ratio" is a shorthand indicator of a company's level of distress. "Book" refers to the company's "book value," that is, the current value of its tangible assets and accounts receivable. It is an indication of the per-share value of the company if it were liquidated. "Market" refers to the current market price of the company's stock. A high book-to-market ratio is an indicator of a distressed company.

Because book values tend to be fairly stable, a high ratio results primarily from a low stock price. A distressed company's stock price is low relative to its own fundamentals, and the ratio is low relative to the general market. Sometimes the ratio is inverted and called "price to book" ratio. In that case a relatively low ratio indicates a distressed company.

Smaller companies tend to be younger and less well established than large companies. In general their status is less reliable and more uncertain.

Playing the lottery is a clear example of uncalculated risk taking.

For only a dollar you can buy a chance to win millions! Somebody wins the lottery. Does that indicate that playing the lottery is a worthwhile endeavor?

The existence of winners proves virtually nothing in regard to the payoff of the system. The system is structured, not for the benefit of the players, but for the benefit of the sponsors. The sponsors intentionally hide the realities and bamboozle the players.

Your chances of winning are not significantly affected by whether or not you have a ticket. In this context there's no real difference between zero and one one-millionth (.000001).

It is unquestionably an overall losing proposition for the players. The payoff is only about half the amount generated by ticket sales. As discussed earlier, the expected value of a ticket is about half what you pay for it. Adam Smith in 1776 was perhaps the first to clarify the folly of lotteries.

> *In order to have a better chance for some of the great prizes, some people purchase several tickets, and others, small shares in a greater number. There is not, however, a more certain proposition in mathematics than that the more tickets you adventure upon, the more likely you are to be a loser. Adventure upon all the tickets in the lottery, and you lose for certain; and the greater the number of your tickets the nearer you approach this certainty.*
>
> Adam Smith,
> *The Wealth of Nations*

Take Smith's advice. If you don't want to be a loser, don't play the lottery. The lottery has been described as a tax on the mathematically challenged. What is the rationale for a special tax on people who don't understand probability? Have we implicitly decided that not understanding probability is a crime? I agree that it's good for people to understand probability, but it's hard to see why people who don't should have to pay what amounts to a fine. Lotteries rely on voluntary exchange, but it's exchange based on cynical and deliberate deception. It's the state's version of active management.

Risk summary

▸ What space and time are to the physical world, risk and return are to the financial world.

▸ Wall Street puts almost all its emphasis on return and virtually ignores risk.

▸ Taking calculated risks is a key to investment success.

► An investor's concern should not just be on the target, but also on the probability of hitting that target.

► Basically, risk is equivalent to uncertainty.

► Since risk cannot be avoided, the next best thing is to manage it for your benefit.

► Accepting the inevitability of risk is one of the keys to being a realistic investor.

► Uncertainty is what makes decision-making such a challenge.

► A primary reason for the success of the market system is that it provides a hospitable environment for risk taking.

► A diversified, robust economy increases our resilience to unpredictable hazards.

► We can't foresee the future, but all outcomes are not equally likely.

► Our knowledge of the world comes in the form of probabilities, not certainties.

► Probability is a major element in the science of decision-making.

► Expected value is simply the combination of payoff and probability.

► In the context of investments, risk essentially translates to the possibility that the realized return will be less than the anticipated return.

► Generally, if you want the opportunity for a higher return, you have to be willing to take more risk.

► An important investor self-awareness question is how much uncertainty are you able to tolerate to give yourself the opportunity for a higher return?

► An investment choice of crucial importance involves only two options—being an owner versus being a creditor.

► It is by way of the debt-equity balance that an investor can make the largest move in the direction of compensated risk.

► The difference between the historical rates of return for stocks and bonds, almost six percent, is called the "equity premium."

► T-bills have an excellent record for maintaining their value, but a terrible record for growing in value.

► Historically, small companies and high book-to-market companies have produced higher rates of return relative to the total market, but also involve greater risk.

► Neither lottery-ticket buyers nor active managers grasp the importance of probability.

CHAPTER 7

Diversification: Why It Matters and How It's Achieved

My ventures are not in one bottom trusted,
Nor to one place; nor is my whole estate
Upon the fortune of this present year;
Therefore my merchandise makes me not sad.
William Shakespeare, *The Merchant of Venice*

Diversification is the cardinal rule of investing and the one most often violated.

Ask most people if they think diversification is a prudent investment strategy and they will probably nod in agreement. As I've talked with and observed investors over the years, however, I've gotten the impression that many of them somehow do not intuitively grasp its importance, nor do they make it part of their behavior. It is almost as though there's a gene that determines whether or not a person is capable of understanding diversification. When I talk to a prospect about diversification, I see one of two different reactions—knowing agreement or bored disinterest.

Even for people who do get it, however, the path to diversification is bewildering and poorly marked. There's a definite tendency for investors to assume they are more diversified than they actually are.

> *James Tobin, upon winning the Nobel Prize in 1981, was asked to summarize the essence of his work. He responded, "Don't put all your eggs in one basket." But as often as this is said, it is not often followed. Despite the indisputable evidence that diversification lowers risk, many investors own very few stocks and indeed put most of their eggs in one big basket.*

> Jeremy Siegel, *Stocks for the Long Run*

Diversification is contrary to the basic belief system of active managers, which is based on confidence in one's ability to predict the future. If you can predict the future, you don't need to diversify. Diversification is for investors who accept the limits of one's ability to predict. The period of 2000-2001 taught many investors and managers of mutual funds hard lessons about the hazards of ignoring diversification.

The well-known experience of Enron employees is an especially painful lesson in why diversification matters. The average employee's 401(k) plan was comprised of 60 percent Enron stock. Not only did their jobs depend on the success of a single corporation, their financial nest eggs did as well. When the company failed, the employees were doubly devastated. Unfortunately, the practice of employees over-concentrating in their employer's stock is all too common.

Investment objectives and performance are best defined in terms of your entire portfolio.

Diversification is one of those concepts that's both simple and complex. Although it has been advocated as a risk-reducing strategy for at least hundreds of years, the first rigorous treatment of diversification did not occur until 1952.

In a path-breaking 1952 article, Harry Markowitz demonstrated the need for a systematic, deliberate approach to diversification. He was the first to place the emphasis on portfolios rather than individual investments. Our current, state-of-the-art investment science is derived from this concept, and it is called Modern Portfolio Theory (MPT). A central element of MPT is the notion that investment objectives and performance are best defined in terms of the risk and return of the entire portfolio. The whole is more important than any of the parts.

One of the central insights of MPT is that, particularly in regard to risk, the whole (i.e. the portfolio) is not the sum of the parts. The variability of the portfolio is not a simple average of the variability of the components. On the other hand, the total return of a portfolio is the weighted average of the components. In mathematical terminology, return is additive, risk is not.

Diversification is not an end in itself.

An important practical application of Markowitz' contributions is what's known as "efficient diversification." Of course, when dealing with the efficiency of something, it's critical to define your objective. To be efficiently diversified, you have to first ask, "What is the purpose of diversification?"

A simple answer is to keep you from losing all your money. The objective of diversification is to reduce the probability of loss. But specifically how does diversification help accomplish that result?

Assume that a population of one thousand investment alternatives has an expected distribution of returns, following a roughly normal distribution from minus 100 percent to plus 100 percent, with a mean of plus 10 percent. If you choose an investment from this population, you might double your money (+100 percent) in a given period or you might lose it all (-100 percent). If, instead, you select a number of investments, your chance of total loss is greatly reduced.

If you distribute your investments among all the stocks in an asset class, you will assure yourself of getting the average rate of return. Diversification pulls you toward the average. In selecting stocks, the outcomes furthest from the average are random and unpredictable. Consequently, the greater the number of events, the greater the probability their divergences will balance out. You effectively reduce the range of results by allowing random outcomes to offset one other. By diversifying, you increase the "probability density" of the uncertain future. Diversification also reduces the cost of an error because you have less riding on any given outcome.

The investments that find themselves on the tails of the distribution are called "outliers." Diversification eliminates the chance you will be an outlier, either on the favorable or unfavorable extremes of the distribution.

The distribution of returns can only be determined retrospectively. The distribution is a historical document. You can think of it as the distribution of prediction errors. Those errors can only be identified with the benefit of hindsight.

The safety you derive from diversification comes at a price, but it's a bargain.

Diversification reduces the possibility of major loss, but it likewise reduces the possibility of major gain. It keeps you away from both tails of the distribution.

Which is better—settling for the average or taking a chance on achieving a better than average result? That depends on both the expected value of taking a chance and your risk tolerance. The right choice depends on the subjective value of the benefits compared to the subjective value of the costs. (The positive value you put on return versus the negative value you put on uncertainty.)

Bear in mind the importance of probabilities. A critical element of successful decision-making is "playing the odds." If you are going to attempt to beat the average, you ought to have some defensible reason why you think the probability of exceeding the average is greater than the probability of doing less than the average. If you have a way to assure yourself of the average (specifically, indexing), attempting to beat the average necessarily involves more uncertainty and, therefore, more risk. Even managers who are confident they can beat the market know they can't guarantee that result. Remember, reducing uncertainty is equivalent to reducing risk.

Because of market risk, there is uncertainty as to what the average will be. Nevertheless, because of the availability of index funds, you can easily eliminate the uncertainty of achieving the average.

Although diversification can't directly increase your expected rate of return, it can achieve an equally valuable result by reducing your exposure to uncompensated risk.

We cannot count on the future being the same as the past. There is a random element in any future event. How do you cope with, or hedge against, the inherent randomness of the future? Your best protection is not allowing too much to ride on any particular outcome. In relation to what you hope for, some outcomes will be unusually favorable to you, while others will be unusually unfavorable. Diversification is based on modesty, on recognition and acknowledgement of our limits. If you have a crystal ball you have no need to diversify. If you recognize and accept your inability to predict, you will want to diversify.

The two basic characteristics you're looking for in an investment are high return and low risk. Any time you get the same return while exposing yourself to less risk, you're better off and a more efficient investor.

In light of our inability to predict, diversification is the most logical and effective choice. Shakespeare had it right (in the quote introducing this chapter). The safest port in a sea of uncertainty is diversification. The Merchant of Venice proclaims that, because of his diversification, "Therefore my merchandise makes me not sad." In other words, he had financial peace of mind.

Since diversification is of such central importance, it only makes sense to approach it seriously, methodically, and deliberately. For such an important principle, however, it's rather amazing how haphazardly it gets treated.

There is stability in numbers.

Suppose you're asked to select from two investment alternatives, A and B, each having returns over the past ten years of twelve percent. Investment A is comprised of a single stock. Investment B is comprised of ten stocks. If you know nothing else about the two options, which should you choose?

You don't need to be an investment expert to recognize that Investment B is superior to Investment A. You could teach yourself a lot by giving some thought to why B is better. Based on the information offered, you can deduce that Investment B is lower risk than Investment A. Why can you make that assumption? The most important reason is that the outcome of ten events is the result of far more factors than the outcome of one event. You don't know what caused the past performance. Even if you did, you couldn't assume that any one factor would persist in the future.

Everyone has heard that there is strength in numbers. Strength is important, but for investors what matters even more is that there is continuity, stability, and persistence in numbers.

Let's take the example a step further. Suppose you had flexibility in selecting the ten investments to include in your portfolio. If you could construct a portfolio of ten investments and you could only select from a population of investments with equal long-run returns, what would be your investment criteria? If you wanted to consider risk as well as return, you would look for a way to diversify.

Efficient diversification is about more than how many investments are in your portfolio.

> *Efficient diversification*—The process of creating diversification in a portfolio by selecting securities in a manner that explicitly considers the standard deviation and correlations of the securities.
> William Sharpe, *et al*, *Investments*, 6th ed.

How do you assure that your investments are, in fact, diverse? You want them to vary in the way they vary. Having a hundred different stocks in your portfolio may leave you woefully under-diversified. If you had owned the "Nasdaq 100" in 2000-2001, your portfolio would have lost about 70 percent of its value. (The Nasdaq 100 consists of the 100 largest companies listed on the over-the-counter market.)

In order to achieve the risk-reducing objectives of diversification, components of a portfolio must have at least a degree of independent behavior. In technical terms, the covariance of the components should be minimized. Covariance measures the degree of parallelism or synchronicity of the components. If the components behave like a school of fish, the main purpose of diversification is lost. The behavior of the portfolio will be no different and no more stable than the behavior of each component.

A school of fish moves in the same direction and changes direction at the same time; its movements are synchronized. The individual fish have a high "covariance" with one another. If a collection of investments behaves in that manner, it will not matter whether there is one investment, ten, or a hundred. The portfolio and each of the parts will perform the same. Stocks of firms in the same industry have a high covariance.

Figure 7-1

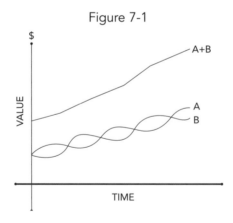

Figure 7-1 illustrates a simple example of the objectives of effective diversification. The graph shows the behavior of two investments, as well as a portfolio comprised of both investments. Both investments have positive long-term rates of return, but their short-term behavior diverges. In this illustration, the ideal case of negative correlation occurs. When investment B goes down, investment A goes up and vice versa. The combined result for a portfolio with both investments is a major reduction in volatility. Figure 7-1 demonstrates the basic logic of efficient diversification and the effects of non-correlated portfolio components.

Failure to diversify is the most easily avoidable mistake an investor can make.

Because the risk-return connection is so strong in the financial world, there's a tendency to assume that higher returns come automatically from taking on more risk. It's not that simple.

Firm-specific risk (which, you'll recall, is the same as business risk and diversifiable risk) is the prime example of uncompensated risk. Insofar as securities markets are efficient, there is no payoff for taking specific risk when investing in stocks. Virtually every form of active management, every strategy having the objective of beating the market, involves uncompensated risk. It would be difficult to overstress the importance of this issue. This again illustrates why market efficiency has such important implications.

In an efficient market, there's no advantage to investing in individual stocks as contrasted with a diversified portfolio of stocks. Why not? When you invest in an individual stock, you expose yourself to at least three times as much risk, but with only the same expected return as compared to investing in an index fund. The only way to make excess returns on individual stocks is by reliability identifying mis-priced stocks, and if markets are efficient, that can't be done with any consistency. The only logical assumption is that every stock is priced such that it has a rate of return equivalent to those of other stocks carrying the same level of risk. That's the equilibrium the market is always heading toward. An explanation of how this happens was presented in Chapter 4 (Figure 4-2 and related text).

Because of market efficiency, the expected return for stocks of similar risk is equal. All stocks with a risk level of X will have an expected return of, let's say, 10 percent. As discussed in Chapter 4, all individual stocks with similar levels of risk gravitate toward the same expected return. Any other situation motivates buying and selling until relative prices reach equal levels of expected return.

When investing in stocks, there is no economic justification for failing to be diversified. Concentration increases your risks without increasing your return.

Figure 7-2:
Risk Components of Owning an Individual Stock

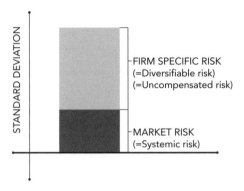

Figure 7-2 shows the two types of risk associated with owning an individual stock: specific risk and market risk. Specific risk is categorized as "diversifiable risk" because it can be avoided by owning a diversified portfolio of stocks from a variety of industries.

Previously it was thought that the risk components of owning an individual stock were about one-third market risk, two-thirds specific risk. However, a recent study (Malkiel *et al*, 2001) found that in the last few decades individual stock prices have become significantly more volatile, while the volatility of the overall market has not increased. For the period 1986-1997, the risk proportions were approximately one-tenth market, nine tenths specific. In other words, investing in an individual stock is now more than ten times riskier than investing in diversified portfolios (a daily standard deviation of .6 for portfolios of two stocks vs. a standard deviation of .05 for portfolios of 50 stocks).

Even those proportions understate the full magnitude of the differences in the two categories of risk. Both specific risk and market risk are measured according to average variability. There is, however, a major *qualitative* difference between the two. There has never been a permanent drop in the stock market in the United States. By contrast, thousands of individual stocks have suffered permanent declines, and many of those declines have been all the way to zero. Market risk is temporary in nature, firm-specific risk can be permanent.

There's a world of difference between a temporary loss and a permanent loss. The money you invest in an individual stock can go down and out. Not so with a diversified portfolio.

The highly important, practical implication is this: when you invest in an individual stock you take significantly more risk (at least three times as much), but you get the same expected return. When you invest in an individual stock or a sector fund, you take a risk for which you get nothing in return. That's the essence of uncompensated risk.

All the magazine articles and TV shows that tell you which individual stocks to buy ignore this basic reality. When you hear some talking head on one of the cable channels telling you which stock to buy, bear in mind he is advising you to take substantially more risk without any compensating reward. Ask yourself, how dumb can he be?

Economists like to point out that there's no free lunch. That's another way of saying that life consists of tradeoffs. Uncompensated risk is worse than getting no free lunch. It's as though you paid for a lunch you were never served.

This is not to deny that you might get lucky when investing in an individual stock. Millions of people have. But that's what's happening—you're being lucky. That is very different from market risk. All the evidence shows that you do get compensated for taking that risk. Market risk is generally and systematically connected with higher returns. Specific risk is not. The expected return of investing in a specific stock is the same as the return for all other stocks in that asset class and, therefore, the same as the average. By being diversified, you position yourself for the same expected return as a single stock, but you expose yourself to far less risk.

With uncompensated risk, there are just as many losers as winners. Unless you value the dollars you win more than the ones you lose, it's a bad idea. Furthermore, the winners and losers are randomly distributed—from one investor to another and from one time period to another.

At the very least, if you're going to invest in individual stocks, face facts about what you're doing. What you're doing is relying on luck. That's your prerogative. Just don't delude yourself into thinking there's some kind of underlying strategy or logic at work. Luck doesn't constitute a strategy.

Enron: what are the important lessons for investors?

The most famous business failure of the past several years was the collapse and bankruptcy of the energy trading company Enron. The news was filled with reports of major losses suffered by investors, who saw Enron's share price fall from $80 to zero in a matter of a few months. News articles asked the question, what could investors do to anticipate these kinds of problems?

That's the wrong question, because no one can ever be aware of the countless possible hazards that can afflict specific companies. Virtually all the major stock research services were giving buy recommendations for Enron until just before the final collapse. However, the Enron debacle was barely a blip on the financial radar screen of any investor who relied on index funds. Anyone who lost a significant amount of money because of Enron was inadequately diversified. It's that simple.

If you agree that passive investing works best, what are the steps you should take to construct a real-world portfolio?

A good way to start thinking about the alternatives to active management is to consider two popular and largely similar alternatives: an S&P 500 fund and a "total market" fund. Index funds consisting of the S&P 500 are the most popular and readily accessible ways to implement a passive management investment strategy. A number of fund families offer only a single index fund, and if they do, it's an S&P 500 fund.

Essentially, the S&P 500 index is comprised of the 500 largest publicly traded U.S. corporations. I say essentially because the list is not strictly a function of size. A corporation's size, or capitalization, is calculated by multiplying the number of its outstanding shares times its current market price. As I write this there are approximately 10 billion shares of General Electric stock outstanding, and its share price is $45. Its market capitalization is, therefore, approximately $450 billion. The total value of all the 500 companies is $10 trillion. General Electric, therefore, gets a 4.5 percent weighting in the S&P 500 index fund.

The challenge of what to include in the listing of the 500 companies isn't with the giants like General Electric, rather, it's at the other end of the listing. Since size depends on share prices and since share prices change constantly, the list would also change constantly if the size criteria were followed religiously. In order to give some stability to the list, a committee at the Standard and Poor's Corporation has the final say. The committee also does not strictly adhere to the all U.S. criterion. About a dozen of the companies in the index are headquartered abroad. In a global economy, whether or not a corporation is foreign or domestic is somewhat arbitrary.

An S&P 500 mutual fund contains all 500 companies selected by the S&P committee, and the companies' weightings within the portfolios are proportional to their size. For example, General Electric's share of an S&P 500 portfolio is 4.5 percent and Home Depot's is .8 percent (at the time I write this). The total value of all the outstanding shares of GE is five times greater than the value of Home Depot's shares. In other words, index portfolios are "cap weighted." Cap weighting means that a company's representation in the portfolio is proportional to its "capitalization." This is appropriate and probably the only reasonable alternative, but there are some important implications of such a policy.

Cap weighting results in most of the value of the portfolios being concentrated in relatively few companies. About 75 percent of the total value of the S&P 500 is concentrated in the 50 largest firms. Furthermore, although there are over 8,000 publicly traded companies in the U.S., the S&P 500 comprises about three-fourths of the total capitalization. The value of all 8,000 publicly traded companies is approximately $13 trillion, $10 trillion of which is accounted for by the 500 largest companies.

Both of these reflections of concentration illustrate why relying totally on either an S&P 500 index fund, or a total market index fund, should be done with a degree of caution. Either alternative is far superior and more diversified than practically any actively managed mutual fund. The main problem, however, is that using either of the most popular indexing options by themselves means that you are essentially restricting yourself to one asset class: U.S large-growth companies. Even with a total market fund, the amount of the portfolio invested in small companies is relatively minor. In the Vanguard Total Market Index fund, only nine percent of the portfolio is in either small or micro-sized companies. The median market capitalization for companies in the S&P 500 is $56 billion. The median capitalization for the Total Market Fund is $33 billion. In other words, on average, the companies are still giant-sized. To be classified as a small company usually means having a size of about $1 billion or less.

The most important implication of these similarities is that there will not be much difference in either the risk or return characteristics between an S&P 500 and a total market fund. The two kinds of index funds will behave approximately the same. Historically, that has been the case. The two types of funds will not have nearly the differences of performance seen in the six asset classes in Table 7-3.

The S&P 500 companies also tend to have relatively low book-to-market ratios. This means they are likely to be growth companies. The practical implication is that there's a relatively small representation of "value" companies. If you want a significant value component in your portfolio you have to go beyond the S&P 500, or even a total market fund.

Another problematic aspect of the total market funds currently available is their virtual lack of non-U.S. stocks. Eventually, there may be "total-global funds." This again, however, raises the issue of the appropriate allocation. About 70 percent of the total capitalization of world equity markets consists of non-U.S. companies. Is that the appropriate allocation? There's no one right answer to that question.

Creating and selecting asset classes: the objective is to find reliable and accessible building blocks with which to construct efficient portfolios.

A central component in the theory and practice of portfolio design is what's known as an "asset class." An asset class is a collection of assets, each of which meets some given definition.

There are, as you might imagine, an unlimited number of asset classes that could be defined. You could, for example, have an asset class of all corporations with names beginning with the letter M. Of course, that would raise the question, why would you want to do that? Obviously, there needs to be criteria or methodology for designing and defining an asset class. It should be something more than the fact that M is your favorite letter. In other words, what are the decision rules for asset class design? Where should you draw the boundary lines for inclusion and exclusion? What you are looking for are reliable and accessible building blocks with which to construct efficient portfolios.

Table 7-3, Rates of Return by Asset Class, shows annual rates of return during a thirty-two-year period for six different asset classes, along with returns for a diversified portfolio made up of the six asset classes. The diversified portfolio has a 20 percent allocation in each of the four U.S. asset classes and 10 percent in each of the two international asset classes. These particular asset classes have been chosen for a combination of reasons. Each has an impressive rate of return for the period. Each is defined broadly enough to include at least 100 different stocks. Each is objectively and quantitatively defined so as to be reproducible and measurable.

The asset class known as U.S. Small Company, for example, contains the smallest 50 percent of publicly traded U.S. companies (with a few minor exclusions). In other words, if you ranked the approximately 8,000 publicly traded domestic companies from large to small, the "U.S. Small" asset class would contain the bottom half of the ranking, the smallest 4,000 companies. Value companies are defined here as the top three deciles, ranked according to book-to-market ratios. The U.S. large growth asset class is the S&P 500.

Table 7-3:
Rates of Return by Asset Class

Year	U.S. Small Company Value	Growth	U.S. Large Company Value	Growth	International Small	Large	Diversified Portfolio
1970	0.3	-11.7	**11.9**	4.0	0.9	-9.6	0.0
1971	14.4	20.4	10.1	14.3	**68.3**	59.9	24.7
1972	7.0	4.2	16.9	19.0	**64.2**	53.2	21.2
1973	-26.0	-36.1	**-1.5**	-14.7	-13.7	-22.3	-19.3
1974	**-18.2**	-28.8	-21.9	-26.5	-28.6	-33.7	-25.3
1975	54.5	56.7	50.5	**37.2**	49.9	**65.3**	51.3
1976	**53.6**	48.3	47.7	23.8	11.5	5.6	36.4
1977	21.8	20.1	-2.2	-7.2	**74.1**	40.6	18.0
1978	21.8	20.5	6.9	6.6	**65.5**	33.2	21.0
1979	38.0	**40.7**	25.9	18.4	-0.8	2.1	24.7
1980	29.1	36.8	18.8	32.4	35.5	**38.5**	30.8
1981	**10.5**	2.5	9.3	-4.9	-4.7	0.9	3.1
1982	**37.7**	25.2	23.9	21.4	0.8	5.2	22.2
1983	**44.2**	30.4	30.9	22.5	32.4	22.2	31.1
1984	5.1	-4.9	**12.0**	6.3	10.1	11.4	5.9
1985	34.7	30.1	29.9	32.2	**60.1**	48.3	36.2
1986	16.9	7.7	18.4	18.5	50.1	**60.0**	23.3
1987	-6.3	-7.1	6.7	5.2	**70.6**	41.4	10.9
1988	**28.8**	24.9	26.8	16.8	26.0	24.8	24.5
1989	19.6	15.9	25.5	**31.5**	29.3	14.7	22.9
1990	-20.8	-19.0	-22.1	**-3.2**	-16.8	-18.4	-16.5
1991	39.4	**46.9**	34.4	30.5	7.1	14.0	32.4
1992	**31.1**	20.4	26.3	7.7	18.4	-9.4	14.3
1993	24.7	17.0	20.3	10.0	33.5	**36.4**	21.4
1994	3.4	-0.1	-4.5	1.3	**12.4**	7.6	2.0
1995	32.1	30.9	**38.4**	37.4	0.5	13.7	29.2
1996	**24.5**	19.1	20.2	23.1	2.6	7.5	18.4
1997	32.3	25.8	28.1	**33.4**	-23.7	-4.4	21.1
1998	-7.3	-5.5	12.0	**28.7**	8.0	15.0	7.9
1999	13.1	25.4	4.8	20.8	20.2	**32.6**	16.1
2000	9.0	2.5	**10.2**	-9.3	-5.7	-14.6	0.5
2001	**22.7**	12.7	3.8	-12.1	-10.7	-21.0	2.3
Compounded Annualized Returns	16.7%	12.6%	15.0%	12.0%	15.4%	13.3%	14.7%

BEST performing asset class each year
WORST performing asset class each year

Source: Center for Research in Security Prices and Dimensional Fund Advisors

Table 7-3 reflects some of the most important realities of investment performance. For each year, the asset class with the best performance for that year is in bold type. The worst return for each year is outlined. One valuable lesson to draw from the table is the randomness of the good and bad relative performances. Random variables can't be predicted.

You will search in vain for any pattern to the relative performance from year to year. You can't foresee which asset class will be the leader or the laggard in a particular year. There is no discernable tendency for good years to follow bad, or vice versa. If you did find a pattern, it would be difficult to determine the likelihood of it repeating itself. Between the years 1999 and 2000 best went to worst and worst went to best.

There is nothing sacred about this particular allocation. Each of the asset classes has had good long-term performance and each is broadly diversified. An important reason to include these particular asset classes is to take advantage of the three-factor model (market, size, and value).

Returns for this 32-year period have been well above average, from a historical perspective, so it would not be surprising if the future averages for the asset classes were well below the performance shown. The returns for the next 32 years might be only half those of the past 32 years. You can't make assumptions. You can, however, design a strategy with a high probability of giving you the best returns possible.

For the period shown, all these asset classes performed well and any one of them would have provided satisfactory results, if you invested long-term. So why not just select any one of them for the future? Past performance, as you often hear, is no assurance of future results. It's entirely possible that any one of these asset classes, even though each is internally diversified, could experience relatively poor performance for extended periods in the future. For example, the S&P 500 (U.S. Large Growth) actually under-performed 30-day Treasury-bill rates of return for the 17-year period from 1965 to 1982 (6.7 percent for 30-day T-bills, 6.3 percent for the S&P 500). Even if you have a long-term perspective, that experience could severely test your patience, nerve, and resolve.

Notice what happened to even the diversified portfolio in 1973-74. Those were the worst two years for the stock market since the Depression. Someone starting in 1970 would have seen his portfolio grow for three years and then lose all the gains over the two-year period. At the end of 1974 he would have had a five-year negative return. However, patience would have been rewarded. He would have recovered all the losses and then some only a year later.

During the years 2000 and 2001, diversification worked just as it's supposed to. The diversified portfolio had a slightly positive return while the S&P 500 had negative returns of –9.3 percent and –12.1 percent. The portfolio held its own because some of the asset classes had positive returns. 1990 was another story, however. Negative returns occurred across all the asset classes. Under such conditions, even diversification isn't enough to shelter you from the storm.

Modern economies are highly dynamic. We have witnessed numerous major changes in the economy. The relative performance of large versus small, value versus growth, or U.S. versus international could be different in the future. Don't make any big bets with your nest egg if there's no reason for doing so.

For the 32-year period a diversified portfolio generated 92 percent of the returns of the best-performing asset class (15.7 percent/17.1 percent=92 percent). This means there is relatively little payoff for "loading up" on any one asset class. In this context, the safety of diversification comes at a low cost. The primary benefit of asset allocation is not increased returns but rather reduced risk.

Another important lesson to draw from the 32-year record is the wide range of asset class performance during many of the years. In the year 2001, for example, the worst performing class had a –21.0 percent rate of return and the best had a 22.7 percent rate of return, a gap of 43.7 percent. This demonstrates the degree of non-correlation among the six asset classes, which is one of the main characteristics you're looking for in constructing efficiently diversified portfolios. Perhaps even more importantly, it shows the potential damage of guessing wrong and the hazards of believing you can predict.

The fundamental purpose of diversification is to reduce the volatility of the portfolio, and that means looking for asset classes with low covariance among the individual components. It's the lack of covariance that contributes to the stability of the portfolio.

The performance record reflected in Table 7-3 can also be used to demonstrate the potential value of having a crystal ball. What if you could predict which of the six asset classes would do best at the beginning of each year? If you could do that and you invested all your money in the highest-performing asset class each year, your compound rate of return for the thirty-two-year period would have been 33 percent. At that rate of return, a $10,000 investment would have grown to $98 million. If you were that smart, you'd be rich!

All that's needed is to pick the one best asset class out of only six, a much easier challenge than picking the best individual stocks out of thousands. On the other hand, the table shows the excellent results possible with no effort spent on either stock selection or market timing. The strategy and asset allocation implied in the table are relatively simple, attainable, and intelligible. Feasibility is a highly desirable feature when choosing a strategy.

What is an adequately long historical record for evaluating an asset class? There is no choice other than to strike a compromise in this regard. What you want to avoid, if possible, is generalizing from too small a sample. Ideally, it would be preferable to have a 100-year track record. However, even if you could get that much data, there would be no assurance that the future would be like the past, and it's the future that matters when it comes to investing. Nevertheless, the longer the historical record, the better. Wall Street's habit of relying on track records of only a few months or one or two years is clearly not enough.

It's also important that what you're measuring over time stays consistent with its original definition. That's one reason why the problem known as "style drift" is so important. Style drift will be discussed in the next chapter.

Furthermore, events or sequences that have recurred repeatedly are more dependable than ones that are historically unique or rare. Ice ages have occurred numerous times in the past. It's not unreasonable to expect them to recur in the future. In 1980 the price of gold exceeded $800 an ounce. It has not come close to that level before or since. We will probably have a very long wait before it gets to that level again, if ever. Gold prices have a low covariance with the stock market, but the long-term real rate of return for gold is essentially zero. Adding gold would add stability to a portfolio but would significantly reduce its return.

Should real estate be considered for an investment portfolio? Possibly, but there are a number of dilemmas inherent in real estate as an investment. Foremost is the difficulty of diversifying. Real estate is a relatively narrow asset class. Most real estate investments are concentrated in a small geographic area. Unlike a mutual fund, there's usually no way to divide them into fractional shares. What has the long-term rate of return been for real estate? No one knows because there's no national real estate market and no meaningful index. Owning rental property typically involves far more of a time commitment than owning a mutual fund, and you don't usually have the protection of limited liability. Real estate investment trusts (REITs) do avoid some of these dilemmas. Nevertheless, even REITs score poorly in regard to true diversification. They basically amount to sector funds.

Building efficient portfolios is a two-tiered process.

Portfolio building through the use of asset classes could be called "maximum feasible diversification." The asset classes are selected so as to ensure that each has at least a degree of independent behavior. Each asset class is itself broadly diversified, with hundreds of companies within numerous industry groups. Investing in this way will prevent the debacle experienced by investors who loaded up on technology stocks in 2000-2001.

Because of the accessibility of passively managed, asset-class funds, it is entirely possible to eliminate uncertainty in terms of achieving average rates of return for the total population of the asset class. The way to assure that you get the average of the population is to purchase the entire population. That's exactly what a passively managed, asset-class fund does. Costs always prevent exactly matching gross rates of return.

However, because the cost of asset-class passive management is only a fraction of the cost of active management, the spread between your gross and net rates of return is quite narrow. For example, the expense ratio for the Vanguard S&P 500 fund is only .18 percent. By contrast, the average expense ratio for actively managed large growth funds is 1.4 percent— more than seven times higher than the passive equivalent. Furthermore, as will become clear in Chapter 8, that 1.4 percent does not fully reflect all the costs of active management.

The practice of asset allocation employing several asset classes combines two of the basic conclusions of Modern Portfolio Theory. First, the use of passively managed asset classes avoids the costly, risky, and futile strategy of attempting to beat the market. Second, using asset classes with non-correlated performance follows the logic of efficient diversification. Actively managed funds will always fall short of passive funds in terms of diversification. The only way to beat an average is to select from a population. If you take the entire population, you'll get the average. Incomplete diversification is an undeniable competitive disadvantage of actively managed funds.

According to Morningstar, large growth mutual funds hold an average of 82 stocks in their portfolios. That's one-fourth the diversification of an S&P 500 index fund. The average number of holdings in small growth funds is 139. The number of companies in the DFA Small Cap fund is over 3,000, twenty times more diversification than the typical active alternative.

Being an efficient frontiersman.

A concept known as the "efficient frontier" represents the best achievable combinations of risk and return. Figure 7-4 illustrates the general shape of an efficient frontier. If an investment portfolio is on what's known as the efficient frontier, it means that higher returns necessitate greater risk. If your portfolio is below the frontier, it implies that you could

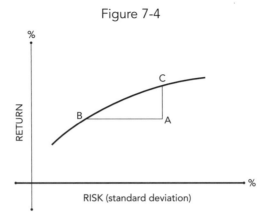

Figure 7-4

get a higher return for a given amount of risk or a reduced risk for a given rate of return. Moving from individual stocks to a diversified portfolio is a move toward the efficient frontier. Because of their higher costs and incomplete diversification, all actively managed mutual funds are below the efficient frontier.

The efficient frontier is more useful as a concept and thinking tool than as a precision instrument. It is a graphic representation of the only two possibilities for increasing investment returns—moving to the efficient frontier by becoming a more efficient investor, and moving along the frontier by deliberately taking more risk. By moving from point A to point B, you decrease your risk without decreasing your return. By moving from point A to point C, you increase your return without increasing your risk. When you go from B to C, you increase your return but you have to increase your risk to do so.

You can't get beyond the frontier. In terms of investment alternatives, it represents the boundary line between what's possible and what isn't. If you got beyond the frontier, it would only mean the frontier was misspecified.

As an investor you have two challenges—getting to the frontier and then deciding at what point on the boundary you belong or feel comfortable. Getting to the frontier is a question of efficiency. However, there is no unique point on the frontier that is optimal for all investors. Deciding at what point you want to be is a matter of risk tolerance. It's a subjective question.

The primary methods for moving to the frontier are diversifying and using passive management. The primary method for moving along the frontier is by changing your allocation between equities and fixed investments. You can move even further along the frontier by allocating more of your portfolio to smaller and distressed company index funds.

Three important investment policy conclusions of Modern Portfolio Theory are these: (1) if you are not fully diversified, you are not on the efficient frontier; (2) if you are relying on active management, you are taking uncompensated risk, incurring unnecessary costs, and you are not on the efficient frontier; and (3) if you are moving along the frontier, you are being compensated for taking more risk (by way of a higher expected return).

Rather than exerting effort optimizing your portfolio, focus on broad diversification.

The process of deciding on the ideal percentage allocations in a portfolio is known as "optimization." Optimization is related to the concept of an efficient frontier. By using computer models, it is possible to identify the asset allocations that would have had the best historical combinations of high return and low volatility.

Optimization, however, should be viewed with skepticism. The outcomes of optimization calculations are highly sensitive to relatively small changes in the historical data. This means that normal variations in relative performance in the future would significantly alter or rearrange the optimal portfolio and necessitate annual alternations in the target investment mix. The optimized portfolio for one year could be quite different from what it had been the previous year, even though nothing unexpected or unusual happened. Figure 7-3 illustrates that changes from year to year are more the rule than the exception.

You might recall from high school math the concept of "significant digits." What, for example, is the product of multiplying .7 times .6? The correct answer, of course, is .4, not .42. You cannot legitimately end up with more accuracy (two decimal places) than you started with (one decimal place). An answer implying two decimal places of accuracy is bogus. Violations of that fundamental logic are incredibly common and usually go unnoticed.

Rather than getting too clever with precisely optimized portfolio construction, a more realistic target is maintaining a broad breadth of diversification. Don't devote a lot of time and effort trying to decide whether one asset class should be 22 percent or 26 percent of a portfolio. It's not an efficient use of your time. Sometimes the use of "round numbers" is the most honest, practical, and realistic option.

Which index funds should you consider?

Although a number of mutual fund families offer S&P 500 funds, at this time only two offer a selection broad enough to do serious asset allocation and efficient diversification—Vanguard and Dimensional Fund Advisors (DFA). Furthermore, DFA and Vanguard are currently the only providers of tax-managed index funds. Morningstar lists 325 index funds, but many of those are index funds in name only. Many of them do, in fact, try to beat the market in the usual ways. One of the funds on the list, for example, had a portfolio turnover in 2001 of 3,603 percent (Profunds Bull Investors). Any fund with a portfolio turnover of 100 percent or more is definitely not passively managed.

Vanguard has been a pioneer in making retail index funds available to ordinary investors. John Bogle, one of Vanguard's founders, has been highly effective and persuasive in spreading the word on the advantages of passive management. Bogle has also emphasized the importance of avoiding unnecessary costs and the problem of hidden costs. His books, *Bogle on Mutual Funds* and *Common Sense on Mutual Funds* have helped spread the word on the benefits of passive management.

Bogle has now retired from Vanguard. While he was there he apparently was not successful in fully convincing the management of the futility of trying to beat the market. Vanguard still offers a number of actively managed funds. As an organization, Vanguard has a split personality. Nevertheless, its passive funds provide investors an excellent selection of alternatives. One gap in its selection the lack of an international small company fund. Nevertheless, in the realm of retail mutual funds, Vanguard is vastly superior to the other well-known families of funds.

The mutual fund group that is by far the most scientific in its approach is Dimensional Fund Advisors of Santa Monica, California. The firm's founders, Rex Sinquefield and David Booth, were both graduate students in the early 1970s at the University of Chicago, the main hotbed of Modern Portfolio Theory and especially the Efficient Market Hypothesis. Eugene Fama, the father of the EMH and a professor at the University of Chicago, is on DFA's board of directors and is an ongoing contributor to their research and methodology.

Sinquefield recalls first hearing about efficient markets in Economics 301 (taught by Merton Miller, a future Nobel laureate). "It was like

*an epiphany—this is so obvious, it has to be the way the world works,"
he says. "My interest quickly became, I want to apply this stuff, because
nobody else was doing it."*

"Indexing Gets a Boost,"
Bloomberg Personal Finance, March 2001.

DFA has only one fund that could be classified as a true index fund
—its "U.S. Large Company" fund that replicates the S&P 500. Its other
funds are asset-class funds, engineered to capture risk and return factors
academic research has shown to be significant—the small company and
value factors in particular. DFA deliberately takes a more focused approach
to these factors. For example, its "large-value" fund has a book-to-market
ratio that is about twice that of Vanguard's corresponding fund. The
average size of the companies in DFA's small-company fund is about half
that of Vanguard's small-company fund. DFA's funds are more distilled
versions of asset classes and as such should capture more of their inherent
risk and return factors. The payoff is a greater degree of independent
behavior and reduced covariance relative to other asset classes. A more
pronounced emphasis on these factors makes it possible to capture more of
the inherent risk and, therefore, higher expected returns.

For various reasons, DFA follows a policy of restricted distribution and
the funds are not directly accessible by most investors. Ordinarily, DFA
requires a minimum investment of $2 million per fund. The funds are
available with much smaller minimums, however, through about 300
investment advisors throughout the United States. One of DFA's basic
beliefs is that investors are better off with an advisor than without.

Spiders, WEBS, and diamonds.

The newest innovations in passive investing are the exchange-traded
funds (ETFs). ETFs represent a number of asset classes, such as S&P
depositary receipts (spiders), World Equity Benchmark Shares (WEBS),
and the Dow Jones Industrial Average (diamonds).

There are a number of technical differences between ETFs and
traditional, passively managed mutual funds. When you buy or sell a
regular mutual fund, the trade price is calculated on the value of the
underlying assets as of 4 p.m. Eastern time following the trade. In other
words, the prices change only once each trading day. ETF prices, on the
other hand, change continuously so you can trade them "intra-day." That
feature, of course, doesn't have much relevance for long-term investors.

Another difference is that ETFs are structured as "closed-end" funds. Regular index funds are "open-ended." Closed-end funds have the potential for trading at discounts and premiums relative to the value of the underlying assets, although that has so far not been a problem with ETFs.

It is too soon to tell if ETFs offer real advantages to the more tried-and-true index funds. So far the potential advantages don't appear to be significant. Because of their relatively short track record, there are still a number of unanswered questions. ETFs are no doubt better than virtually any form of active management, but for now the even better alternative continues to be the older kid on the block—asset-class index mutual funds.

Consider taxes before making a switch to passive investing.

If you are persuaded about the advantages of passive management, the next question is whether you should switch your investments immediately. The answer is yes, with one proviso—first consider the tax implications.

Before you liquidate your existing positions, estimate what the capital gains will be. That's particularly true if your existing portfolio consists of individual stocks and you've been lucky or you've been a long-term buy-and-hold investor.

Diversification and passive management are definitely superior, prudent investment policies. If converting immediately to those alternatives means a large tax liability, however, that cost needs to be taken into account. You have no choice but to trade-off one objective for another.

If you have investments in a pension plan, there will be no capital gains problem if you decide to switch to passive management. Within qualified plans—IRAs, corporate pension plans, 401(k)s—it's not necessary to report capital gains as long as they remain within the plan. You can choose the best alternative without worrying about the IRS.

Do the terms indexing, passive management, and asset class investing all mean the same thing?

Three terms frequently used in the context of passive investing need clarification: index funds, asset-class funds, and passively managed funds. Although closely related these terms have distinctions worth noting.

The Dow-Jones Industrial Average (DJIA) is known as the "senior index" and is the one you hear cited most often. Its senior designation is because of its age, not its accuracy. It has been around since the nineteenth century, but includes only thirty stocks. That's a relatively small sample from a diverse population of several thousand. The specific thirty stocks are rather arbitrarily chosen. General Electric is the only company that's been included from the start. There are index funds that replicate the DJIA, but because of their lack of diversification they're not a good choice for investors.

A far more representative index is the S&P 500. The sample size is more than sixteen times that of the DJIA. The index funds that replicate the S&P 500 attempt to keep as close to the index as possible. Their primary focus is to minimize "tracking error."

An asset-class fund isn't directly affected by the existence (or lack of) a specific index. Dimensional Fund Advisors has been the primary innovator in the field of asset-class funds.

The creation of an asset-class fund commences with the identification of factors that evidence shows have a persistent connection with either risk or return in the market. It's important that the factors can be quantitatively defined. One of the objectives of an asset class fund is to eliminate any reliance on subjectivity.

An asset-class strategy allows more flexibility in comparison to a strict index emphasis. Once you define an asset class, it will not much matter whether or not every single stock of that class is continuously included in the portfolio. There might be, for example, 300 stocks that fit a given criterion. If 95 percent of the population is in the portfolio (285 stocks), there will be only a small tracking error relative to 100 percent of the population. If the portfolio managers have difficulty finding sufficient quantities of a stock at a particular time, they can just wait until the availability is better, rather than being forced into a distress purchase.

The term passive management is perhaps the most generic and inclusive term of its type. Passive management basically means choosing not to attempt to beat the market. Index funds and asset-class funds are both passively managed, as are most exchange-traded funds. The objective is to duplicate returns of some segment of the market rather than to generate excess returns.

Perhaps the main drawback to the practice of passive management is the connotation of the word passive. In most contexts, active is better than passive. In communication, the active voice is usually more efficient than the passive voice. "I love you" rather than "You are loved by me." Active participation in an activity is usually more admirable than passive participation. In regard to investing, however, your real choices are between passive management and active mismanagement.

What if everyone indexed?

A question that sometimes occurs to people when they hear about the advantages of indexing is, what if everyone indexed? Doesn't there need to be an ongoing search for bargains for the market to remain efficient?

The short answer is, don't worry about it, it's not going to happen in your lifetime. The logic and evidence supporting passive investing have been around for decades, and widely available passive investments have been around for at least ten years. Still, only about ten percent of the market is passively invested. How long will it take to reach 50 percent or 90 percent?

No one knows for sure, but it would probably take no more than five percent of the players looking for incorrectly priced securities to keep prices efficient. There is no question that there is enormous redundancy of efforts to beat the market and over-investment in market research. Mark Carhart estimates that the benefit-cost ratio for market research is about .05 (Carhart, 1997). In other words, for each dollar spent on market research, there's about a nickel's worth of value. There could be a tidal change in the active-passive division among the players without any reduction in market efficiency.

Among the forces that keep prices reflective of intrinsic values is the buying and selling of stock by the company itself. For example, in the aftermath of the attack on the World Trade Center, when the market declined abruptly, there was an unusually high level of companies buying back their own stock. The companies could see that the prices were out of sync with reality.

It's not clear exactly what the extreme-case scenario would be. Suppose all the money entering and exiting the market were indexed. Would that mean that relative stock prices would be frozen in place? As long as there is less than 100 percent indexing, relative prices would have freedom to shift. When that happened, all the rest of the participants in the market would have to adjust their portfolios. It's conceivable that prices would adjust to news even faster than they do now.

Possibly the thought of passive management makes you feel guilty about "free-riding" on the research of others. Maybe you feel an obligation to participate in keeping markets efficient. Forget about it. That's what's known as unearned guilt.

Rebalancing is about maintaining diversification.

If you've chosen asset classes properly, they will not all grow at the same rate each year. Suppose you decide on an allocation similar to the diversified portfolio of Figure 7-3 (page 145):

Figure 7-5

U.S. large growth	20 percent
U.S. large value	20
U.S. small growth	20
U.S. small value	20
International large companies	10
International small companies	10
Total	**100 percent**

Suppose that, in the first year, U.S. large growth has a 15 percent rate of return and U.S. small value has a minus 10 percent rate of return. At the end of the year, your allocation will not be what it was at the beginning. U.S. large growth will be over-weighted and small value will be under-weighted. One option would be to just leave them that way.

A policy of "rebalancing" involves re-establishing the original percentage allocations. In the above scenario, this would mean selling some U.S. large growth and buying more small value.

Rebalancing imposes a counterintuitive discipline on the decision process. It involves selling winners and buying losers. That tends to go against the grain of human nature.

Rebalancing has been described as the only market-timing system that actually works. There may be some truth to that, but saying that rebalancing is market timing is a stretch. It makes more sense simply to think of it as a system for maintaining diversification.

If you don't rebalance periodically (once a year, for example) your portfolio will become overly concentrated in the asset classes with the best recent performance. There should be logic to your original allocation, and unless something has happened to change your rationale or you have new information, the best policy is to maintain that allocation.

Unequal asset class performance is something you should expect. It's happened in the past (that's a big part of the reason why you selected those asset classes), so why shouldn't it happen in the future? Unless something has happened that's beyond what you expected, why alter your plan?

Whether or not you should rebalance every year is partly determined by tax considerations. If your funds are in a retirement account you can rebalance with no tax implications. However, if your account is a regular taxable account, rebalancing could result in some taxes. In that case, you may want to rebalance less often.

How important is asset allocation?

The most famous study on the value of asset allocation was done by Gary Brinson, Gilbert Beebower, and Randolph Hood, initially conducted in 1986 and updated in 1991 (Brinson, *et al*, 1986). Their best known conclusion is that, in the pension plans they studied, asset allocation accounted for 92 percent of the variability of performance. The remaining 8 percent was the result of security selection and market timing. The inference taken from their study is that asset allocation accounts for 92 percent of investment performance.

Two caveats are worth noting. First, the BBH conclusions were focused on annual variability of performance, not absolute long-run performance, which is what investors should care about. The second is that they only considered three general asset classes—stocks, bonds, and cash equivalents. That is not the kind of asset allocation that's been examined in this chapter, nor is it the main focus of Modern Portfolio Theory. As stressed in this chapter, asset allocation is much more of a risk issue than a return issue. Unfortunately, the BBH study focused on the lesser objective of asset allocation.

Diversification summary.

▶ Diversification is the cardinal rule of investing and the one most often violated.

▶ Investment objectives and performance are best defined in terms of the risk and return of the entire portfolio.

▶ The variability of the portfolio is not a simple average of the variability of the components.

▶ To be efficiently diversified you first have to ask, what is the objective of diversification?

▶ By diversifying you narrow the range of possible outcomes of the uncertain future.

▶ Diversification increases the probability that you will receive rates of return equal to the average of the asset class.

▶ Although diversification can't directly increase your expected return, it can have an equally favorable result by reducing your exposure to uncompensated risk.

► Diversification is based on modesty and on recognition and acknowledgement of our limits.

► The safest port in a sea of uncertainty is diversification.

► Efficient diversification is not simply a function of the number of investments in a portfolio.

► In order to achieve the risk-reducing objectives of diversification, components of a portfolio must have at least a degree of independent behavior.

► Investing in an S&P 500 index fund is superior to and more diversified than practically any actively managed mutual fund.

► Investing in several asset-class index funds is a way to implement the logic of efficient diversification.

► The primary purpose of asset allocation is not to increase expected returns but rather to reduce risk.

► Rather than getting too clever with precisely optimized portfolio design, a more realistic objective is maintaining broad diversification.

► The only honest statements we can make about the future are probability statements.

► There is no fixed relationship between risk and return. Some risks are rewarded while others are not.

► Virtually every form of active management, every strategy having the objective of beating the market, involves uncompensated risk.

► Investing in individual stocks generates the same expected return but at least three times as much risk as investing in an index fund.

► Failure to diversify is the most easily avoidable mistake an investor can make.

► When you invest in individual stocks, you're relying on luck.

► A concept known as the efficient frontier represents the best achievable combinations of risk and return.

► The primary purpose of rebalancing is to maintain diversification.

CHAPTER 8

Active Management: The Costs Are Hidden, the Returns Exaggerated, and the Risks Ignored

꽃

If these guys were race horses, they'd be glue.

Rex Sinquefield

This chapter spells out the numerous reasons actively managed funds create irresolvable problems and dilemmas for investors, and why active management delivers lower returns along with heightened risk. There is only one reason to use active management—the remote hope of beating the market. On the other hand, there are numerous reasons not to use it.

By pursuing excess returns, you will actually diminish results.

The pursuit of excess returns will likely diminish returns but by how much? Although Wall Street hates to admit it, the damage done averages over three percent a year. The magnitude of the decreased performance varies widely from one fund to another and from one investor's experience to another. As we will see also, the lower return is accompanied by an increase in risk exposure—that is, greater uncertainty in a number of dimensions.

As the following table shows, a simple comparison of performance between active and passive management results in a difference of roughly two percent.

Figure 8-1

	5 Year	10 Year
S&P 500	14.5%	15.1%
Large blend funds	12.1	13.2
Difference	2.4	1.9

Source: Morningstar Performance Closeups. Period ending 6/30/01

As you can see, the performance difference is 1.9 percent for a ten-year period. Does that mean trying to beat the market involves giving up 1.9 percent a year on average? Unfortunately, for active managers and their clients, the actual damage is even worse.

Burying their mistakes and rewriting history.

In order to evaluate and compare mutual fund historical performance, something known as "survivor bias" has to be taken into account. For a research service like Morningstar to measure a ten-year performance record, the fund has to exist both at the beginning and end of the ten-year period. That simple fact has interesting implications.

Mutual funds have a mortality rate greater than zero—each year some of them are put out of their misery. Mark Carhart estimated that about 3.5 percent of funds go out of existence every year (Carhart, 1997). Over a ten-year period, that would mean about 30 percent of the funds that started the period would be gone by the time it ended. If they were distance runners, they would be listed as "DNF" (did not finish).

Which ones would you guess failed to make the distance? Unlike a fund's intermittent ability to beat the market, mutual fund mortality is not random. As with the quiz show "The Weakest Link," the poor performers are banished, never to be heard from again. When the poor performance records of these failed funds get dropped from the data, it provides the industry an opportunity to rewrite its own history.

There's something statisticians call the "Texas sharpshooter fallacy." That's the process of shooting holes in the side of a barn and then, after the fact, drawing bull's eyes around the holes. This is the basis for the favorite advertising tactic of mutual fund families—advertise the performance of your best performing fund without mentioning the other 25 funds in the family that did poorly. Survivor bias is equivalent to having a target before the shooting starts, but papering over the holes farthest from the bull's eye.

> *Mutual funds that have taken bets against the market that proved to be unsuccessful do not tend to survive. It is extremely difficult to sell a mutual fund to the public that has a poor track record. Mutual fund complexes (that run large numbers of funds) will typically allow the fund to suffer a painless death by merging the fund into one of the more successful funds in the complex, thereby burying the fund's bad record with it.*
> Burton Malkiel, "Returns from Investing in Equity Mutual Funds 1971-1991," *Journal of Finance*, June 1995

Malkiel estimates that survivor bias overstates the performance of actively managed funds by approximately 1.5 percent a year. Therefore, if the reported long-term historical performance difference is 1.9 percent a year, the actual difference is over 3 percent.

When attempting to beat the market, a price must be paid.

Attempting to beat the market inevitably involves higher costs and higher risks. Higher costs are necessitated by the fact that attempting to beat the market simply requires more effort than does replicating market rates of return.

You can, if you like, choose to believe that beating the market is possible. You cannot, however, deny that the attempt costs something. The extra costs aren't debatable, although active managers prefer to gloss over their magnitude. In order for market-beating attempts to be worthwhile, you must do more than just exceed the asset class rates of return. You must exceed them by more than the associated extra costs.

The unnecessary costs involved in active management accounts for its lower rates of return. About nine-tenths of the money invested in the stock market is actively managed, either by way of mutual funds, professional money managers, or individual investors. In other words, about nine-tenths of the invested money is attempting to beat the market. The gross average rate of return on this money is virtually equal to the average rate of return for the market as a whole. As explained in Chapter 4, all funds cannot beat the market—that's a logical impossibility. Since the active managers are competing among themselves, they cannot all be above average. On the other hand, their gross average returns cannot be far below the market either.

Therefore, if there is a difference in the net return between active and passive management, it's mostly due to cost differences. Estimating how much active management retards performance is primarily a matter of getting a fix on the total costs of attempting to beat the market. Indeed, the studies show that the percentage difference in performance between active and passive management is generally equal to the cost differences.

You are paying roughly four percent a year for your attempt to beat the market.

A major and frustrating problem with active management is the fact that there is no way to measure all the extra costs. Four percent is only a conservative, educated guess of the average extra expense.

Most investors, if they think about it, realize there are costs associated with mutual funds. However, it's a rare investor who has anything but a vague idea of what those costs are. Even the comprehensive research services such as Morningstar are unable to do a complete accounting of all the costs of active management. Some are impossible to measure directly and can only be estimated or deduced.

We'll start with the costs that are relatively easy to identify and then examine the ones that are not. Three accessible sources for basic expense ratios are mutual fund annual reports, the *Wall Street Journal* monthly mutual fund summaries, and Morningstar. According to Morningstar management fees for stock mutual funds average 1.4 percent per year. Included in management fees are the typical administrative costs you would expect for any financial organization—record-keeping, rent, staff, reports to shareholders, advertising, and so on. Investors might assume the management fees are the only costs they're paying. Unfortunately, that is not the case.

I've spoken to numerous investors who were surprised to learn there are any costs involved when investing in mutual funds. That's not too surprising. Those costs are never brought to their attention by the mutual funds. True, they're reported in the funds' annual reports, but you have to know where to look to find them. Fees do not show up anywhere on the regular account statements, and these are often the only documents investors choose to inspect.

High portfolio turnover is the source of most of the extra and totally wasted costs associated with active management.

The average annual portfolio turnover of actively managed large growth funds during the 1990s was 97 percent, and in 2000 it was 162 percent (Morningstar, Inc.). A 100 percent turnover rate means that each year virtually all of the stocks in the portfolio are sold and replaced with other stocks. In comparison, a 20 percent turnover would equal an average holding period of five years.

High portfolio turnover causes major additional costs. These costs are an absolute dead weight burden on returns—all costs, no benefits. Bear in mind this critical reality—as a general strategy, portfolio turnover cannot help overall average performance. The mutual fund managers are, after all, buying from and selling to each other. One manager's gains are another manager's losses and vice versa. In game theory, this is called a zero-sum game. In reality, however, because of transactions costs, it's a *negative*-sum game. There is considerable friction in the system, and just as mechanical friction produces heat, turnover generates costs. Both cause a dissipation of energy and reduced efficiency.

One study of 143 funds over a twenty-year period found that portfolio turnover diminished a fund's net return. The study ranked the mutual funds into five groups according to turnover and return. There was a perfect inverse relationship between performance and turnover—perfectly bad for the perpetrators. High turnover was robustly associated with poor performance (Elton, *et al*, 1993).

High portfolio turnover further demonstrates both the arrogance of active managers and their instinct for self-preservation. Although portfolio turnover is doomed as a general strategy, each active manager justifies his use of it because he thinks he is smarter than the others. He continues to believe this even as he perennially under-performs the market. High portfolio turnover rates also are needed to justify the manager's existence. If he follows a buy-and-hold strategy, his board of directors will wonder why he's needed. They are likely to ask: "What have you done for us lately?" High turnover rates are probably the most counterproductive and self-serving larcenies perpetrated by active managers on the investing public.

There's an old story of an isolated army outpost. The men stationed there were frustrated because they were always short of money to spend at the canteen. One of them came up with a solution. Rather than each of them doing his own laundry, they would hire each other and pay to have the laundry done, giving them all an extra source of income. Portfolio turnover makes as much sense and has about the same hope of success.

An interesting mystery is why portfolio turnover has increased dramatically in recent years. The 162 percent rate translates to an average holding period of just seven months. The numbers for the year 2000 could be attributed to panic, but 1999 was a good year for the market, and that rate was also relatively high—123 percent.

Figure 8-2:
Annual Portfolio Turnover, Percent

	'91	'92	'93	'94	'95	'96	'97	'98	'99	'00
Large Growth funds	92	87	88	85	93	105	96	105	123	162
Technology funds	240	190	171	116	93	106	191	160	121	217
Vanguard S&P 500	5	4	6	6	4	5	5	6	6	9

Source: Morningstar, Inc.

Figure 8-2 also shows the average turnover percentages for technology sector funds. Through August 2001, the average turnover had already reached 404%!

All the evidence supporting market efficiency points to the folly of portfolio turnover.

If stock prices reflect all available information about the relative values of companies, it is impossible to reliably identify and buy a stock at a bargain price or sell it for more than its intrinsic value. An important practical conclusion of market efficiency is that the best long-term investment strategy is buy and hold—assuming you're well diversified.

"Trading" is the name given to strategies based on frequent buying and selling. The success of that approach hinges on identifying and buying bargain-priced stocks and selling them when they rise to or above their true value. It is based on the rather arrogant belief that the trader knows more than the buyers and sellers with whom he is trading. Why would someone sell him the stock for less that its intrinsic value, and why would someone else buy for higher than the right price? The answer must be in part the unfounded overconfidence and conceit of those playing the game.

Portfolio turnover also indicates the time horizon of the portfolio manager. Does he identify, buy, and keep good companies? As mentioned earlier, a 100 percent turnover translates into an average holding period of 12 months. That means the manager's time horizon is 12 months. That's how long, on average, he thinks it takes for whatever's supposed to happen to happen. The average active manager indicates by his actions that he is definitely not a long-term thinker. The Rydex Leisure Advisors fund had a turnover of 5,734 percent in 2000. That translates to an average holding period of less than one week. It basically amounts to the mutual fund equivalent of day-trading. That level of hyperkinetic activity makes you wonder why it's called the Leisure Advisors fund.

John Bogle describes transaction-related costs as the "invisible cost" of money management. They result from sales commissions and differences in the "bid" (sale) price and the "ask" (purchase) price inherent in the market. Those costs are estimated to be approximately one percent for each 100 percent of turnover in a portfolio.

But wait, there's more! Portfolio turnover creates the additional burden known as market impact costs. "Market impact is what happens when a mutual fund buys or sells a large block of stock. The fund's purchase or sale causes the stock to move beyond its current bid (lower) or offer (higher) price or ask price, increasing the cost of trading" (Swedroe, 2000).

Market impact has the effect of raising the cost when buying a stock and decreasing the proceeds when selling a stock. It's been described as causing the price to move away from the trader. It increases the cost of each roundtrip. High turnover means lots of roundtrips.

The potential for market impact costs is one of the reasons mutual fund managers give for not fully and promptly disclosing their strategies and activities. That's because telegraphing their stock picks could cause their buys to be bid up even more if other market players attempt to piggyback on their research.

According to Swedroe, "Using the most conservative estimates, market impact costs can be assumed to add at least one percent to the costs active managers must beat to achieve above market returns." In general, the larger the size of the mutual fund, the greater the magnitude of market impact costs. Even when the percentage of these costs is low for each transaction, the cumulative cost is significant over time when the turnover rate is high.

Keep in mind that market impact and other turnover costs are not included in the reported management fees of mutual funds. The SEC does not require reporting of transaction costs. Because of their nature, they are virtually impossible to identify and measure accurately. Regardless of whether they are difficult to identify, however, these costs have real and substantial impacts on net rates of return.

The combination of commissions, the bid-ask spread, and market impact costs add up to at least 2 percent on average. Add that to the average expense ratio of 1.4 percent and the costs of active management begin to come into focus. By contrast, the average total costs of a passively managed fund average about one-half a percent and often even less.

> *Given their poor performance, how do actively managed funds get away with charging high fees and incurring large costs? It's simple: Investors let them. Investors aren't focused on costs, partly because the markets have done so well in recent years. In addition, investors don't receive a bill labeled management or trading costs—their fees are deducted from the fund's total assets and never show up on an account statement.*
> Larry Swedroe, *Journal of Accountancy*, January 2000

Concealed costs do more potential damage than obvious, out-in-the-open costs. Choosing among alternatives should involve a comparison of costs and benefits. If the costs are impossible to identify, how can you make effective decisions?

Most defenders of active management will argue that the costs of attempting to beat the market average less than four percent. Because of all the hidden and inconsistent costs, however, it's impossible to get a precise fix on the average costs. For the sake of argument, let's say it's closer to two percent than four percent. Even if that's what it is, two percent is far too much to pay when you are getting nothing in return. If it's two percent, that's still at least four times what passive management costs. If market returns in the future are less spectacular than those of the '80s and '90s, the impact of the excessive costs will become much more of a burden on performance.

The average investor arrives after the party's over. Unfortunately, he suffers the hangover anyway.

Dalbar, an investment research firm (dalbar.com), has done one of the more intriguing studies on mutual fund investors. It concluded that from 1984 though 2000 "the average equity-fund investor realized an annualized return of 5.3 percent compared to 16.3 percent for the S&P 500 Index." Now, you might be asking, how in the world could investors have done 11 percent worse than the market?

According to Dalbar the main culprit seems to be the relatively short holding period for mutual fund investors. According to the data, in 2000 the fund retention average was 2.6 years.

The short holding period would not, by itself, cause so much damage, but the impact is aggravated by the practice of chasing recent returns, sometimes referred to as "track-record investing." Investors tend to flock to funds having impressive recent performance. This causes the fund's size to swell after the high returns. If there is any reversion to the mean, or if the returns were the result of taking excessive risk (a reasonable assumption), the fund will likely have below average performance when it's managing the most money. A mutual fund's performance calculations are time-weighted, not size-weighted. In other words, the performance experienced by the average investor is likely to be below the fund's average.

The Dalbar findings reveal what is possibly the major component of the costs of active management. The hype-and-casino atmosphere of the beat-the-market game results in investors being at the wrong place at the wrong time. It is yet another reason why active management means lower returns, higher risks, and reduced financial peace of mind. The cost of being in the wrong place at the wrong time never shows up in the funds' annual reports, Morningstar, or the *Wall Street Journal*.

There is probably no way to fully measure the costs of chasing returns. It varies widely from one investor to another. It has the effect of transferring wealth from the unlucky to the lucky, an effect that would not show up in a measure of aggregate results. What you see is the average performance, not the magnitude of diversions away from the average. The published performance numbers do not reflect how much wealth was redistributed as a result of some investors being unlucky or victims of bad timing. It's difficult to fully measure the perils of hot pursuit.

The IRS has to love active managers.

Another under-reported cost of active management is the tax impact of high portfolio turnover. Mutual fund companies follow a strict policy of passing through all the taxable income and capital gains each year to the individual shareholders. There's a good reason for such a policy. If they did not do so, they would subject their shareholders to double taxation—once at the mutual fund company and a second time when the income and gains were paid out to the shareholders. Obviously, that would not be a good idea.

Investment tax efficiency relates primarily to the issue of capital gains distributions. A capital gain (or loss) is the net difference between an asset's purchase price and its sales price.

A crucial aspect of the capital gains tax is that it is applied only when the gain is realized, that is, when the asset is actually sold and converted to cash. "Paper profits" are not subject to the tax. A paper profit is when something you own goes up in value but you haven't cashed in on the gain.

This not-due-until-realized aspect of the capital gains tax applies to both individuals and mutual fund companies (as well as all other tax-paying entities such as trusts and corporations).

As you might guess, the realized portion of capital gains is affected by the rate of turnover in a portfolio. Higher turnover means that the stocks in the portfolio are being bought and sold more frequently, and sales trigger the realization and taxation of the gains.

When turnover rates are 80 percent or even higher there is very little tax deferral. The average holding period is only 15 months so capital gains are deferred barely longer than when annual taxes are paid. About one-fourth of your gains would be deferred but only for one tax year.

For index funds, by comparison, the annual turnover rates are between 5 and 30 percent. A 5 percent turnover rate translates to an average holding period of twenty years. Tax deferral is equivalent to an interest-free loan, so the longer holding periods provide many years on average of interest-free loans. Even if you ultimately pay the same amount of tax, postponing the tax gives you a longer period to use and control the money.

The short average holding period for active funds means the pain is more than just paying taxes sooner rather than later. When gains are realized on stocks held less than a year, the tax rate can be twice that for long-term (a year or more) gains. Long-term capital gains are treated favorably by the IRS in calculating taxes. Short-term gains, however, are taxed as regular income. Under current law the maximum federal tax rate for long-term gains is 20 percent. Currently the maximum federal rate for regular income (including short-term gains) is 38.6 percent.

A particularly maddening aspect of the tax inefficiency of active funds is the unpredictability of the reported gains. For example, the volatile year 2000 produced numerous situations in which funds with significant negative performance reported large capital gains distributions. That's adding tax insult to performance injury.

You might be saying to yourself that tax-efficient funds don't necessarily lead to permanent tax savings. You could argue that mutual fund tax efficiency is really more about tax deferral than permanent tax avoidance.

Potentially as important as permanent tax savings is the increased ability to control the timing of when your investments are taxed. If you can choose the year you realize gains you may be able to match them with capital losses or a drop in your other income.

Actively managed funds are virtually the polar opposite of tax control.

Paying taxes is always painful, but when you're caught by surprise the pain is worsened. It is a given that active managers pay no attention to tax considerations as they manage the portfolios. It's another manifestation of their total focus on raw rates of return. Just as they avoid mentioning risk, they avoid mentioning taxes. Their efforts are not judged on the basis of tax efficiency. Except for municipal bond funds, taxes are rarely mentioned in mutual fund advertisements.

On the other hand, because of their relatively low portfolio turnover, index funds are inherently tax efficient. The annual taxable distributions of an index fund are significantly less than that of an active fund.

Tax-managed index funds go a step further. For example, at the end of each calendar year the stocks with imbedded losses are harvested, that is, sold so as to realize losses to help offset any realized gains. What is more, tax-managed funds are careful to avoid short-term capital gains, which are taxed at the same high rates as ordinary income. Tax-managed index funds minimize sales of stocks that have been in the portfolio for less than a year.

Actively managed funds are only 95 percent committed.

The cash portion of actively managed stock funds averages between 5 and 6 percent. This means that when you use active funds, you do not have the option of being 100 percent invested in the market. Index funds, in contrast, keep an average of only about one-half a percent in cash or approximately one-tenth as much as active funds.

An equity mutual fund's cash balances are invested in the same kinds of assets as those of money market mutual funds—Treasury bills, bank certificates of deposit, and short-term (typically 30-60 day) commercial loans. The cash balances are like having a money market fund within your stock fund. Such investments do better than the market when it's going down, worse when it's going up, and worse in the long run since the market goes up more of the time than it goes down.

For the past 77 years the S&P 500 has generated a rate of return of 10.7 percent and 30-day treasury bills have returned 3.8 percent. A portfolio of 95 percent equities, 5 percent cash equivalents would have generated a return of 10.4 percent, a difference of about .3 percent. This drag on performance increases the damage already done by higher costs.

There are a variety of reasons why active funds maintain relatively large cash balances, none of them particularly beneficial to shareholders. Partly it's a reflection of the active management view of the world—the managers want the capability of taking advantage of "buying opportunities." Cash can also build up if the managers have failed to discover stocks that meet their buying criteria. If stock markets are efficient, those kinds of dilemmas are absurd and nonsensical. No one has demonstrated the ability to reliably identify such buying opportunities. A buying opportunity is simply another term for a mis-priced security.

Cash balances are also maintained as a way of meeting the need for unpredictable liquidations of shares. Index fund managers, by contrast, maintain much smaller cushions but still manage to meet those contingencies. This is possible partly because most index fund investors think longer term and are less likely to liquidate during market turbulence.

Cash balances of ten percent or more are prima facie evidence of a closet market-timing strategy. The mutual fund manager might believe that the overall market is over valued and is waiting on the sidelines to get back in when the market corrects.

There's nothing wrong with having part of your money in a money market fund, if that's your intention. However, it should be a decision you control. The appropriate alternative is a separate money-market fund. Furthermore, the administrative costs of a money market fund are only about .2 percent, compared with 1.4 percent (plus hidden costs) for an actively managed stock fund.

Attempts to beat the market have non-monetary costs such as the time you spend on research.

If you take mutual fund selection seriously, you're going to have to devote some time to the process. The amount of information available on mutual funds is vast. There is no limit to how much time you could spend sifting through the numerical data and attempting to identify the best funds, but at what point do you stop? At what point do marginal costs equal marginal benefits?

The time-consuming nature of active management is an additional cost of that form of investing. Most people feel that time is their scarcest resource. Some people feel they have enough money, but do you know anyone who feels he has enough time? Time is the great equalizer. None of us has more than 24 hours in a day.

Here's a guaranteed way to become wealthy—invent something that saves people a significant amount of time or makes them more time efficient. Why, for example, is air travel so much more popular than trains or buses?

Anything that puts extra demands on your time should be justified by corresponding extra benefits. If you believe in active management, how much do you think it adds to your rate of return? As you spend time screening funds, how much are you earning hourly? What is the probability that your efforts will be successful?

Some people, of course, actually enjoy doing mutual fund research. The question is how much are you willing to pay for that form of entertainment? In general, active management generates rates of return four percent below passive management, and it increases risk. That much difference in a compound growth rate will have a dramatic impact on long-term results. To say the least, it is not an efficient form of recreation.

Furthermore, attempting to beat the market requires periodic monitoring to determine if you are, in fact, succeeding. This is yet another extra cost of active management. With passive investing, on the other hand, you own the entire asset class so you already know you're getting asset-class rates of return.

Active management is inherently unintelligible.

How does a mutual fund manager attempt to beat the market? How does a mutual fund portfolio manager match the market? An answer to the first question is far, far more complicated and opaque than an answer to the second. It is, therefore, harder to understand. In fact, it's probably impossible to understand. Attempting to understand active management will give you a brain hernia.

The approach active managers use in their attempts to beat the market is usually some variation of securities selection, or what is more popularly termed "stock picking." An alternative, though less often used method, is market timing, but most portfolio managers' efforts are devoted to securities selection. How specifically do they decide to select one stock and reject others? Explaining this is much like trying to explain art—not an easy thing to do.

I think it's safe to say that none of the investors in any given mutual fund comprehends the methodology used by the portfolio managers in selecting one stock and rejecting others. I certainly have never even heard of one who did.

Relying on active management essentially amounts to faith-based investing. There's nothing wrong with relying on faith in religious matters, but it's not something you want to make part of your investment policy statement. If you can't understand or define something, how can you use it to build an internally consistent and logical investment strategy? It simply can't be done.

In most cases the portfolio manager does not have a consistent methodology or discipline, but few of them would admit that. I've heard hundreds of portfolio managers describe their approaches and, generally speaking, I would characterize their remarks as vague, confused, rambling, and unintelligible. What they say sounds impressive as long as you don't listen too closely. For scores of examples, read *Wizards of Wall Street: Market-Beating Insights and Strategies from the World's Top-Performing Mutual Fund Managers* by Kirk Kazanjian or *The Market Gurus: Stock Investing Strategies You Can Use from Wall Street* by John Reese and John Glassman. The fact that these traders and fund managers are trying to beat the market against overwhelming odds casts serious doubt on their status as wizards or gurus.

For the most part, active managers provide few details about the methodology, logic, or discipline that governs their strategies. The managers have a number of plausible explanations for why they can't divulge their strategies and methodology. "Fund firms, especially the largest, contend that revealing holdings too soon would be (like) releasing a football team's playbook before the game is over" (*Wall Street Journal*, June 28, 2000).

In mutual fund advertisements, the emphasis is definitely on track record. Emphasizing track records diverts attention from the methodology supposedly used to achieve those particular results. The message is: "Pay attention to what I accomplished, but don't ask me to explain how I did it."

Granted, results are ultimately what matters most. (That, in fact, is one of the primary themes of this book.) The same or better results, however, can be achieved by way of fully illuminated, intelligible techniques. What are the benefits of secrecy? Apparently, the real purpose of the secrecy is to perpetuate the mystery of their expertise—the same reason the Wizard of Oz hid behind a curtain.

By contrast, index funds come about as close as possible to being fully illuminated and transparent. A major benefit of index funds is "what you see is what you get."

Largely because of being clearly defined, asset-class, index funds also score high on consistency and reliability. When investing in index funds, it's far easier to relax and assume they will remain true to character. A small-company index fund will be just that next month, a year from now, and indefinitely.

Active management fails in two dimensions—lower returns accompanied by increased risk.

The best throw of the dice is to throw them away.

English proverb

On average, actively managed mutual funds match market averages, minus all the wasted additional costs associated with that style of management. That handicapped rate of return is not the full extent of the problem, however. There is also considerable dispersion away from that reduced mean. In other words, there is a significantly greater degree of uncertainty inherent in the use of active management.

One undeniable source of increased risk is that active management necessitates incomplete diversification. The only way to exceed asset class rates of return is to select from the class. On the other hand, buying the entire universe will result in a replication of the average return.

No one knows, of course, what the market or asset class rates of return will be for the next one, five, ten, or fifteen years. However, by investing in index funds, you can assure yourself of capturing asset class rates of return (net of associated costs). If, on the other hand, you go the active management route, your range of possible outcomes—including many you would prefer to avoid—is considerably expanded. Because of the virtually complete lack of persistence of performance, you can only assume your future returns will be somewhere within the frequency distribution. Active management severely aggravates the problem of uncertainty.

Because of market risk, you don't know what the market rate of return for the given period will be from this time forward. That's what market risk means. There is no known way to avoid that uncertainty if you invest in equities. On the other hand, there is a simple and accessible method for eliminating the additional uncertainty of deviations away from asset class rates of return—invest in index funds. There is an enormous difference in the degree of uncertainty between active and passive management.

By necessity, the average rates of return received by active investors equals the overall market rates minus all the associated costs. There is no such consolation when it comes to risk. Striving for excess returns creates a net addition to total risk as experienced by the total population of active investors.

Imagine two contrasting investor populations. The first is one in which each investor owns a single stock. In the second population each investor owns an index fund containing all the stocks in the economy.

Both populations own the same set of stocks, but they own them in different ways. In the aggregate the two populations will get the same rate of return. There will be a dramatic difference, however, in the variability of performance experienced by the individuals in the populations.

In the single-stock-portfolio population some investors will do great, others will be wiped out if the single stock they own is an Enron. In the index-fund-portfolio population no one will be wiped out unless there is a wide-spread economic meltdown. The total amount of uncertainty and stress experienced by the single stock population will be far greater than the index-owning population.

In other words, there's no fixed aggregate amount of uncertainty to be shared among the universe of investors. It can be either a negative-sum-game or positive-sum-game. By their actions investors can either create or destroy the amount of uncertainty, at least in terms of variance and subjective uncertainty. As more investors switch to passive management, the amount of stress experienced by investors will decrease and there will be a net improvement in financial peace of mind.

Just how smart is your portfolio manager?

Besides track record, another theme of mutual fund marketing is emphasizing the credentials of the portfolio manager. For example, how much experience does he have? What is his education? In an efficient market, however, the credentials of the portfolio manager are no more useful than past performance. Even a portfolio manager who approaches genius cannot hold or process as much information as the entire market. No matter how much research a person does about a given stock, what he knows is miniscule compared to the amount of total information embodied in the stock's price.

Credentials sound impressive and in most circumstances mean something. We have a natural and logical tendency to attach significance to someone's training and accomplishments. However, in the context of an efficient market, what counts is *comparative* advantage. If a large number of the players have impressive credentials, the issue of credentials loses its significance.

Furthermore, because of the competitive realities of the market, an active manager needs to explain more than how smart he is. He also needs to explain why he's smarter than the other active managers. The fact that you're a fast runner doesn't mean you will win the race. In a competitive situation, what matters is your speed relative to the other runners.

More importantly, it's not just competence relative to other managers, it's competence relative to the market. The impressive credentials of so many managers only goes to make the entire market more efficient. The high level of competence and competition only raises the bar for everyone and effectively self-cancels.

The beat-the-market gang also fails to recognize that it only takes one or a small number of other players to eliminate their bargain-hunting opportunities. If a single player knows that a stock is bargain priced, his rational course of action is to keep buying it until it's no longer a bargain.

> *The potential for self-cancellation shows why the game of investing is so different from, for example, chess, in which even a seemingly small advantage can lead to winning by the person with a slight edge…Investors implicitly lump the market with other arenas of competition in their experience.*
> Mark Rubenstein, "Rational Markets: Yes or No?"
> *Financial Analysts Journal*, May-June, 2001

Given that securities markets are efficient, there are basically only two reasons portfolio managers would attempt to beat the market: (1) they don't realize that markets are efficient. In other words, they don't know what they're doing, or (2) they recognize that markets are efficient but are perpetrating a deliberate fraud. The members of the first group, no doubt, are convinced that their performance resulted from skill and hard work. In an efficient market, however, anything they accomplish will be due to luck. How could active managers ever admit that, even to themselves?

Aren't you forgetting about Peter Lynch?

But, you might be saying, what about Peter Lynch? Didn't he beat the market during his twelve-year tenure as portfolio manager of Fidelity's Magellen Fund? While he was there the annualized return for the fund was 29 percent as compared to 15 percent for the S&P 500. Most of that difference, however, occurred in the first six years while the fund was still relatively small. During the second half of his tenure he barely beat the market. Relatively few of his investors actually realized the unusually high returns.

Even more telling is his record since he left Magellen. Since 1993 Lynch has written an investment column for *Worth* magazine. Steve Kichen and Michael Maiello calculated the return on his recommended stocks.

We calculate that Lynch's Worth picks bought and held would be valued today, on average, at 27 percent less than identical sums put into the S&P 500. Lynch may have sold some of his picks, but his column offers no such suggestions. Following him, your money would've doubled. Unfortunately, the S&P-invested money would've tripled…So credit Lynch with a superb final trade: his May, 1990 exit from Fidelity, record intact. Because of that, his record stands forever.
"Quit While You're Ahead," *Forbes*, February 7, 2000.

In his 1993 book *Beating the Street* Lynch offers "25 Golden Rules." The eighth says the following:

Owning stocks is like having children—don't get involved with more than you can handle. The part-time stock picker probably has time to follow eight to twelve companies and to buy and sell shares as conditions warrant. There don't have to be more than five companies in your portfolio at any given time.

In case you missed his point, the fourteenth rule includes the following: "By owning too many stocks, you lose the advantage of concentration. It only takes a handful of big winners to make a lifetime of investing worthwhile." Apparently he doesn't think there are any disadvantages to concentration. Obviously, Lynch has no regard for the role of probability in making choices or designing strategies. In his book the word risk is mentioned only once. Wizards never need to doubt themselves so there's no point in being concerned about uncertainty.

If there's a poster boy for active management, it has to be Peter Lynch. If the guy they hold up as their number one genius has so little regard for diversification and risk, it's an indictment of the entire active-management industry. The fact is Peter Lynch is just another active manager who had a hot streak—and now the streak is over. Luck comes and goes. However, even if Lynch had beaten the market through skill, what would that prove? The extreme rarity of such achievements is confirmation of market efficiency, not evidence against it.

Infidelity funds: Even without all the other problems of active management, "style drift" would be enough to reject it as a viable alternative.

A mutual fund operates within certain boundaries, as defined in its prospectus. However, a mutual fund's latitude within these restrictions is effectively quite broad. Usually, the prospectuses are written so as to give the portfolio managers maximum flexibility. Reading the typical fund's stated objectives is like reading your horoscope in the daily newspaper —all you get are vague invitations to wishful thinking. The words say less than meets the eye. For all practical purposes, the portfolio manager can pursue virtually any strategy he desires. He can switch from a value strategy to a growth strategy or switch from small companies to large companies. He can generate whatever rate of useless portfolio turnover he desires.

Limits or restrictions are contrary to the basic philosophy of active management. Why hamstring the talented portfolio manager with constraints? If he can pick winners, don't hold him back—let him go where he sees opportunities. Don't clip his wings—let him soar.

The free hand exercised by portfolio managers leads to a problem known as "style drift." Conscientious investors build their portfolios according to certain criteria—for instance, small, medium, large, growth, blend, or value. But what happens when a mutual fund they've chosen changes its approach and applies a new and different criteria for stock selection? This is, in fact, a widely recognized occurrence in the world of actively managed funds.

Suppose you decided to buy a dog. Being a careful consumer and responsible pet owner, you would do research on the characteristics of various breeds to make sure you got the dog that was right for you. Let's say you decided a dachshund was for you and were happy with your choice. How would you feel if a year later your dachshund had morphed into a cocker spaniel? That's the reality of the style drift in mutual funds.

You definitely cannot design and implement a logical and consistent investment plan using active management.

Style drift makes it impossible to accomplish effective and lasting asset allocation—the single most important step investors must take to achieve efficient diversification. Because of style drift, active management makes it impossible to control diversification, and, therefore, impossible to manage risk. You cannot know how much diversification you have now or how much you will have in the future. There may be considerable overlap in your portfolio, and this has the effect of diminishing your diversification. Because of the ongoing need to monitor, the job of an active funds investor is never done.

You abandon any hope of reliability when you opt for active management. Neither the track record nor the nature of the fund can be depended upon, and any exceptional performance will be transitory. Like milk, above average performance is a perishable good. Unlike milk, no one tells you the expiration date.

Passively managed index funds eliminate the problem of style drift. Once you've decided on your allocation among asset classes, you can rest assured your allocation will remain true to its original blueprint. Once you've set your course, you know you will stay on course.

This stands in sharp contrast to investing in actively managed funds, which is like driving a car with play in the steering wheel—you must do a lot of extra steering to stay in your lane. Fortunately, for even less cost, you can get a car whose steering mechanism has no play at all.

If you get more information about your actively managed funds and get it more often, what are you supposed to do with it?

One of the ongoing controversies in the mutual fund industry is how much information should be provided to shareholders and how promptly to provide it. There's more to this issue than what appears on the surface. As is often the case, what's not said is even more interesting than what is said.

Current regulations require mutual funds to publicly disclose their portfolios twice a year with no more than a sixty-day lag. However, some investor advocates have demanded more frequent disclosures.

> *But financial advisors and activists contend that disclosure only twice a year gives a fund too much chance to stray from its investment objective. Funds...can operate more freely in an environment with less disclosure, with the investor never aware of how gains are truly achieved...Investor advocates want people to know exactly what they own through their stock and bond mutual funds.*
> *Wall Street Journal,* June 28, 2000

This issue illustrates still another active management dilemma. Suppose investors got more information and got it more often. What, exactly, are they supposed to do with it? Do they need to review it each time? How much time would that take? Review it with what objective in mind? If they need the information, it means they don't trust the managers. If that's true, why invest in that fund in the first place? What, specifically, are the payoffs for suffering all these frustrations, stresses, and time commitments? All the evidence points in the direction of a negative payoff—in the form of extra risk and below-market rates of return.

"Our whole approach was flawed. I feel enormous remorse."

Although it's difficult enough to determine what goes on in an ordinary actively managed mutual fund, the real princes of darkness are the so-called "hedge funds." Burton Malkiel and J.P. Mei define hedge funds as follows:

> *Basically hedge funds try to exploit temporary differences between similar types of securities. They buy a security that appears "cheap" in the market while selling an equivalent amount of another security that appears to be relatively "overvalued."*
>
> "Hedge Funds: The New Barbarians at the Gates,"
> *Wall Street Journal*, September 29, 1998

Hedge funds, in other words, are designed to exploit supposed market inefficiencies. Actual hedge funds, however, drift far from the above definition. In a cover story in *Forbes* magazine the authors could find very few common traits in their actual operation. The best definition they could offer was: "A hedge fund is any investment company that is unregulated, has limited redemption privileges and charges outrageous fees." (Clash, *et al.*, 2001).

The *Forbes* article starts with the following question: "What do Barbra Streisand, Senator Robert Torricelli, and Bianca Jagger have in common? They have all lost money investing in hedge funds." The article is a mind-boggling litany of what hedge-fund managers get away with. The names mentioned above are people with significant wealth. They can afford to hire competent advisors.

The following is a headline from a front-page *Wall Street Journal* article.

Portrait of a Loss

Chicago Art Institute Learns Tough Lesson About Hedge Funds

Small Dallas Firm Promised Security; Should Trustees Have Known the Risks?

At Least $20 Million Gone

Wall Street Journal,
February 1, 2002

Because of the losses, the museum is suing the investment company and its owner, Conrad Seghers.

> *The money managers deny doing anything wrong. Mr. Seghers argues in a counter suit filed in mid-January that his contract with the museum gave him carte blanche. His attorney, Lawrence J. Friedman, says in an interview that like most hedge fund managers, Mr. Seghers "could have bet on the Super Bowl if he wanted" with clients' money.*

Based on what I know about hedge funds, Mr. Friedman is entirely correct, and I wouldn't be surprised if some hedge-fund manager has done just that.

Hedge funds are only available to so-called accredited investors. To be classified as an accredited investor you must have a net worth of $1 million or more, not including your residence. Having such a restriction on their investors allows hedge funds to operate with virtually no Securities and Exchange Commission oversight. The SEC's basic philosophy is that when you have that kind of net worth, you can take care of yourself. The net worth requirement has the additional effect of giving the investment a kind of snob appeal. They get to say, "We don't let just anybody invest in these, you know." Furthermore, they have turned even their lack of disclosure into a marketing advantage.

> *But many funds feel little obligation to offer additional information, because they have no trouble attracting clients. "We don't have the need to take all comers," says David Webb, who manages a $300 million hedge fund for Shaker Investments, Cleveland, Ohio. "We only want people who agree with our strategy."*
>
> "Mystique of Fast Growing Hedge Funds Starts to Tarnish," *Wall Street Journal*, February 22, 2001.

Mr. Webb did not explain how his investors would know they agreed with the strategy. If no one told them the strategy, how would they know whether they agreed or disagreed?

The largest hedge fund was called Long-Term Capital Management and was managed by John Meriwether. In 1998, according to the *Wall Street Journal*, "global stock and bond markets nearly seized as Long-Term Capital lost a stunning $4 billion in a matter of months, teetering on collapse, only to be rescued in a $3.6 billion bailout by a consortium of 14 Wall Street firms pulled together by the Federal Reserve." In an August 2000 interview with the *Wall Street Journal*, Meriwether admitted, "Our whole approach was flawed. I feel enormous remorse" ("Long-Term Capital Chief Acknowledges Flawed Tactics," *Wall Street Journal*, August 21, 2000).

I doubt his enormous remorse makes all those who lost money feel much better. Furthermore, Mr. Meriwether's remorse didn't keep him from attempting to establish another hedge fund. ("Investors May See 'LTCM, the Sequel,'" *Wall Street Journal*, May 20, 1999.) Hope springs eternal, especially among slow learners.

Like other hedge funds LTCM defiantly kept investors in the dark about its strategies. According to the *Journal*, "Mr. Meriwether's troops kept lenders at arm's length and even treated their own investors with disdain at times, sharing little of their strategy and charging high management fees." Hedge funds have been the hot investment among sophisticates in the past several years. Perhaps you can tell me why supposedly sophisticated investors would put up with that kind of abuse and arrogance, but I don't get it. In retrospect, it's crystal clear that the Long-Term Capital managers had absolutely no justification for their conceit or secrecy.

It is obvious now that the managers were grossly incompetent. They were certain that the kind of financial catastrophe they did in fact create could never happen. The professionals who trusted them should have known better than to place so much trust in an unknown entity. They gave Long-Term Capital their clients' money without knowing any specifics of the investment. Unfortunately, this ill-advised approach is not unusual.

An irony of the hedge fund fiasco is that they've been sold as risk-reduction vehicles. Generally, that's what hedging is supposed to be about.

THE WALL STREET JOURNAL

"We find the defendant not guilty of fraud. In fact, the jury would like to invest in his *next* stock venture."

What does it mean, after all, to hedge your bet? Obviously, labels are important, whether or not they're fraudulent and totally misleading. In a blind attempt to reduce risk, investors bought into something they knew nothing about.

The hedge-fund story, like that of the Beardstown Ladies, is important mainly for the general lessons it teaches. It speaks volumes about the gullibility and vanity of people who should know better.

Money Magazine's "Swimsuit Issue."

Mutual fund research has become a serious undertaking for many investors. The most readily available and comprehensive research provider is Morningstar, Inc. in Chicago. Morningstar compiles data on over 12,000 mutual funds.

Because of its cost—about $400 a year—relatively few mutual fund investors subscribe to the Morningstar research reports. The most popular source of information for mutual fund investors are the periodic reports in publications such as *Money* magazine, *Forbes*, *Business Week*, and *Worth* magazine. At least once a year each of these magazines publishes an issue highlighting the "best mutual funds." Usually, these are the fastest-selling issues for the entire year. These best-funds issues are the financial media's equivalent to *Sports Illustrated's* annual swimsuit issue, which is perennially the hottest issue of any periodical on the market.

> *Like the swallows returning to Capistrano, the publication of mutual fund performance surveys by prominent business magazines is an eagerly awaited annual event…Despite all the hoopla surrounding the surveys, empirical evidence casts strong doubt on the naïve application of past performance to the selection of investment managers.*
>
> William Sharpe, *et al, Investments* (2nd ed.)

The fund rankings are almost entirely a matter of track records. Among the variables they consider are rates of return, consistency and longevity of rates of return, and volatility of share prices.

No two mutual funds are exactly the same, but the differences are usually much less significant than the similarities. For the most part, mutual funds within a given asset class are like granules of sugar. No two granules are identical, but for all practical purposes, they are the same. There are now over 12,000 mutual funds. In what ways are they different? In what ways are they similar? Are there meaningful and reliable ways to categorize them?

Attempting to determine which active manager is best is an example of asking the wrong question or what could be called the *smaller* question. The *larger* question is this: Is active management a viable strategy? If the answer is no, there is no reason to quibble over particulars, especially if the indicators are notoriously unreliable. If attempting to beat the market is, in general, a bad strategy, what is the likelihood you will successfully identify the exceptions? If the entire population is inferior, don't waste your time searching for the outstanding individual. The better solution is to abandon that population altogether. The search for the best active fund is like looking for diamonds in a pile of broken glass. You will not find diamonds but you might well end up with bloody fingers.

Efficient markets are amazingly tolerant of incompetence.

Efficient markets produce curious ironies. The strategies used by the practitioners who try to beat the market fly in the face of the theory and empirical conclusions of academic research. If the academic model is the best available description of reality, then active managers do not understand how markets work. Is someone who demonstrates through his actions a lack of understanding of a system likely to beat that system?

A related irony of the market stems from the fact that an efficient market is amazingly tolerant of incompetence. The evidence shows beating the market is not a realistic possibility. Fortunately for active managers, however, it's also fairly difficult to drastically under-perform the market, so long as you maintain a reasonably diversified portfolio. Of course, many active managers spurn diversification and, in the end, pay the consequences—along with their investors. In most cases, the same market efficiency that makes active management so futile also saves most active managers from themselves.

If performance is more a function of luck than skill and if that reality is not generally appreciated, there are likely to be some curious consequences. The people who generate abnormal returns will interpret the outcome as resulting from their skill. Some of the people who are lucky may rank far below normal in knowledge and understanding yet will perceive themselves as extremely clever. Believing you beat the market is a heady experience. Among other things, it creates a situation that offers ideal growing conditions for charlatanism and mischief.

A general problem in interpreting the world around us is confusing correlation with causation, sometimes termed the *post hoc* fallacy. If you expend effort in attempting to generate excess returns and you succeed, the natural conclusion is that your intellect and effort led to the result. Believing that you've beaten the market says nothing about your intelligence or your research skills. In fact, if it says anything, it isn't favorable. If you were smart, you wouldn't be trying to beat the market in the first place. Furthermore, it's highly doubtful you did beat the market. Did you take into account the extra risk? What's the probability you can repeat those results?

Being an active manager is a racket similar to that of the rainmakers who once preyed on desperate farmers in drought-stricken regions. The rainmakers placed themselves in a no-lose situation. They offered rain to

DILBERT reprinted by permission of United Feature Syndicate, Inc.

people upon seemingly reasonable terms—they would only be paid if it actually rained. This placed the rainmakers in the enviable position of profiting from the forces of nature. If one-fourth of active managers appear to beat the market in a year, a large number of them will look like successful rainmakers. Because of rising markets, it usually rains. Active managers are like rainmakers in a rain forest who get paid whether or not they had anything to do with it raining, and whether or not the rainfall is above or below normal.

Active managers who fail always have ingenious, convincing stories to explain why it wasn't their fault. Their explanations often make them sound even smarter than they were before. They're older and wiser, and they'll never make that mistake again!

All the frustrations of active management are easily avoidable. The availability of passively managed, asset-class index funds have made active management obsolete. Active managers are vinyl records in an age of digital music. You have no reason to suffer all the scratches, skips, and hisses.

Active management summary.

- ▶ In order to evaluate and compare mutual fund performance data, something known as "survivor bias" has to be taken into account.
- ▶ The basic reason active management generates lower rates of return is unnecessary costs.
- ▶ Estimating how much active management retards performance is primarily a matter of getting a fix on the costs of attempting to beat the market.
- ▶ Mutual fund companies never like to focus investors' attention on costs.
- ▶ Concealed costs do more damage than obvious, identifiable costs.
- ▶ As a general strategy, high rates of portfolio turnover are doomed to failure.
- ▶ An important practical conclusion of market efficiency is that the best long-term strategy is "buy-and-hold"—assuming you're well diversified.
- ▶ Portfolio turnover rates indicate the time horizon of the portfolio managers.
- ▶ Investors tend to flock to funds having impressive recent performance.
- ▶ The hype and casino atmosphere of the beat-the-market game results in investors being in the wrong place at the wrong time.
- ▶ Published mutual fund performance numbers do not reflect how much wealth has been redistributed as a result of some investors being unlucky or victims of bad timing.
- ▶ When you use actively managed funds, you do not have the option of being 100 percent invested in the market.
- ▶ Anything that places extra demands on your time ought to be justified by corresponding extra benefits.
- ▶ If you're relying on the brilliant-portfolio-manager route to success, you are counting on a strategy you can never truly understand.
- ▶ One undeniable source of the increased risk of active management is that it necessitates incomplete diversification.
- ▶ Investing in index funds assures that you capture asset class rates of return.

- ► Active management severely aggravates the problem of uncertainty.
- ► The beat-the-market gang fails to recognize that it only takes a small number of other players to eliminate their bargain-hunting opportunities.
- ► Style drift makes it impossible to accomplish effective and lasting asset allocation.
- ► Is active management a viable strategy? If the answer is no, there is no reason to differentiate among the particulars.
- ► If the entire population is inferior, don't waste your time searching for the outstanding individual.
- ► Ironically, an efficient market saves active managers from themselves.
- ► Believing that you've beaten the market says nothing about your intelligence or research skills. In fact, if it says anything, it isn't favorable.

CHAPTER 9

Major Long-term Determinants of Market Performance

And I am sure I have never read any memorable news in a newspaper. If we read of one man robbed, or murdered, or killed by accident, or one house burned, or one vessel wrecked, or one steamboat blown up, or one cow run over by the Western Railroad, or one mad dog killed...we need never read of another. One is enough. If you are acquainted with the principle, what do you care for a myriad instances and applications?

Henry David Thoreau, *Walden*

With the exception of weekends and holidays, the one thing you can be sure of seeing on every evening news program is a report about what happened to the stock market that day. During the day, news reports provide breathless, hour-by-hour performance updates. Anything reported that often must be important, right? Unfortunately, what the media focus on most actually has the least value and significance to investors.

The media don't concern themselves with whether or not you have a successful long-term investment experience. Thinking long-term isn't the way they approach the news. Why should they? They have no incentive to focus on the long run.

There's no point in getting angry with the media, but it is important, for your own benefit, to keep in mind that their agenda is quite different from yours. Be aware that listening to the media will give you investment myopia. Don't look to someone with a short-range focus to give you long-range guidance.

"Those are the headlines, and we'll be back in a moment to blow them out of proportion."

If you're a long-term investor, short-term performance is irrelevant. Short-term factors matter only if you are a trader, that is, if you enter and exit the market frequently. And that, of course, is a recipe for failure. If you do enter and exit on a daily basis, you will not be an investor for long. The random nature of daily changes will do you in.

What really matters is what happens between the time you enter the market and the time you exit the market. The intermediate path the market follows has no real or lasting impact on you. If you aren't trading on a daily basis, daily performance is totally irrelevant. Paying attention to daily stock market reports is corrosive and will destroy your financial peace of mind.

Virtually every item of news relating to daily, monthly, or quarterly investment performance is noise, not information. What's worse, noise isn't innocuous; it drowns out information. Noise pollutes your brain and distracts your attention from what is useful. Unless you have a surplus of unused time in your life, filter out all the predictions you hear about what the stock market is going to do tomorrow, next month, and any period other than your own investment time horizon.

No doubt some people listen to daily market reports in the same way they look at weather reports. What kind of mood is the economy in today? The fact is, the economy's diurnal mood swings are irrelevant, and even if they were relevant the Dow Jones Industrial Average is an extremely poor indicator of their true nature.

Most analysis of short-term market behavior is absurd and arrogant.

Usually, when the stock market averages change more than about two percent on a given day, news reports will provide explanations for what happened. There is almost never a hint of skepticism about the validity of these explanations.

When there are thousands of variables buffeting the position of something, how can anyone pinpoint any specific, dominating factor as the cause of a change in its position? Such glib, nutshell explanations are gross oversimplifications of complex reality. We're still arguing about the factors that caused market behavior decades ago—the crash of 1929, for example. Even with the benefit of that much hindsight, no final conclusions are possible. If that can't be done, what does it say about the validity of instant analysis?

Some stocks are increasing in value, others decreasing. With the price of each there are hundreds, even thousands of factors affecting the outcome. Decisions are made by millions of people. Who can read the mind of any single person, let alone millions? The experts accomplish this challenge instantaneously and from great distances. Who can say what factors dominate investors' decisions? Who is smart enough to summarize all those factors? Even if someone could, it's not clear what value, if any, it would have. The whole exercise is absurd when you think about it. The following are typical examples:

> *Stocks withstood a day of fluctuating prices and managed a modest advance yesterday as investors tussled with worries about the strength of the economic recovery and a profit warning from Bristol-Myers Squibb.*
> *San Francisco Chronicle*, April 5, 2002

Shaking off a profit and revenue warning from IBM, stocks bounced back from a sharp early drop yesterday and ended mostly higher as investors regained their confidence about a business turnaround.
San Francisco Chronicle, April 9, 2002

Some of the explanations are absolutely rote and predictable. Anytime the market goes down for a few days and then has an up day it was because of "bargain hunters." When it goes up for a few days then down, it was because of "profit takers." Predictable statements have no information content.

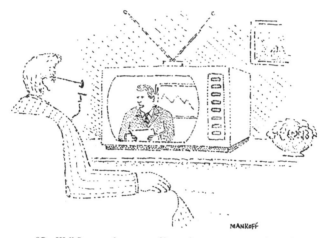

"On Wall Street today, news of lower interest rates sent the stock market up, but then the expectation that these rates would be inflationary sent the market down, until the realization that lower rates might stimulate the sluggish economy pushed the market up, before it ultimately went down on fears that an overheated economy would lead to a reimposition of higher interest rates."

It's not easy staying focused on the long-term, but that is what's important for investment success.

In the long run, what propels the stock market? You hear daily what supposedly causes short-term changes. On the other hand, you rarely hear analyses of longer-term market performance.

It's not easy keeping a long-term perspective. You need some protection as you run the gauntlet of media hype. Knowledge of the long-term determinants is one of the best defenses against being led astray and made unnecessarily fretful by the short-term obsession of the media.

To achieve long-term investment success, focus on the horizon, not on your feet. Professional driving instructors advise focusing down the road as far as you can see, not on the car in front of you. When you do, you drive more safely and smoothly and you have more time to react to potential hazards.

In the long run, it's the economy that drives the stock market.

For the past 75 years, the period of time for which there is especially good data, the stock market has produced a compound rate of return in excess of ten percent, assuming reinvestment of dividends. A thousand dollars invested in 1925 would have grown to over $2 million today. Look at the SBBI graph on page 125. The long-term performance of the stock market reflected by that graph is perhaps the most amazing financial achievement in all of human history. An awareness and appreciation of the main reasons for it should be part of every investor's general education. Ironically, offerings of such information are surprisingly rare. An important question for investors is: how has that phenomenal performance been possible?

To put it in the fewest possible words, the stock market depends on the economy. The stock market reflects ownership of a major portion of the economy. The market has done well because the economy has done well. Why has the economy done well?

The question of why some economies grow and others do not is one of the most important and challenging issues addressed by economists. It was Adam Smith's primary focus in his *An Inquiry Into the Nature and Causes of the Wealth of Nations.* Smith emphasized factors such as free trade, specialization, and especially the "invisible hand" inherent in a voluntary-exchange, free-market system. Over 200 years have passed since Smith's first explanations of the wealth of nations, but still no simple or final conclusions have been reached.

Ultimately, a nation's—and its population's—wealth and income are limited by productivity. It's not possible to consume and enjoy more than you produce for long. So what are the important factors that affect productivity?

Productivity growth is the single most important economic indicator. It determines how fast living standards can grow. The reason why the average American is seven times better off than his counterpart at the turn of the century is that he is seven times as productive.

The Economist, September 21, 2000

Figure 9-1:
Taking off
World GDP per person, 1000=100

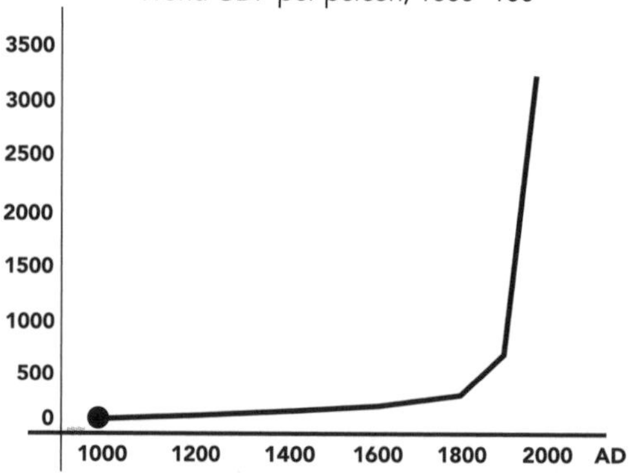

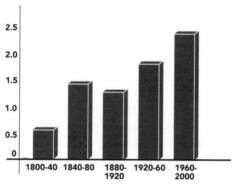

Source: Angus Maddison; *The Economist*, Sept. 21, 2000

Figure 9-2:
Bigger and better
US GDP per person, annual average % increase

Source: Angus Maddison; *The Economist*, Sept. 21, 2000

The "capital-labor ratio" has a large impact on how much the average worker produces. Someone operating a backhoe will obviously move much more earth than someone using a shovel. Someone using an electronic calculator or computer will complete computations far more quickly than someone using only paper and pencil. Investing is the process of adding to our total capital stock. Securities markets play a key role in the investment process and thereby enhance our wealth and income.

Many economists are convinced that the foremost explanation of increased productivity is our ever-expanding stock of knowledge. Picture a car manufactured in 1925 next to one manufactured in 2000. Those two pieces of machinery encapsulate much of the explanation of why we've had 75 years of impressive economic and stock market growth. Both have four wheels and are self-propelled, but the similarities don't go much beyond that. Consider, especially, the incredible difference in the embodied technology. The advances we've made in chemistry, physics, electronics, and numerous other fields is staggering.

All of those advances result in cars being safer, faster, more comfortable, and more dependable, as well as being more affordable. Car prices, in terms of how many hours we have to work to earn the money, have actually declined. Measured in terms of 1997 wage units, the price of a 1908 Model T Ford was $61,008. The price of a new 1997 Ford Taurus was $17,995 (Simon and Moore, 2000).

The skills, education, and training embodied in the population (human capital) are other major factors in an economy's productivity. Try to imagine how much training and knowledge is embodied in the total population of the U.S.

It's all about earnings.

The influence of corporate earnings on the stock market is greater than that of any other factor, both in the short and long-term. That is because a stock's price is roughly equal to the discounted value of its expected future earnings stream. In general, what's good for earnings (profits) is good for the stock market.

"Discounted value" takes into account the fact that a benefit received in the future isn't worth as much as a current benefit. One important reason for this is the inherent uncertainty of the future. Tomorrow is guaranteed to no one.

The total net income in a market economy comes in the form of wages, salaries, interest, rent, and profits. The total amount of profits depends on overall national income and the portion going to profits. Those are the macro factors that will determine the base upon which stock values are built. The total value of all stocks will be some multiple of that base. The relationship is known as the price-earnings ratio.

Each stock's price is some variation of the average price-earnings ratio, the relationship between a stock's market price and the current annual earnings per share of the company. The historical average price-earnings ratio for U.S. stocks has been approximately 15. In other words, you have to pay about $15 to buy annual earnings of $1. At any given time, however, there is a wide variance away from that average. Some stocks have a price-earnings ratio of five, while others have ratios as high as 200.

The usual explanation for the wide range of ratios is that they are measured in terms of current (or recent) earnings. The market is always looking forward. If a company's earnings are expected to increase, its price-earnings ratio will be above average and often far above average, e.g., 200 rather than the market average of 15. In fact, it's not uncommon for a company's price-earnings ratio to be mathematically undefined. That will happen any time a company is losing money, for example. The price-earnings ratio for a company with negative earnings isn't measurable because you can't have a ratio of a negative to positive number. Furthermore, you can't have a ratio of a positive or negative number and zero. If a company is breaking even, it has no meaningful price-earnings ratio.

For stock market forecasters, by far the most popular early-warning signal for a stock market peak is an average price-earnings ratio of historically high levels. That's the vital sign they point to most often when they profess that the market is "over valued" and ripe for a "correction." Unfortunately for the forecasters, this signal is notoriously unreliable, especially in regard to its timing. The ratio can remain high for extended periods or low for extended periods.

Ultimately, the price of a stock will be determined by the interplay of supply and demand.

The stock market is, among other things, a collection of prices. When it comes to understanding pricing behavior, there's nothing so useful as supply and demand analysis. Approaching the problem as a question of supply and demand can help in understanding past, present, and future stock market performance.

In Chapter 3 we discussed some of the forces driving both the supply and demand of stocks. For example, current owners sell (supply) stock to raise capital for expansion, and investors buy (demand) stocks in the expectation that it will lead to an increase in their wealth.

To understand the rise and fall of prices, you have to look at shifts in supply and demand and what causes them. What are some of the factors that lead to changes in supply and demand for stocks? An increase in the demand for something puts upward pressure on its price. An important source of the increased demand for stocks has been the growth of pension plans, such as the popular 401(k) profit-sharing plans. These arrangements generate a continuous infusion of new funds into the securities markets.

The demand for stocks has been rising because average incomes have grown dramatically.

When your income increases, your demand for goods and services increases, and what's true for you individually is true in general. Not only does the demand for current consumption goods increase, the demand for investments increases as well. In fact, investments fall into a category of expenditures economists call luxury goods. The word "luxury" has a broader meaning here than what is commonly understood. In economics, a luxury good is one for which an increasing proportion of a person's income is spent as his or her income increases. If you make $20,000 a year, you may save a very small fraction of that income. On the other hand, if your income is $100,000, you're likely to save a larger fraction. In most cases, saving money is not a necessity.

Half the households in America now have stock market-related investments and the percentage is growing. In 1929 only three percent of the population owned stocks. As recently as 1980 the number was only 13 percent (Wattenberg, *et al*, 2001).

Interest rates have a powerful effect on stock markets, and a lot can be learned by understanding why this is so.

Rising interest rates tend to depress stock prices, falling rates stimulate stock prices. This generalization, however, is only true *ceteris paribus* (meaning "assuming other factors don't change" or "other things are constant"). But why do changing interest rates have an impact on the market? The main thing to remember is that investing is fundamentally a process of choosing among alternatives or a series of portfolio decisions. Each of the alternatives has costs and benefits, pluses and minuses. The primary positive of an investment is its return; the primary negative is its risk.

In the U.S. economy there are more examples of interest rates than you could count—Treasury bill rates, long-term government bond rates, mortgage rates, credit card rates, auto loan rates, prime rates, and federal funds rates, to name just a few. When we say that interest rates affect the stock market, we mean interest rates in general. Even though all interest rates never move in perfect tandem, there is, nonetheless, a large element of common behavior. Long-term corporate bond rates are always higher than long-term government bond rates (because corporate bonds are riskier), but they both tend to rise and fall in a similar manner.

When investors choose among investments they implicitly or explicitly consider their relative returns and risks. One basic choice is between stocks as a group and fixed investments as a group, such as bank certificates of deposit or municipal bonds. When interest rates rise, the return on fixed investments increases. That tends to tilt investors at the margin toward fixed investments and away from stocks (equities). When the demand for stocks drops, the equilibrium price declines. That's the basic chain of causation from rising interest rates to falling stock prices.

Over the past 50 years, interest rates on ten-year government bonds have ranged from 2.4 percent (1953) to 13.9 percent (1981). The rate in January of 2002 was 5.0 percent. The current rate is higher than it was in the 1940s, '50s, and '60s, but lower than the '70s and '80s. What's it going to be for the oughts, teens, and twenties? No one knows. Interest rates, however, are definitely subject to "reversion to the mean."

If you're a long-term investor, interest rates in the relatively distant future are what should concern you. If they go up and back down between now and then, there's no significant net impact as long as they have returned to the same approximate range when you cash in your investment.

Note that the interest rate effect is quite different from the economic growth effect. Increased productivity essentially goes in one direction. It's a progressive, building, and cumulative process. Our total stock of knowledge is always growing. Interest rate effects are more like a pendulum. There is no real opportunity for taking advantage of the pattern in the long run. Except for the interest income, your gains and losses will balance out. Likewise, there is no real reason for worrying about changing interest rates having a negative long-term impact on your portfolio. What you lose as interest rates rise you will gain back as they fall and vice versa.

Note that rising interest rates have a negative impact on both bonds and stocks. If you're a long-term investor, the reason to diversify away from stocks is to reduce the volatility of your portfolio. Long-term bonds in particular are flawed vehicles for accomplishing that objective. Cash equivalents (money market funds, for example) and short-term bonds (one to five years) hardly change in response to interest rate fluctuations. They are, therefore, a far more effective way to reduce portfolio volatility.

The rate of return for long-term maturity bonds has not been appreciably higher, than short-term rates. For the period of 1964 to 1995, the difference between rates of return on one-year and 20-year government bonds was only .1 percent (7.5 percent for one-year bonds, 7.6 percent for 20-year bonds). The prices of 20-year bonds are far more volatile than one-year bonds, however. In other words, there is not a good risk-return tradeoff. Of the three traditional asset classes—stocks, bonds, and cash—

you can prudently disregard long-term bonds. If you want growth, invest in stocks. If you want safety and liquidity, invest in cash equivalents—money market funds and short-term bonds.

A change in interest rates also changes the rate at which future earnings are discounted. The value of a dollar received in ten years is reduced as the rate of discount increases and vice versa. That's another way rising interest rates depress asset values. At a three percent discount rate, $100 ten years from now is worth $74 today. At a five percent discount rate, it's worth only $61.

Like all factors affecting the stock market, interest rates by themselves do not dictate market performance. For example, in Japan for most of the 1990s, interest rates were extremely low. Rates on certificates of deposit there have commonly been below .5 percent. Nevertheless, the Japanese stock market has performed poorly. One of the realities of low interest rates is that they are generally the result of anemic business conditions.

The impact of inflation on stocks is another important example of the difference between short-term and long-term effects.

In his book *Stocks for the Long Run*, Jeremy Siegel states, "In the short run, stocks are not good hedges against inflation—but neither is any financial asset. In the long run stocks are extremely good hedges against inflation, while bonds are not."

What are the explanations for these relationships? Part of the answer can be found by looking at the impact of inflation on interest rates. Inflation and inflationary expectations have a powerful influence on interest rates. Lending money is a voluntary exchange activity. If you want to borrow money from me, one of the things I'm going to consider is the purchasing power of the dollars you repay me with. During inflationary periods, the purchasing power of a currency declines. Borrowing money takes place in one time period and repayment happens in another time period.

The so-called "real interest rate" is the stated or nominal rate minus the rate of inflation. That's the real compensation you receive for lending someone your purchasing power. During periods of zero inflation, the real interest rate is equal to the stated or nominal rate of interest—what you see is what you get.

During inflationary periods, on the other hand, you are likely to demand and the borrower is likely to willingly offer a higher rate of interest. You will want to be compensated for the erosion of the purchasing power of the dollars during the period of the loan. Otherwise, the voluntary exchange is unlikely to happen.

The inflationary premium component of interest rates is one of the clearest examples of "rational expectations," a topic discussed in Chapter 4. Expected events affect corresponding prices, and interest rates are simply another kind of price. Actual inflation may be more or less than the expected inflation, but market-determined rates of interest are usually good predictors. Prediction errors are about evenly distributed above and below what actually transpires.

During the early 1980s in the United States, interest rates on, for example, certificates of deposit and money market funds climbed to 16 percent. The primary reason lenders were able to charge those rates, and that borrowers were willing to pay them, is that the U.S. was experiencing double-digit inflation, the worst peace-time inflation in the country's history.

During such periods, lenders demand a higher interest rate because they anticipate reduced purchasing power of the repayments. Borrowers are willing to pay higher rates because they expect the price or value of the purchase or investment to increase. It's better to buy something now before the price increases, even if you have to pay a high rate of interest to get the money.

Neither of the parties in the voluntary exchange ignores the environment around them. Ignoring inflation would be a "systematic error." Furthermore, it is not necessary for all or even most lenders and borrowers to observe and react to inflationary expectations. As with stock prices, only those at the margin are required to affect the market rates that apply to all participants. When someone refinances his home, the mortgage rate he pays is the same whether or not he takes into consideration the impact of inflation.

We have already seen why higher interest rates negatively affect the market. It's the inflation-interest-rate-stock-price sequence that explains why inflation creates short-run indigestion for the stock market. Inflation pushes interest rates up, and higher interest rates depress stock prices.

But this doesn't explain why there is less of a long-term problem in regard to inflation. In the long run, stocks are considered a good hedge against inflation, especially in comparison to other securities and financial assets such as bonds. When you buy a stock, you become a part owner of an operating enterprise. Inflation, of course, causes higher costs for these businesses—higher prices for raw materials, supplies, equipment, rents, wages, and salaries. But also during inflationary times there is excess demand and, therefore, businesses can raise the prices of their products. Especially during periods of mild inflation, inflation has a more or less neutral long-term impact on the stock market.

In the long run the greatest threat inflation poses for the market is that higher levels can be detrimental to productivity. A small but representative example of this type of damage could be seen during the high inflation in the early 1980s, when catalog prices were quickly rendered invalid. The need for frequently revising catalogs and price lists is a dead weight loss for the economy. The lack of a stable currency reduces the efficiency of an economy. Money becomes less efficient in its roles as a medium of exchange and store of value. Inflation puts sand in the machinery of voluntary exchange and corrupts the informational role of prices.

The business cycle is an unpleasant but short-lived economic fact of life.

No developed economy has ever experienced totally stable growth rates. Since WWII in the U.S. there have been eleven recessions (recession is defined as two consecutive quarters of zero or negative growth).

Recessions invariably have a negative impact on the stock market, but the connection is not a simple one. The stock market is used as a "leading indicator" by economists in their forecasts. The market tends to go down preceding recessions and begins to recover before the recession is over. However, as Paul Samuelson observed many years ago, "the stock market has predicted nine out of the last five recessions."

The market's reaction to recessions is understandable in one sense and not in another. Recessions obviously hurt corporate earnings and national income. Nevertheless, all our past recessions have been temporary. The market seems to react as though there's never before been a recession and that the current one will last forever. Insofar as investors have long-range objectives, it's not clear why they should become concerned with short-lived problems.

What about the future?

With all the factors that can affect the market, there is no way to really know what the long-range performance will be. What's an investor to do? Should the attitude be optimism or pessimism, confidence or fear?

One of the themes of this book is that prediction is not a worthwhile endeavor. I'm not going to violate that advice, but I can explain a few of the reasons I'm a long-range optimist.

An important component of my optimism is the belief that the main explanation for our growing wealth and productivity is our expanding stock of knowledge. That stock of knowledge continues to increase and, if anything, the rate is accelerating. Knowledge builds on itself and propagates. Whole new fields of knowledge open and cross-fertilize existing ones. "Invention breeds invention," is how Ralph Waldo Emerson expressed it.

Another force driving our income and wealth upward is ambition. It's been said that Americans are too ambitious, and maybe that's true. Nevertheless, our tendency never to be satisfied is a big part of the reason we are so productive and wealthy. Human nature changes slowly, if at all. Economists believe the main reason behaviors change is that rewards, costs, or incentives change. It's possible that we may become so wealthy we lose our drive. That prediction has been made in the past, but there's no sign of it happening yet. If it ever does happen, it will probably be far in the future, and some other change might very well counterbalance it.

Perhaps the most interesting recent work that's been done regarding the prospects for economic growth has been by Stanford economist Paul Romer, who has been described as the father of "the new growth theory."

> *Romer believes that the rate of growth has increased over time because of increasing returns to knowledge. Knowledge builds upon itself. The more that mankind discovers, the better it gets at the process of discovery.*
> *The Economist, September 21, 2000*

Another factor Romer emphasizes is that technological innovation is endogenous, not exogenous. In other words, technological advance is not something that comes from outside the system. The critical role of incentives has been emphasized several times in this book. The rate at which we make new discoveries is not a given. The better the incentives for making those discoveries, the more discoveries we'll have. When thinking about public policy, we need to be extremely careful not to discourage innovation. Many of our regulations do just that. Over-regulation is the greatest threat to economic improvement. An economy needs flexibility in a rapidly changing world. Regulations cause economic arthritis.

The reality is that no one really knows what the economy or the world will be like 10, 20, or 30 years in the future. There is inescapable uncertainty about the long-range prospects for the economy. One consolation is that that's the main reason there's an equity premium.

Since there is no way ultimately to foresee the long-range future, I'm going to end this chapter with my "Fiscal Fitness" column first published in the January 1997 *North Coast Journal.*

The Logic of Optimism

The beginning of each year is a time when our attention is almost automatically focused toward the future. Even more important than any specific plans we have is our attitude about the future.

I guess I'm an optimist by nature. My blood type, in fact, is B-positive. Nevertheless, whether or not optimism and hope are natural tendencies, optimism is more logical than pessimism.

Consider the profound questions about the future. Should we be hopeful or fearful about the future of mankind? People are concerned about overpopulation, global warming, loss of species, and a long list of similar problems. Many seem to believe that one or another of these problems will lead to our demise.

The threat posed by any one of these problems is debatable, to say the least. How serious will they be in 25, 50, or 100 years is even more debatable. You can't really know what the future has in store, so essentially you have to make an assumption. You can assume that we will create ways to deal with these problems, or assume we will fail.

Here's where the logic of hope and optimism comes in. Suppose you decide to work on the assumption that mankind will fail to solve the mega-problems. That means you live your life in some degree of despair.

Even if you live to see your pessimistic predictions come true, there is no payoff. Your prediction came true, but you were probably miserable in anticipation of it. Your only consolation is you can say, "See, I was right!"

If mankind succeeds, it means you were wrong. You can breathe a sigh of relief, but much of your own life was wasted in unnecessary worry. One of the truest quotes in all of literature is "Cowards die many times before their deaths, the valiant never taste of death but once." (William Shakespeare, *Julius Caesar*) Couldn't it also be said that pessimists "die many times before their deaths"? Personally, I'd rather die only once.

Here's another reason why it makes sense to have hope. Consider two "populations": the population of problems and the population of solutions.

It's clear that as our stock of knowledge and information grows, the population of solutions grows. The more we know about the world—chemistry, biology, medicine, electronics, genetics, psychology—the greater is our problem solving ability.

We've learned, for example, that many mental problems are the result of imbalances in blood chemistry. Millions of people have achieved dramatic relief through the use of a growing number of pharmacological treatments. That's just one example of how greater knowledge has reduced human suffering.

On the other hand, what has been happening to the population of problems? Some people have the attitude that every new solution creates a new problem. They belong to the "there's-no-hope" school.

Solutions do cause change, and with change there are gains and losses. The clearest and most significant achievement of science and economic growth is our increased life expectancy. This advance, however, has caused Alzheimer's disease to be far more common than it used to be. I would argue that the population of problems is almost static, that most of the large problems and challenges of the human condition have been with us for thousands of years.

Besides logic there is also historical support for optimism. Pessimists and doomsayers have been with us throughout recorded history. Every kind of catastrophe imaginable has been predicted and practically none has come to pass. Society keeps on muddling through. Of course, present day pessimists maintain that "this time it's different." All the previous pessimists said the same thing.

One well-known doomsayer is Paul Erlich. In his 1968 book *The Population Bomb* he warned, "The battle to feed humanity is over. In the 1970s the world will undergo famines—hundreds of millions of people are going to starve to death." Repeatedly, Erlich's dire predictions have failed to materialize. Strangely, people keep buying his books and listening to what he says.

Pessimisim's only real advantage is that, in the short run, it's easier to be pessimistic than optimistic, and cynicism is the cheapest way to act sophisticated.

The greatest damage done by pessimism is what it does to our youth. I'm troubled hearing children relate what they learn in school regarding insurmountable problems facing mankind. In most cases I'm sure it's unintentional, but destroying a young person's hope is a terrible, terrible thing to do. In fact, giving our children hope should be one of society's highest priorities.

Major long-term determinants summary.

► What the media focus on most has the least value to investors.
► The media don't concern themselves with whether you have a successful long-term investment experience.
► If you're a long-term investor, short-term performance is irrelevant.
► To achieve long-term investment success, focus on the horizon.
► In the long run, the stock market depends on the economy.
► The question of why some economies do well and others do not is one of the most challenging and important questions addressed by economists.
► Ultimately, a nation's wealth is limited by its productivity.
► Many economists are convinced that the foremost explanation of increased productivity is our ever-expanding stock of knowledge.

- ► The factor most directly linked to the stock market is corporate earnings.
- ► To understand changes in prices you have to look at what causes changes in supply and demand.
- ► Rising interest rates tend to depress stock prices; falling rates stimulate stock prices.
- ► When investors choose among investments, they implicitly or explicitly consider their relative returns and risks.
- ► Rising interest rates have a negative impact on both bonds and stocks.
- ► During inflationary periods, you as a lender are likely to demand and the borrower to offer a higher rate of interest.
- ► The inflationary premium component of interest rates is one of the clearest examples of rational expectations.
- ► Inflation puts sand in the machinery of voluntary exchange and corrupts the informational role of prices.
- ► The market tends to go down before recessions and go up before the recession is over.
- ► The market seems to react as though there's never before been a recession and that the current one will last forever.
- ► Knowledge builds on itself and propagates.
- ► The better the incentives for innovating and inventing, the more innovations and inventions we'll have.
- ► There is inescapable uncertainty about the long-range prospects for the economy.
- ► Optimism is more logical and efficient than pessimism.

CHAPTER 10

Efficient Decision Making

*It's our choices, Harry, that show who we truly are, far more than
our abilities.*

        J.K. Rowling, *Harry Potter and the Chamber of Secrets*

Opting for passive investing will give you the opportunity to focus on the decisions that matter.

Deciding to use passive management resolves numerous investment
dilemmas. It will save you time, money, taxes, frustration, and reduce your
risk exposure. You will no longer waste your time and effort on the vain
and costly pursuit of beating the market. It is not, however, the last
financial decision you'll ever have to make. The good news is that the time
and energy you save will be more than enough to deal with the decisions
that really can make a difference.

Financial planning is both simple and complex. Fortunately, the most
important decisions are relatively simple. The fundamental decisions
provide the foundation and prerequisites for all the others. These decisions

are, more often than not, a choice between only two alternatives, or involve striking a balance between two alternatives. For example:

- What fraction of your income do you want to save?
- Do you want to be an owner or a creditor?
- Do you want to concentrate your investments on certain stocks or market sectors, or do you want to diversify?
- Do you want to be a do-it-yourself investor or seek professional advice?
- Is the primary objective of your investment portfolio entertainment, or attaining maximum risk-adjusted rates of return (excitement or financial peace of mind)?
- What do you want to happen to your wealth after you're gone?
- What is going to be your methodology for deciding what works and what doesn't?

As we will see, saying that these choices are simple is not to say they are easy to make. Nevertheless, making them in a conscious and well-considered way is worth the effort.

When the advisors at our firm first meet with a new client or prospect, we explain the "secrets" our firm employs in managing money. We advise them to diversify and take a long-range perspective. We explain the risks and rewards of owning relative to lending and review the reasons why trying to beat the market is ill advised. We outline our methodology for distinguishing between what works and what doesn't—we carefully examine the evidence and employ the scientific method.

Clients who have followed these recommendations are highly satisfied and have financial peace of mind. Keeping our clients focused on the fundamentals is probably the main way we add value in our relationships with them and why they are willing to pay us for our services. We didn't invent nor do we have copyrights over these strategies. They are in the public domain, available to everyone, but they're ignored far more often than they're followed. These principles will work for you, too.

Decision-making efficiency cannot be achieved by giving you a list of questions and answers.

There's no way anyone can anticipate all the financial questions you'll encounter in the future. What's more useful in the long run is having a decision-making framework.

Making choices is a major challenge and responsibility in our lives. To a great extent, the quality of our lives and the success we attain are the result of the choices we make. Making choices isn't easy and none of us is as well equipped to do so as we would like to be, but since choice making has so much to do with success in life, doesn't it make sense to treat it systematically and seriously?

Thinking about your decision-making methodology is one of the greatest time and effort savers you could imagine. It is essential if you want to avoid wasting time going in the wrong direction and moving away from your intended objective.

Decision-making efficiency only makes sense relative to your objective. If you haven't decided what your objective is, there is no way to evaluate your choice. I am always surprised at how much it clarifies my thinking and actions if I stop to ask myself, "What exactly is my real objective here? What specifically am I trying to accomplish? Would the action I have in mind actually move me toward my objective?"

Your ultimate objective is your reference point. All subsidiary decisions are mostly about means, not ends. Decisions have to be evaluated relative to your ultimate purpose. In the absence of a goal, you cannot measure whether you are going in the right direction or not. As Yogi Berra observed, "If you don't know where you're going, you'll end up somewhere else."

Attempting to avoid making a decision usually doesn't work. Choosing not to decide is itself a choice. You have the freedom to choose among a wide range of alternatives but, ironically, you can't choose not to choose. Trying to avoid decisions is another example of the high cost of attempting the impossible.

Using decision rules can be thought of as making decisions wholesale.

One helpful tool for achieving decision efficiency is making use of "decision rules." What are they? One good example is the famous "triage" system first applied under battlefield medical situations. The wounded are categorized into three groups: those who will probably live whether or not they receive medical attention, those who will survive only if they get attention, and those who will probably die regardless of the care they receive.

The scarce medical resources are then focused on the middle group. Following that decision rule will result in the maximum number of lives saved with the resources at hand, and the maximum payoff for the medics' efforts. In other words, it leads to a more efficient use of scarce resources.

Bear in mind that the medics can't know for sure if their judgments are correct about who goes in which group. All they can do is make their best estimates of probabilities based on their experience. They have no other available choice.

A decision rule can also be thought of as a process of categorizing choices, thinking about the whole category and then, as specifics arise, looking at whether a specific case fits one of the categories. Decision rules are major time savers. Devoting time to establishing them is itself a kind of investment. As Stephen Covey emphasizes in his best-selling *Seven Habits of Highly Effective People*, "there is always time to sharpen your saw." The time you spend sharpening will be returned several times over in the subsequent time you save. Cutting wood goes much faster when you're using a sharp saw.

The next time you're having trouble making a decision, stop and ask, "What is the general nature of this question or situation?" You can get more mileage from your deliberations if you derive principles to apply to similar questions in the future. That way you will not have to start at the beginning with each new choice.

It's best to frame important questions in the largest possible context.

Making choices in isolation is an all too common decision-making error. Each of us has proximate, local objectives and general, more "global" ones. We need to keep our global objectives well in view. The adage "to cut off your nose to spite your face" illustrates the sacrifice of a large objective in the pursuit of a single, smaller, short-term one.

One of the commonest traps we all fall into is "ends-means displacement." We become so focused on means that we start believing they are ends. For example, I'm sure you've known people who behave as if making money is their primary purpose in life. Well-balanced people, of course, recognize that money is a means rather than an end. Making money just for the sake of making money is a useless endeavor. Money's importance stems from its role in helping us achieve other objectives.

You have numerous objectives, but they are not all equally important. Another book by Stephen Covey, *First Things First*, makes the case for the importance of thinking carefully and systematically about setting priorities. The idea of "first things first" is itself an example of a decision rule. It recognizes that some objectives are more important than others and that your efforts should go first to the most important ones. That's another way of being more efficient with your limited time and energy.

Setting priorities involves establishing a hierarchy of objectives. Because some objectives move us much farther toward our ultimate goals than others, they deserve much more of our time and effort.

Covey advocates devoting time and thought to determining your personal "true north"—the direction or goal that guides your personal compass. That step will make every other significant decision in your life both easier and more efficient. As Roy Disney, Walt's brother, observed, "Decisions are easy when your values are clear." Spend time on clarifying your values and priorities, and decisions will come easier. The corollary of what Disney said is also true—decisions are difficult when your values are vague and poorly defined. You cannot truly rank priorities without reference to your ultimate goals.

Another type of decision-making error is the failure to make preliminary or prerequisite decisions. For example, deciding on your time horizon is a prerequisite to deciding how to allocate your portfolio between equities and fixed investments.

A helpful prerequisite decision is to clarify your basis for deciding what works and what doesn't. Are you going to base your decisions on evidence, intuition, advertising, advice from a friend, trial and error, or what? Spending time establishing whether or not a particular strategy will work can avoid an enormous amount of wasted effort. It's amazing how often we fail to address that critical question.

One reason these fundamental questions are worth serious attention and an investment of time is that, when you've settled on the answers that are right for you, those answers tend to be long-lasting. Once you've spent time focusing on and coming to conclusions about these questions, there's little need to revisit them frequently. Making the big decisions first will, in many cases, allow you to make them just once, with only minor adjustments over time. The conclusions you reach are themselves like investments—a current expenditure having future benefits. Below are some examples of the big, defining decisions in the context of personal financial planning.

Striking a balance between enjoying yourself now versus later.

How much of your resources should be invested in your future? This is the pivotal financial-planning decision and a good example of the benefit of making the large decisions first. This is the decision that will determine how much of your income you need to save and then invest. It is also a prime example of the fundamental lesson of economics—life involves tradeoffs.

Think about the now-versus-later balance. Decide your allocation between spending and saving—one that you can live with. Do it and then stop thinking about it—at least don't think about it again until conditions change (you win the lottery, for example) or you have new information. I'm sure you know people who go to one of two extremes—they either give no thought to the future and save little or nothing or worry so much about having enough for retirement that they can't enjoy themselves now.

I'm not suggesting that it's an easy decision. There are a number of related issues that play a role in the choice. For instance, at what age do you want to retire? What are your expectations about the growth of your income? Do you want to pre-fund your children's college expenses? At what rate are you paying off your indebtedness—student loans or home mortgage, for example? What rate of return do you expect on your investments? Is there a possibility you will inherit money?

Even though the now-versus-later decision is not easy, it has to be made before your other decisions can make sense. You don't want to be in the position of the guy who said, "I have plenty of money to last me the rest of my life, providing I don't live more than six months."

Our tax laws purposefully bias the decision toward enjoying yourself later. Up to the limit of your retirement plan eligibility, what you save reduces your current tax liability. What you consume currently is done with after-tax dollars. The money you put into individual retirement accounts or 401(k) plans is done with before-tax dollars. The lawmakers don't think we will save as much as we should if left to our own devices, so they nudge us in that direction. We're given an increase in our allowance if we behave properly.

Keep in mind that retirement planning is about more than investments. Besides diversifying your investments, it's also important to diversify your interests. Furthermore, it probably isn't a good idea to wait until retirement to begin cultivating hobbies and developing your leisure interests. If you only live to work, it will be difficult to have a satisfying life after retirement no matter how much money you have. If working makes you happiest, maybe you want to work until you die and don't need retirement funding.

It's best not to wait too long to make use of your investments. It doesn't make sense to save your money for the purpose of traveling until you're too old to enjoy it. Enjoying life involves a combination of ingredients—time, good health, companionship, money, and peace of mind, for example. If you want to travel with your children, you might want to do it before they're teenagers. By then they may not enjoy your company, and the feeling might be mutual. Take advantage of opportunities before they slip away.

Should you be an owner or a lender?

As an investor you must either be an owner or a creditor. If you buy a General Electric common stock, you become an owner. If you buy a General Electric bond, you become a creditor. Although there are literally thousands of investment alternatives to choose from, an investment choice of crucial importance involves only two options—being an owner versus being a creditor, or equities versus debt.

Ownership is the way you can make yourself a beneficiary of economic progress. Your financial success is only partly your own creation. Any individual's wealth is largely the result of all the other participants in the economy, especially the people who develop new technologies and systems for making the economy more efficient. Put yourself in alignment with and in a position to share in the continued progress of the economy and our ever-expanding wealth of knowledge and advancing technology. Get on the gravy train—there's still plenty of room.

Another example of a prerequisite question is: do you think we will continue to experience economic growth? Are you a long-term optimist or pessimist? The answer to that question—as well as your time horizon—largely determines your appropriate equities/fixed investment allocation.

Advice about advice.

Should you be a do-it-yourself investor or seek professional advice? This is a decision most people make, more or less, but the way they go about it is often haphazard. It's an important decision that warrants contemplation and careful review. There are advantages and disadvantages to either choice.

As you've learned, passive management is much simpler conceptually and practically than active management. If you believe that markets are efficient, do you even need an investment advisor? What can an investment advisor do for you in the context of passive management?

Just as is the case with you as an investor, abandoning the futile quest for beating the market allows an advisor to focus on those issues that can actually make a difference. A financial advisor who uses passive management can focus on asset allocation, risk management, tax planning, retirement planning, and estate planning, for example. The relevant questions are these: Is the value of his services greater than the amount of his fees? Does his advice enhance your peace of mind? Can he reduce your risk exposure? Does he take care of the details and save you valuable time? Does he suggest "third alternatives" (alternatives you hadn't thought of)? Does he help you simplify your financial affairs?

On average, index funds save you two-to-four percent a year compared to actively managed funds. You can reallocate those savings and apply them to true, value-added advice.

I'm a strong believer in professional guidance. Although there have been times when I received counterproductive professional advice, those have been the exceptions. For any important decision, situation, or dilemma, I always seek the advice of an experienced professional.

Perhaps the foremost benefit of using professional advice is simply that it is an efficient form of "access to information." We live in what's been called, appropriately, the Information Age, and the efficient use of information has been a common theme throughout this book. Using professional advice is an excellent way to be more efficient with information. As Aesop put it long before the Information Age, "Better to be wise by the misfortunes of others than our own." One of the reasons professionals can add value is they've witnessed and learned from the misfortunes of others.

In Chapter 2, I used a quote from the first page of Adam Smith's *Wealth of Nations*. It referred to the benefits of "the division of labor," or what we now call specialization. That is the fundamental reason I advocate professional advice, not just for financial matters but for writing a will or trust, filing a tax return, learning to ski, play golf, or resolving marital or family discord. There is no way amateurs can know all that a professional knows about his or her field of expertise, particularly in regard to any complex topic. I wouldn't even consider doing my own income tax return.

Tiger Woods is the world's best golfer. Nevertheless, he relies heavily on his coach, Butch Harmon. Why does Tiger feel he needs a coach? What are the benefits he's deriving?

A professional can also give you a more objective, disinterested perspective than you can give yourself. This is especially significant in the investment realm. Emotions don't ordinarily interfere with legal or tax questions as much as with investment questions and choices. Legal or tax issues aren't as subject to the psychological pitfalls discussed in Chapter 5—hindsight bias, regret avoidance, over-confidence, etc.

> *Even though many sophisticated investors eschew advisors, it's a rare individual who shouldn't have a good advisor in some capacity. If nothing else, they keep you from doing something stupid, from giving in to impulses to make unwise investments.*
> Rex Sinquefield, *Bloomberg Personal Wealth*, March 2001.

The greatest challenge in seeking professional advice is locating and identifying competent advisors who are right for you. However, the time and effort you spend doing this is an investment with a high rate of return.

One highly desirable goal of a relationship with an advisor is that it be long-term. This is the main road to developing trust, and the longer you know one another, the better your working relationship will be. Working with someone who knows you, your situation, and your objectives is a powerful time saver and a source of peace of mind.

A major disadvantage of being a do-it-yourself investor can be seen in how often it necessitates relying on little more than "800 numbers" for assistance. The reality of 800 numbers is that whomever you reach on the other end of the line knows virtually nothing about you. Technology is great, but it has its limits. In most situations you still benefit from having a real person to work with.

Compensation and conflicts of interests.

If you decide to hire an investment advisor, you will discover that there are two methods of compensation—fees or commissions. Fees are usually a percentage of the value of the portfolio—typically one to two percent a year. No compensation structure has ever been invented that is totally free of potential conflicts of interest. However, commissions are much worse in this regard than fees. Commissions result in an incentive to generate transactions, and that's not usually in the best interests of the investor. Transaction-based compensation is a major contributor to Wall Street's dysfunction.

A fee structure eliminates that artificial incentive and comes closer to a harmony of interest between the advisor and the investor. Both benefit if the account grows in value. A fee structure also provides compensation and an incentive for ongoing service, something that's lacking from what's essentially a point-of-purchase commission structure.

Possibly you would like to compensate your investment advisor on an hourly basis. You will have difficulty finding one willing to do so. One reason this manner of payment hasn't worked in investment advising is that it doesn't take into account the greater degree of responsibility inherent in larger portfolios.

Investment advisors who advocate passive management are still relatively rare. If you're working with an investment advisor you like, but who still believes in trying to beat the market, see if he can be educated out of his counterproductive and obsolete beliefs. If he insists on attempting to beat the market, it's time to look for another advisor. If you can't find one, being a do-it-yourselfer is probably the better option.

The whole idea of anyone advising another person about how to beat the market is inherently illogical. A reliable market-beating strategy would be immensely valuable. However, it's a private good, not a public good. The benefit can accrue to only one user. If you had such a strategy and hired yourself out rather than using it, then you probably need to have your head examined. On the other hand, it does make sense that someone would give advice about ways to match the market and reduce risk exposure.

If you think your current advisor is open-minded, consider getting him to rethink what he's doing by using the Socratic method. Ask him a few of the following questions.

Twenty questions for anyone who advocates attempting to beat the market:

- What is your definition of "beating the market?"
- Is there additional risk involved in your strategy? If yes, what is it?
- Is beating the market a strategy that works in general?
- Most investors attempt to beat the market. Do they succeed?
- Why is it that most players who try to beat the market fail?
- If most players fail, how are you different, specifically?
- Is beating the market a matter of identifying the most promising companies?
- Is the right company the right investment regardless of the price of its stock?
- Is it possible for a company with great potential to be overpriced? If it is possible, how can you tell when it's so?
- Beating the market is about making superior predictions. What is your predictive model?
- What determines relative stock prices (each stock's price relative to other stock prices)?
- How can you assume that the stock you're recommending is mis-priced?
- If a large number of other investors used this strategy, would it still work?
- What is the probability your strategy will succeed?
- Your strategy sounds good; do you have any evidence it actually works?
- If you're winning, who's losing? If you're above average, who's below?
- Do you think that diversification is important? If so, how do you plan to achieve it?
- When someone makes excess returns, how do you know it was because of skill rather than just luck? Does it matter?

- Is return more or less important than risk? Why or why not?
- Why are you sharing this advice rather than keeping it for yourself and exploiting it for your own benefit? Doesn't sharing it dilute its potential benefit for you?

Market efficiency is the standard in the classroom and in the courtroom.

Another good decision principle is making sure you're well grounded when you make important choices. To illustrate what that would mean, consider a document with the ungainly title *Restatement of the Law Trusts* from the American Law Institute in Washington, D.C. The forward to *Restatement* says

> *This work restates the basic rules governing investment of assets of a trust, known as the prudent investor rule. Along with this reformulation are revisions of related rules concerning the conduct of a trustee in the management of a trust… This Restatement is a guide for practitioners of law, trustees, and investment advisors as well as a source of legal authority.*

Included in the *Restatement* is a summary of Modern Portfolio Theory, including sections on pricing and risk, market efficiency, risk and the duty to diversify, practical passive strategies, and active strategies. The *Restatement* strongly recommends passive management. It emphasizes that any trustee who chooses a beat-the-market strategy is asking for trouble.

> *[With active management] there will be new expenses of investigation and analysis, increases in general transactions costs, and additional risks such as may result from judgment calls involved and from an acceptance of specific risk…Realistic, cautiously evaluated return expectations of active management programs must justify these extra costs and risks. The greater the trustee's departure from one of the valid passive strategies, the greater is likely to be the burden of justification and continuous monitoring.*

In other words, if you find yourself in the role of a fiduciary and choose active management, you better hope no one sues you. If you want to have the weight of accepted legal opinion on your side, choose passive management. Passive management is the best alternative, no matter whose money is at issue. Nevertheless, if you're making decisions about money that belongs to someone else, attempting to beat the market is just foolhardy. At last count, the *Third Restatement* has been formally incorporated into the legal codes of twenty-eight states, including New York and California. For a complete analysis of the *Third Restatement*, see Scott Simon's *The Prudent Investor Act: A Guide to Understanding.*

Investment advisors are fiduciaries; stockbrokers are not.

A further legal protection you can and should take advantage of is choosing an investment advisor who is registered as such with the Securities and Exchange Commission. Registered Investment Advisors are classified as fiduciaries when they provide advice to their clients. A fiduciary is "a person having a legal duty, created by his undertaking, to act primarily for the benefit of another in matters connected with his undertaking" (*Barron's Law Dictionary*).

It is important to recognize that stockbrokers are not fiduciaries. The brokerage industry's deliberate avoidance of that classification is an indication that it has value. Whenever you consider someone for investment advice, ask him if he will be defined as a fiduciary. If he says yes, get it in writing. If he says no, look elsewhere. There is no reason why you should forego that extra degree of protection. You are entitled to that standard whenever you trust anyone with your life savings.

Common sense—a much underutilized but important tool in making financial choices.

In his book *Winning the Loser's Game*, Charles Ellis makes the case that avoiding mistakes is more critical to investment success than brilliance. Judging from what I've observed, the best defense against devastating errors is common sense. A few all too typical situations will illustrate what I mean.

You've probably read in the news more than once about someone being cheated out of his life savings by someone promising a guaranteed, risk-free 20 percent rate of return. If these people had simply applied common sense to such a promise they would have recognized it as too good to be true. They would have rejected it out of hand and would still have their life savings.

In the discussion on the importance of diversification, we noted that the employees of corporations often put large parts or even all of their retirement funds into the employer's stock. Doing so makes them especially vulnerable because both their job and nest egg are dependent on the continued good fortune of a single entity. If they heeded their common sense, they would realize that's not a good idea.

Unfortunately, employers often put psychological pressure on employees to show their commitment to the company. Nevertheless, you have to keep in mind that your primary responsibility is to yourself and your family. Your employer is not an objective financial advisor.

Sometimes the pension plan is structured so that you have no choice. In that case, all you can do is attempt to convince your employer to change the plan and offer more options.

Ironically, attempting to bolster the price of the stock by having employees increase demand isn't a strategy that will work in the long run. Market efficiency will bring the stock to the appropriate level regardless of employee participation. If upper management thinks the stock is underpriced, let them use their own money to buy it.

Also discussed previously was the epidemic of hedge-fund fiascoes. Half a trillion dollars has been invested in these black boxes that maintain an arrogant and totally unjustified policy of secrecy. Intelligent, well-educated people commit large amounts of their money to enterprises they know virtually nothing about. They actually invest their money with people who say, "Give us your money and don't ask questions." Common sense alone should be enough to cause investors to take their money and run.

Decision-efficiency summary.

- Deciding to use passive management resolves numerous investment dilemmas.
- Financial planning is both simple and complex. Fortunately, the most important decisions are relatively simple.
- To a large extent, the quality of our lives and the success we attain result from the choices we make.
- Devoting time to thinking about your decision-making methodology is a great saver of time and effort.
- A decision rule could be thought of as making decisions wholesale.
- A common error in decision making is that choices are made in isolation.
- The idea of "first things first" is itself an example of a decision rule.
- "Decisions are easy when your values are clear."
- Determine your time horizon before you decide how much of your portfolio should be allocated to equities and how much to fixed investments.
- Answering the fundamental questions is worth an investment of time since the answers tend to be long lasting.

► Using professional advice is an excellent way to be more efficient with information.

► Market efficiency is the standard in the classroom and the courtroom.

► It's important to insist that your investment advisor be classified as a fiduciary.

► Make common sense a common element of your decision making.

CHAPTER 11

A Recap of Why You Now Know More Than the Experts

❦

Civilization advances by extending the number of important operations which we can perform without thinking about them.

Alfred North Whitehead

The goal of this book has been to make you a more efficient and successful investor. The recommendations have followed the premise that investment efficiency comes from an understanding of investment realities. Your efficiency is closely intertwined with the issue of market efficiency, the most accurate picture yet derived of how markets work.

The important good news of market efficiency is that investing is far easier than you've been led to believe. Matching market rates of return is less stressful, lower cost, more tax efficient, and more intelligible. Passive, asset-class investing offers the only realistic chance for financial peace of mind. In the context of efficient markets, lazy is good.

The recommendations offered are not freestanding. They follow from a prerequisite decision—how do you decide what works and what does not? How do you derive the most accurate picture of reality? The path that's been followed here is to rely on the scientific method—definition of a problem or puzzle, formation of hypotheses, collection of evidence, testing of hypotheses, and analysis of internal consistency and logic. We look to the scientific method for guidance in determining what works because history shows that the scientific method itself works. The scientific method works better than any alternative we know of, and whatever's in second place isn't even close.

At the very least, now that you've read this book, your knowledge of fundamental investment terms and concepts has been enhanced. It would not surprise me that you had never before heard of terms such as the Efficient Market Hypothesis, rational expectations, unbiased estimators, expected value, survivor bias, asset-class investing, and uncompensated risk, but I hope you've been pleasantly surprised by how useful these seemingly arid and arcane concepts can be. I hope I have given you new things to think about and increased your appreciation for the power of ideas. John Maynard Keynes was right—in the long run, ideas are more powerful than vested interests. I can't expect you to love economics as much as I do, but I hope I've softened your resistance a bit.

You now have a more rigorous and clearer understanding of the importance of concepts already familiar to you—voluntary exchange, efficiency, diversification, equilibrium, probability, incentives, information, relativity, risk, and uncertainty. These realities are far more pervasive and relevant than you may have realized.

You now know what is meant by market efficiency and see why the issue has such far-reaching implications. You see why the dimensions of prices and information define the nature of the contest. You know now why the vast majority of information presented in the media is redundant and why redundant information is absolutely useless. The incessant discussions in the media about the prospects for specific companies have no excess-return potential, and now you understand that following their advice will, at the very least, triple your risk exposure.

If stock prices promptly and effectively embody information, the efforts of millions of investors are misguided. Market efficiency means that attempting to beat the market, either through stock selection or market timing, is doomed to failure. It means that attempting to distinguish among actively managed mutual funds is a frustrating waste of effort. Market efficiency means that the high rate of portfolio turnover generated by most mutual funds is an absurd exercise in futility.

Most stock analysts incorrectly assume that the key to earning excess returns is identifying superior companies. However, if generating excess returns were possible, the secret would be in identifying pricing errors. The dogs of Wall Street are barking up the wrong tree.

Active management is fundamentally illogical. Anyone having the ability to confidently achieve excess returns would be crazy to give away or sell that extremely valuable information. In the unlikely event someone invented a system for winning the lottery, you wouldn't see him offering it for sale.

People who attempt to beat the market rarely stop to define what that means. Active management practitioners assume that abnormal returns are equivalent to beating the market. This ignores the fact that attempting to beat the market necessitates more risk and that excess returns are virtually always the result of luck rather than skill. Active managers show up at work every day without ever stopping to clearly define what they're trying to do.

You now know there is no persistence in mutual fund performance. Lack of persistence is the DNA of luck-based performance. Evidence that active managers know they're relying on luck not skill is their willingness to sell their supposedly market-beating secrets. If they believed it were skill, they would use those secrets rather than sell them. Active management is little more than a gigantic con game.

The importance of the luck versus skill question stems from this basic reality—investing is about the future. Luck is random and random variables cannot be predicted. There's no information applicable to the future in historical, luck-based performance (unlike the case with skill-based historical performance).

You now see why you should only be investing in the stock market if your financial objectives are long-range—at least five years and ideally ten or more. Your time horizon is an important factor in all the rest of your financial choices. Wall Street would prefer that you be a hyperactive investor, trading frequently and switching funds often in hot pursuit of abnormal returns. Wall Street and the media hype the importance of daily and hourly changes in the market. You may now give yourself permission to tune out the daily stock market reports. The market's short-term behavior is a useless distraction for anyone not entering and exiting the market frequently. Taking a long-range perspective will help in keeping your financial emotions under control.

By its nature, investing is about the future and about long-range goals. If you're not thinking long term, you shouldn't be investing in the first place. If financial peace of mind is important to you, you have to make the choice to take a long-range focus. Doing so has a result similar to diversification—it narrows the range of possible outcomes. The longer you're invested, the more time there is for the short-run, random fluctuations to balance out.

You now are able to see why risk is at least as important as return. The topic of risk is not conducive to Wall Street's number one priority—marketing. When you're trying to sell something, you accentuate the positive (return) and pretend that the negative (risk) doesn't exist. Investment success, however, isn't achieved by totally ignoring or avoiding risk, but by consciously managing it. Reducing risk is a far more achievable objective than making excess returns.

When you understand risk and that it is equivalent to uncertainty, you can use it to your advantage. You now know the basic principles of how to do that.

Risk is the same as uncertainty, and uncertainty is managed by considering probability. If you don't believe that probability matters, you might as well use winning the lottery as the base of your retirement planning, and, of course, some people do just that. Their success rate is not significantly different from zero.

The foremost opportunity for managing risk is through diversification. In an efficient market, diversifying reduces risk without sacrificing expected return. To diversify effectively, you must understand the objective of diversification as well as the techniques for achieving efficient diversification. You can now recognize and avoid uncompensated risk—the greatest unnecessary detriment to your financial success.

Uncertainty is about the range of possible outcomes, and the best way to narrow that range is through diversification. Efficient diversification is about more than the number of investments you have. Equally important is the behavior of those investments relative to one another. Efficient diversification is achieved through the use of "non-correlated" investments and the avoidance of uncompensated risk.

The central message of this book is that truly beating the market is impossible. Is that an overstatement? Let's say that it is. Who can really say what's possible and what's not? However, even if you grant that beating the market is a theoretical possibility, it doesn't matter from a practical perspective. At a bare minimum, beating the market is an extreme long shot. The probability is overwhelmingly against you. The "expected value" of the attempt is extremely small. (Recall that the expected value of an event is the amount of its payoff times the probability of it happening.)

Except for the entertainment value, the only reason not to invest in asset-class, index funds is to attempt to beat the market. That one possibility is the only potential benefit of active management. All the other aspects of active management are negatives—higher risks, higher costs, unreliability, lack of control, higher taxes, more confusion, and more frustration. The single potential benefit shrinks to nothingness the instant probability is taken into accounts. When you make the choice to use active management, you create all kinds of dilemmas and challenges, such as "style drift." What's the point of going there? What's the probability of a payoff? When you're trying to decide what target to select, one of your major considerations should be the probability of actually hitting the target.

If the logic and evidence have convinced you to take the passive management route to investing, you will continue to be in the minority for many years to come. The logic and evidence are not new, yet only about ten percent of regular investment funds are directed toward passive management. All of the realities addressed in Chapter 5, "Against All Odds: Why Do So Many Keep Trying to Beat the Market?" will persist. Don't lose sleep worrying about the question, "What if everyone indexed?" If you want to worry about something, consider asteroids or another ice age, either of which is about as likely as every investor switching to indexing in our lifetime.

If you decide to be a scientific method, evidence-based investor you will be going against the grain. Don't expect it to be easy to stay the course. Virtually the entire investment industry is aligned against you.

You are now far better equipped to withstand the allure of attempting to beat the market. You know the logic of why it's a hopeless endeavor. This is the reason this book has devoted so much space to explaining the theory and evidence of market efficiency. You need to understand something before you can really make it part of your belief system.

The trend that started several years ago will go on. There will continue to be a slow conversion from active to passive management. Reality doesn't just go away, it persists. As Aldous Huxley observed, "Facts do not cease to exist because they are ignored." Reality isn't optional. The active management gang will find it increasingly difficult to live in denial and deceive their customers.

Although this book has addressed itself primarily to investment success, it has also been about maintaining perspective. Financial peace of mind is important, but it's only one aspect of living. One hundred and fifty years ago, Ralph Waldo Emerson asked, "What is success?" and provided the following memorable answer:

> *To laugh often and love much;*
> *To win the respect of intelligent persons and the affection of children;*
> *To earn the approval of honest critics and endure the betrayal of false friends;*
> *To appreciate beauty;*
> *To find the best in others;*
> *To give of one's self without the slightest thought of return;*
> *To have accomplished a task, whether by a healthy child, a rescued soul, a garden patch or a redeemed social condition;*
> *To have played and laughed with enthusiasm and sung with exaltation;*
> *To know that even one life has breathed easier because you have lived,*
> *This is to have succeeded.*

Money and wealth are not included in Emerson's definition of success. Money is a means rather than an end. Its importance is in helping us achieve the kinds of things listed above. Asset-class, passive management is a way to be more efficient in managing the mundane responsibilities all of us have. It is a way of liberating the time and energy required to "laugh often and love much."

Suggestions for Further Reading

I hope that reading this book has whetted your appetite for learning more about investing and financial economics. The following are some of the best books and other sources on the topic.

- *Random Walk Down Wall Street*, Burton Malkiel
- *Bogle on Mutual Funds,* and *Common Sense on Investing,* John Bogle
- *Index Mutual Funds,* W. Scott Simon
- *What Wall Street Doesn't Want You to Know,* Larry Swedroe
- *Capital Ideas* and *Against the Gods,* Peter Bernstein
- *Winning the Loser's Game,* Charles Ellis
- *Searching for Safety,* Aaron Wildavsky
- "Getting Going" columns by Jonathan Clements, each Wednesday in the *Wall Street Journal*
- indexfunds.com website

Besides these suggestions I recommend you review the bibliography for other possibilities that might grab your interest.

About the Author

꙳

Ron Ross Ph.D. is a Certified Financial Planner and investment advisor with Premier Financial Group in Eureka, California. A former professor of economics (Humboldt State University, Arcata, California), he has provided investment advice to individuals, pension plans, and trustees for the past 23 years. He lives with his wife, Jan, in Arcata. Besides financial economics, his interests include running, golf, gardening, and motorcycling.

To contact the author:
    e-mail: rossecon@aol.com or pfg@premieradvisor.com
    725 Sixth Street, Eureka, California, 95501
    707.443.2741

For additional copies of The *Unbeatable Market* contact:
    Bookmasters, 800.247.6553 or atlasbooks.com (for individual orders)
    or order@bookmasters.com (for wholesale orders).

    Orders may also be placed through amazon.com,
    Barnes & Noble (bn.com), or Books-A-Million (bamm.com.)

    For information on quantity discounts contact Premier Financial Group, 707.443.2741, 725 Sixth Street, Eureka, California, 95501

Bibliography

❧

American Law Institute. 1992. *Restatement of the Law Trusts: Prudent Investor Rule.* American Law Institute Publishers.

Barber, Brad M. and Terrance Odean. 2000. "Trading is Hazardous to Your Wealth: The Common Stock Investment Performance of Individual Investors." *Journal of Finance,* 55, 773-806.

Barber, Brad M. and Terrance Odean. 1999. "Too Many Cooks Spoil the Profits: The Performance of Investment Clubs." unpublished paper, Graduate School of Management, University of California, Davis. Available at www.gsm.ucdavis.edu/~bmbarber.

Barber, Brad M., Reuven Lahavy, Maureen McNichols and Brett Trueman. 2001. "Can Investors Profit from the Prophets? Security Analysts Recommendations and Stock Returns." *Journal of Finance,* 56, 531-563.

Beebower, Gilbert L., Gary P. Brinson, and L. Randolph Hood. 1986. "Determinants of Portfolio Performance." *Financial Analysts Journal,* 39-44.

Bernstein, Peter L., 1993. *Capital Ideas: The Improbable Origins of Wall Street.* The Free Press.

Bernstein, Peter L., 1996. *Against the Gods: The Remarkable Story of Risk.* John Wiley and Sons.

Black, Fischer, 1986. "Noise." *Journal of Finance,* 41, 529-543.

Black, John, editor. 1997. *Oxford Dictionary of Economics.* Oxford University Press.

Bodie, Zvi, Alex Kane and Alan J. Marcus, 1996. *Investments,* 3rd edition. McGraw-Hill.

Bogle, John C. 1994. *Bogle on Mutual Funds: New Perspectives for the Intelligent Investor.* Dell.

Bogle, John C. 1999. *Common Sense on Mutual Funds.* John Wiley and Sons.

Brown, Stephen J. and William N. Groetzmann. 1995. "Performance Persistence." *Journal of Finance,* 50, 679-698.

Bronowski, Jakob. 1973. *The Ascent of Man.* Little Brown and Company.

Carhart, Mark. 1997. "On Persistence in Mutual Fund Performance." *Journal of Finance,* 52, 57-82.

Clash, James M., Robert Lenzner, Michael Maiello, and Josephine Lee, 2001. "The $500 Billion Hedge Fund Folly." *Forbes,* August 6, 2001. 70-75.

Clements, Jonathan. 1998. *25 Myths You've got to Avoid—If You Want to Manage Your Money Right: New Rules for Financial Success.* Fireside.

Cootner, Paul H. 1964. *The Random Character of Stock Prices.* MIT Press.

Covey, Stephen R. 1989. *The Seven Habits of Highly Effective People.* Fireside.

Covey, Stephen R., A. Roger Merrill and Rebecca R. Merrill. 1994. *First Things First: To Live, To Learn, to Leave a Legacy.* Simon and Shuster.

Davis, James. 2001. "Mutual Fund Performance and Manager Style." *Financial Analysts Journal,* 57, 19-27.

Ellis, Charles D. 1998. *Winning the Loser's Game: Timeless Strategies for Successful Investing.* McGraw-Hill.

Ellsberg, Daniel. 1961. "Risk Ambiguity and the Savage Axioms." *Quarterly Journal of Economics,* 75, 643-699.

Elton, Edwin, Martin J. Gruber, Sanjiv Das, and Matthew Hlavka, 1993. "Efficiency with Costly Information: A Reinterpretation of Evidence from Managed Portfolios." *Review of Financial Studies,* 6, 1-22.

Elton, Edwin, Martin J. Gruber, Sanjiv Das, and Christopher R. Blake. 1996. "The Persistence of Risk-adjusted Mutual Fund Performance." *Journal of Business,* 69, 133-157.

Fama, Eugene F. 1965. "The Behavior of Stock Market Prices." *Journal of Business,* 38, 34-105.

Fama, Eugene F. 1965. "Random Walks in Stock Market Prices." *Financial Analysts Journal,* September/October, 55-59.

Fama, Eugene F. 1970. "Efficient Capital Markets: A Review of Theory and Empirical Work" *Journal of Finance,* 25, 383-417.

Fama, Eugene F. 1991. "Efficient Capital Markets: II." *Journal of Finance,* 46, 1575-1617.

Fama, Eugene F. 1995. "Random Walks in Stock Market Prices." *Financial Analysts Journal,* 75-80.

Fama, Eugene F. 1998. "Market Efficiency, Long-term Returns, and Behavioral Finance." *Journal of Financial Economics,* 49, 283-306.

Fama, Eugene F. and Kenneth R. French. 1992. "The Cross Section of Expected Stock Returns." *Journal of Finance,* 47, 427-465.

Fama, Eugene F. and Kenneth R. French. 2001. "The Equity Premium." Center for Research in Security Prices, Working Paper No. 522

Friedman, Milton. 1953. "The Methodology of Positive Economics." *Essays in Positive Economics,* University of Chicago Press. Reprinted in *The Essence of Friedman,* Kurt R. Leube, editor, 1987, Hoover Institution Press.

Gandar, John; Richard Zuber, and Ben Russo. 1988. "Testing Rationality in the Point Spread Betting Market." *Journal of Finance,* 43, 995-1007.

Gibbons, Vera. 2000. "Sorry, Wrong Number." *Smart Money.* January 2000, 113-119.

Hayek, F.A. 1945. "The Use of Knowledge in Society." *American Economic Review,* 35, 519-530. Reprinted in F.A. Hayek. 1948. *Individualism and Economic Order.* University of Chicago Press.

Henderson, David R., editor. 1993. *Fortune Encyclopedia of Economics.* Warner Books.

Hirshleifer, Jack and John G. Riley. 1992. *The Analytics of Uncertainty and Information.* Cambridge University Press.

Jaffe, Jeffrey F.; and James M. Mahoney, 1999. "The Performance of Investment Newsletters." *Journal of Financial Economics,* 53, 209-307.

Jeffrey, Robert H.; and Robert D. Arnott, 1993, "Is Your Alpha Big Enough to Cover Your Taxes?" *Journal of Portfolio Management,* 15-25.

Jensen, Michael C. 1978. "Some Anomalous Evidence Regarding Market Efficiency." *Journal of Financial Economics,* 6, 95-101.

Jensen, Michael C. 1968. "The Performance of Mutual Funds in the Period 1945-1964." *Journal of Finance,* 23, 389-416.

Jones, Steven L. and Jeffry Netter. 1993. "Efficient Capital Markets." *Fortune Encyclopedia of Economics.* David R. Henderson, editor. Warner Books.

Kahneman, Daniel, Slovic, Paul, and Tversky, Amos, eds. 1982. *Judgement Under Uncertainty: Heuristics and Biases.* Cambridge University Press.

Kahneman, Daniel; and Mark Riepe. 1998. "Aspects of Investor Psychology: Beliefs, Preferences, and Biases Investment Advisors Should Know About." *Journal of Portfolio Management,* 24, 1-22.

Kaneman, Daniel and Amos Tversky. 1981. "The Framing of Decisions and the Psychology of Choice." *Science,* 211, 453-458.

Keynes, John Maynard. 1936. *The General Theory of Employment, Interest, and Money.* Harbinger.

Landsburg, Steven E. 1993. *The Armchair Economist: Economics and Everyday Life.* Free Press.

Leroy, Stephen F. 1989. "Efficient Capital Markets and Martingales." *Journal of Economic Literature,* 27, 1583-1621.

Lomborg, Bjorn. 2001. *The Skeptical Environmentalist: Measuring the Real State of the World.* Cambridge University Press.

Lorie, James H. and Mary Hamilton, editors, 1973. *The Stock Market: Theories and Evidence.* Irwin.

Lynch, Peter. 1993. *Beating the Street.* Fireside.

Maddison, Angus. 2001. *The World Economy: A Millennial Perspective.* Organization for Economic Co-operation and Development.

Malkiel, Burton G. 1995. "Returns from Investing in Equity Mutual Funds 1971 to 1991." *Journal of Finance,* 50, 549-572.

Malkiel, Burton G. 1999. *A Random Walk Down Wall Street.* W.W. Norton and Company.

Malkiel, Burton G., John Y. Cambell, Martin Lettau, and Yexiao Xu. 2001. "Have Individual Stocks Become More Volatile? An Empirical Exploration of Idiosyncratic Risk." *Journal of Finance,* 56, 1-43.

Markowitz, Harry M. 1952. "Portfolio Selection." *Journal of Finance,* 7, 77-91.

Markowitz, Harry M. 1959. *Portfolio Selection: Efficient Diversification of Investments.* John Wiley and Sons.

Merton, Robert C. 1983, "Financial Economics." in *Paul Samuelson and Modern Economic Theory,* E. C. Brown and Robert M. Solow, editors. MIT Press.

Merton, Robert C. 1987. "On the Current State of the Stock Market Rationality Hypothesis." in *Macroeconomics and Finance: Essays in Honor of Franco Modigliani,* Stanley Fischer, et al, editors. MIT Press.

Pagano, Marco; Fabio Panetta and Luigi Zingales. 1998. "Why Do Companies Go Public?" *Journal of Finance,* 53, 27-64.

Peck, M. Scott. 1978. *The Road Less Traveled: A New Psychology of Love, Traditional Values and Spiritual Growth.* Touchstone.

Pearce, David W. editor. 1996. *The MIT Dictionary of Modern Economics.* MIT Press.

Poterba, James M. and John B. Shoven. 2002. "Exchange Traded Funds: A New Investment Option for Taxable Investors." MIT Department of Economics Working Paper Series. Social Science Research Network Paper Collection at http://papers.ssrn.com/paper.taf?abstract_id=302889

Roberts, Harry V. 1964. "Stock Market Patterns and Financial Analysis: Methodological Suggestions." in *The Random Character of Stock Prices,* Paul H. Cootner, editor. MIT Press.

Rubinstein, Mark. 2001. "Rational Markets: Yes or No? The Affirmative Case." *Financial Analysts Journal,* 57, 15-29. Available at in-the-money.com.

Samuelson, Paul H. 1965. "Proof That Properly Anticipated Prices Fluctuate Randomly." *Industrial Management Review,* reprinted in *The Collective Scientific Papers of Paul Samuelson.* 1972. Robert Merton, editor. MIT Press.

Sargent, Thomas J. 1993. "Rational Expectations." *Fortune Encyclopedia of Economics.* David R. Henderson, editor. Warner Books.

Sauer, Raymond D. 1998. "The Economics of Wagering Markets." *Journal of Economic Literature,* 36, 2021-2064.

Sharpe, William F. 1998. "Morningstar's Risk-Adjusted Ratings." *Financial Analysts Journal,* 54, 21-33.

Sharpe, William F. 1966. "Mutual Fund Performance." *Journal of Business,* 39, 119-138.

Sharpe, William F.; Gordon J. Alexander and Jeffrey V. Bailey 1999. *Investments,* 6th edition. Prentice Hall.

Sheffrin, Steven M. 1996. *Rational Expectations.* Cambridge University Press.

Sherden, William A. 1998. *The Fortune Sellers: The Big Business of Buying and Selling Predictions.* John Wiley and Sons.

Siegel, Jeremy J. 1998. *Stocks for the Long Run: A Guide for Selecting Markets for Long-Term Growth.* McGraw-Hill.

Simon, Julian and Stephen Moore. 2000. *It's Getting Better All the Time: 100 Greatest Trends of the Last 100 Years.* Cato Institute.

Simon, W. Scott. 1998. *Index Mutual Funds: Profiting from an Investment Revolution.* Namborn Publishing.

Simon, W. Scott. 2002. *The Prudent Investor Act: A Guide to Understanding.* Namborn Publishing.

Skinner, David C. 1995. *Introduction to Decision Analysis: A Practitioner's Guide to Improving Decision Quality,* 2nd ed. Probabilistic Publishing.

Smith, Adam. 1776. *An Inquiry into the Nature and Causes of the Wealth of Nations.* Modern Library.

Summers, Lawrence H. 1986. "Does the Stock Market Rationally Reflect Fundamental Values?" *Journal of Finance,* 41, 591-602.

Swedroe, Larry E. 2000. "The Quest to Outperform." *Journal of Accountancy,* January 2000, 32-39.

Swedroe, Larry E. 2001. *What Wall Street Doesn't Want You to Know: How You Can Build Real Wealth Investing in Index Mutual Funds.* St. Martins.

Thoreau, Henry David. 1854. Walden. Reprinted in *Walden and Other Writings.* 2000. Modern Library.

Tully, Shawn. 1998. "How the Really Smart Money Invests: Nobel Prize Winners Entrust Their Nest Eggs to DFA, Where Investing is a Science, Not a Spectator Sport." *Fortune,* July 6, 1998.

Warwick, Ben. 2000. *Searching for Alpha: The Quest for Exceptional Investment Performance.* John Wiley and Sons.

Wattenberg, Ben J., Theodore Caplow, and Louis Hicks. 2001. *The First Measured Century: An Illustrated Guide to Trends in America, 1900-2000.* American Enterprise Institute.

Wildavsky, Aaron. 1988. *Searching for Safety.* Transaction Publishers.

Index

Summers, Lawrence, 68
supply, 28
survivor bias, 160-161
Swedroe, Larry, 165-166
systematic errors, 60-61
taxes and mutual funds, 167-169
technical analysis, 71-73
Texas sharpshooter fallacy, 160
Thoreau, Henry David, 187
time as a cost of investing, 170-171
Tobin, James, 131
Tritsch, Shane, 92
turnover, portfolio, 163-166
unbiased estimator, defined, 59
unintelligibility of active management,
    171-172
Value Line, 70
Vanguard mutual funds, 141, 147, 150-151
voluntary exchange, defined, 21
Wall Street, defined, 3
Warwick, Ben, 87-88
Wattenberg, Ben, 201
Whitehead, Alfred North, 219
Wildavsky, Aaron, 113-114
Woods, Tiger, 82-83, 212